HOW THE WORLD BECAME A STAGE

HOW THE WORLD BECAME A STAGE

Presence, Theatricality, and the Question of Modernity

William Egginton

State University of New York Press

Published by
State University of New York Press, Albany

© 2003 State University of New York

All rights reserved.

Printed in the United States of America

No part of this book may be used or reproduced in any manner whatsoever without written permission. No part of this book may be stored in a retrieval system or transmitted in any form or by any means including electronic, electrostatic, magnetic tape, mechanical, photocopying, recording, or otherwise without the prior permission in writing of the publisher.

For information, address State University of New York Press,
90 State Street, Suite 700, Albany, NY 12207

Production by Michael Haggett
Marketing by Anne M. Valentine

Library of Congress Cataloging-in-Publication Data
Egginton, William, 1969–
    How the world became a stage : presence, theatricality, and the question of modernity / William Egginton.
       p. cm.
    Includes bibliographical references and index.
    ISBN 0-7914-5545-9 (alk. paper) — ISBN 0-7914-5546-7 (pbk. : alk. paper)
       1. Theater—Europe—History—16th century. 2. Theater—Europe—History—17th century. 3. Theater and society—Europe—History—16th century. 4. Theater and society—Europe—History—17th century. I. Title.

PN2171 .E37 2002
792'.094'09031—dc21   2002070717

10 9 8 7 6 5 4 3 2 1

CONTENTS

Acknowledgments	vii
Introduction: The Legend of Saint Genesius	1
1 Actors, Agents, and Avatars	9
Avatars	10
Performativity	13
Theatricality	20
2 Real Presence, Sympathetic Magic, and the Power of Gesture	33
Magic	36
Presence	42
Performances	47
Religious Spectacle	51
Political Spectacle	56
Seeds of Theatricality	60
3 Saint Genesius on the Stage of the World	67
Diderot's Paradox	69
Metatheater	74
Actors and Martyrs	80
4 A Tale of Two Cities: The Evolution of Renaissance Stage Practices in Madrid and Paris	85
Italian Innovations	87
Theories and Theaters in Paris	91
Theories and Theaters in Madrid	99
Tales from the Crypt	105
True Pretense: Lope's *Lo fingido verdadero* and the Structure of Theatrical Space	113
5 Theatricality versus Subjectivity	123
Philosophical Subjectivity	125
Political Subjectivity	140
Aesthetic Subjectivity	153
Theatricality and Media Theory	164
Epilogue	167
Notes	171
Index	205

ACKNOWLEDGMENTS

Thanks are owed first to the professors at Stanford who guided me during the writing of my dissertation, upon which this book is based: to Hayden White, who always knew of one more author to read; to Valentin Mudimbe, who asked questions so profound that sometimes they could not be answered, and whose conversation over lunch always inspires; to Robert Harrison, who understood deeply and immediately what I intended and whose suggestions never failed to improve my work, his friendship is among the things I remember best from Stanford.

Now I come to the most important person involved in the years of schooling, research, and writing that this project represents. It is customary for a dissertation advisor to be thanked and acknowledged. But Sepp Gumbrecht deserves more than custom. He is, indeed, much more than a dissertation advisor. He is a dear and caring friend, who has always been there for me, for any problem, great or small. He is a thinker of extraordinary imagination and subtlety. And he is, quite simply, the best teacher I have ever had.

My work benefited greatly from my friends and colleagues at Stanford and elsewhere: David Castillo, my earliest colleague, with whom I began thinking about this topic; Kevin Heller, who keeps my writing in shape; Peter Gilgen, collaborator and confidant; Jeffrey Schnapp, whose Dante is as extreme as his skiing; Joshua Landy, whose tough reads always gave me something to work on; Tim Lenoir, for being interested in everything; Anston Bosman, who was with me from the ground floor; Nick Spadaccini, who first taught me the Golden Age.

The first year of research for this project took place while I was a fellow at the Stanford Humanities Center, 1996-97. My thanks go to all those who made that year possible, especially Keith Baker and Susan Dunn, the director and associate director of the Center, and my colleagues that year, especially Melissa Goldman, Paul St. Amour, Brendon Reay, Angus Locklear, and Richard Rorty. Thanks as well to the Julian Park Fund at UB, for a grant supporting this project.

During the process of reworking the dissertation into its present form, I have been fortunate enough to be in a new department and university with colleagues as supportive as they are insightful. Further thanks are due to those, both at Buffalo and elsewhere, who were generous enough to read and comment on the manuscript: Henry Sussman, Czeslaw Prokopczyk, Richard

Rorty, John McCumber, Edward Friedman, Jorge Gracia, Angus Locklear, David Glass, Kevin Heller, and my editors, Jane Bunker and Michael Haggett.

Thanks go also to my family: my mother, Margaret Maguire, my father Everett Egginton, my stepmother Wynn Egginton, and my mother-in-law Elisabeth Wegenstein (1934-2001). Their love of learning and of me has given me all the support I could need for the seeming eternity of education, which I am, of course, continuing. They are, each in their own way, role models for me, and if I have managed over the years to become, even in some small way, more like them, then these years have been a success.

To my life's companion and intellectual partner, Bernadette Wegenstein, I give my thanks not only for her wondrous presence in my world, but also for all the conversations and debates we have had, readings we have shared, and criticisms she has given me on my work. No single aspect of my existence would be the same without her. This book is dedicated to her.

For Berna

Introduction:
The Legend of Saint Genesius

Every profession, no matter how unholy, must have its patron saint. The patron saint of actors is the legendary Genesius, who, as legend has it, performed the role of a Christian martyr for the emperor Diocletian so convincingly that he himself became a Christian in the very act of his performance. Unbeknownst to the admiring emperor and his entourage, at some point in the performance Genesius's playacting, his parody, intended to provoke derision and laughter, became the real thing. When the fact of his conversion was finally realized—when, we might speculate, emperor and entourage finally tired of his performance and asked him to stop—Genesius met his fate in the most appropriate of ways: a real martyrdom on the very stage on which he had just been prepared to fake it.

Genesius's life and martyrdom may be the stuff of legend, but it is also, and more essentially, the stuff of theater. At least this is what several playwrights in the seventeenth century believed. For what could be more appropriate to an age obsessed with theater than the story of the martyrdom of the patron saint of the theater, played out in the theater? And how better to stage this story than with recourse to the age's most characteristic technique, the stage within the stage, where actors portray characters who in turn portray actors playing characters? This is indeed the technique chosen by Lope de Vega and Jean Rotrou, the most famous and influential poets to write Genesius's story in early modern times. The fact that they chose this technique is not, nor should it be, surprising. What is perhaps more surprising is that when the same story was performed several hundred years earlier in France, in the form of a *mystère*, no such technique was used. In this version, Genesius's conversion occurs already in the first quarter of the play and is brought about merely by his conversations with Christians. The notion that he is an actor is barely alluded to, and the bulk of the play is devoted to Genesius's scholastic debates with Diocletian over Christian doctrine, as well as to an extended and rather detailed performance of his martyrdom when he fails to convince the emperor.

What is happening here? Did the medievals simply lack imagination? Were they so dedicated to the dry exposition of doctrine that the notion of dramatic enactment, of seizing this perfect opportunity to dramatize the conversion of a saint, just never occurred to them? Such a conclusion is not far from the traditional interpretation of the medieval drama as a dry, impoverished version of what finally achieved its grandeur in the exalted works of Shakespeare, Lope, and Corneille. My hypothesis is rather different: The medieval performance of Genesius's death *could not* have been staged in the metatheatrical style of a Lope or a Rotrou, because that style is the essence of a completely different cultural practice than that of medieval spectacle—namely, theater. Theater, in turn, is itself the central cultural practice of a different world from that of the Middle Ages, a world in which the most fundamental of phenomena, the very experience of the space one inhabits, had radically changed. For lack of a better word, we have chronocentrically called this world modern. With this book I am hoping that we will change that, and simply call it *theatrical*.

This is a thesis, then, about the modern world, about what distinguishes it as modern, and about what might have come before it. Even now, as I put these words down, there are aspects of this formulation that strike me as absurd: the notions, for example, that one can say anything at all about a swath of time 500 years in length that would be generally true of it without flying in the face of both scholarly research and common sense; or that if there were specific and broad-ranging commonalities among the multiplicity of styles, practices, industries, and ideas that constitute what we vaguely call "western culture," then most or all of these elements might have conspired to change at a narrow enough interval in time to create the historical distinction that we call modernity. But even if one overlooks the surface absurdities of such a claim, another kind of objection springs into view. Ever since the Renaissance's self-christening as the phalanx of modernity, historians have constantly tried to explain what distinguishes the modern world, and have located that distinction at more or less the same time I do. My project, then, would seem to have the misfortune of suffering from what should be mutually exclusive disadvantages, namely, being both untenably ambitious and starkly unoriginal. So where does that leave me?

I will confront this potential accusation head on, by pointing out that it is only in the scope of its ambition that the project lacks originality and, therefore, that it is precisely its unoriginality that renders tenable its ambition. For to note that between the sixteenth and the seventeenth centuries the western world changed—and perhaps in a more fundamental way than it had for several centuries before and would for several centuries after—is to make a claim of startling generality. Claims of this generality usually do not stand or fall on the research of one scholar alone, but rather rely on generations of accumulated data and interpretations of that data. And what is true of claims of this sort in general is equally true of this particular claim. Its ambition is supported by its unoriginality. What is original about my project, on the other hand, can be seen in a much more modest light—as a proposal for a change in the vocabulary used to describe the distinction of modernity.

A dominant tendency in historicism has been to attribute much of the perceived change at the origins of modernity to the concept of subjectivity—a legacy of Hegel's categorization of the world and of history in terms of greater and lesser degrees of self-consciousness. One specific goal of this book—perhaps the central goal—is to argue that the vocabulary of subjectivity is inadequate to the expectations placed on it, and to replace that vocabulary with a new one. I hope that the new vocabulary I am proposing will explain, better than subjectivity does, those elements of change that the vocabulary of subjectivity purports to explain, elements that have been interpreted, in other words, as the emergence of one subjectivity manifested in a variety of philosophical, political, and aesthetic practices.

The vocabulary I am proposing revolves around the concepts of *presence* and *theatricality*, and while it is impossible to try to clarify completely their significance in the opening pages (that, after all, is what the book is for), I will nonetheless clarify from the outset what they emphatically *do not* mean. Both concepts already have a variety of uses, but the use I am proposing is not precisely the same as any of the prior or generally-accepted uses. When I speak of presence, for example, I do not refer at all to the "metaphysics of presence" that has been the nemesis of so much twentieth-century thought. Much closer to my meaning is presence in its theological sense, as in the Real Presence of the body of God. Of course, I do not mean it in precisely this way either, because to accept the descriptive value of this vocabulary ought not to (nor in fact could it) commit one to a specifically Catholic belief system (although, I would claim, it should help modern people like ourselves translate into a belief system that is, in fact, no longer of our world). Rather, by presence I refer to that experience of space that subtends such diverse experiences as the participation in a ritual invocation of the seasons, certain shamanistic cures, "voodoo death," and the miracle of transubstantiation.

Theatricality, on the other hand, should not be understood as the quality of engaging in overt performance, or as emotiveness, or as being self-conscious of one's status as actor. Nor, as I explain in chapter 3, should it be equated with the notion in art criticism of the overflowing of borders (although it is deeply connected with this artistic effect). And though still maintaining some of its root meaning, "of or having to do with the theater," it departs from this definition insofar as it is used as a *phenomenological* notion. For while everything that is theatrical still does, in a distant sort of way, have to do with the theater, the "theater" in this formulation has undergone a transformation as well, and has become *that medium of interaction whose conventions structure and reveal to us our sense of space or spatiality*. The spatiality so revealed is theatricality.

One way to understand the relation of the new vocabulary to the old is to think of it as being the product of a shift in methodology, from what one could call an *epistemological* approach to a *phenomenological* one. In other words, if the discourse of subjectivity is concerned with describing the appearance in the world of a new or different form of self-consciousness, and with showing how the relation between this self and the "world out there" is exhibited in philosophy, political organization, and art and literature, then the phenomenology I am proposing attempts to describe what Heidegger would call the "worlding" of the world, that is, how ideas of selfhood are found alongside the various skills and practices that constitute human existence. What I am claiming to be doing is thus a kind of ontology, albeit in the only way that Heidegger believed ontology could be done: namely, as phenomenology, as a description of how, in different times and different places, the world worlds.

Heidegger, then, is a point of reference in this work, and what is most pertinent in my appropriation of Heidegger is his notion of spatiality. Briefly, Heidegger's trope, which is at the core of his version of phenomenology, is to move the notions of space and time from "inside" the perceiving being, where they had been since Kant—the forms of intuition, *in which* all perceiving occurred—to the "outside," to make them the most fundamental of phenomena.[1] Individuals, then, do not order their world within the confines of a pre-given but neutral *space*, but rather this pre-given but neutral space is one historical manifestation of the individuals' *spatiality*: the experience of space that underlies their interactions in the world and that is specific to their own (culturally and historically specific) world. The individuals' experience of space, their specific spatiality, comes to them via the ordinary, everyday practices and conventions peculiar to their world.

The underlying assumption of this book is that among the practices and conventions most constitutive of spatiality are those associated with spectacle. Thus, if it is to be noted, as it has been time and time again, that there is something fundamentally different about the form of spectacle in the modern age from those of previous ages (see chapters 2 and 3), then the history of spectacle might be the place to go for further analysis of that spatiality that is specific to modernity and that hence subtends much of modern experience. The purpose, then, of this book is to propose a new vocabulary through a description of the practices and conventions of spectacle and an analysis of how those practices and conventions change from the Middle Ages to the early modern period. Because this approach focuses so exclusively on the experience of spectacle, it should be understood not as exclusive of other approaches and other vocabularies, but rather as contributing a new conceptual tool, one that will certainly be of more help to some than to others. Moreover, because it focuses on the history of spectacle, the book also provides another way of making sense, in a particular historical context, of the often radical changes marking the development of the theater in the sixteenth century.

The scope, then, is of necessity limited. In the pages that follow I do not discuss colonialism; the discovery/conquest of the New World; the plethora of technological developments throughout the modern period that have nothing to do with spectacle; changing gender relations in the sixteenth century; or, for that matter, the undeniable influence of capitalism and the emerging market economies of the same period. By excluding them I am not saying they are not important, not connected, or not causal; I am only saying that I cannot cover everything. Furthermore, this book is a phenomenology, not an etiology. As I discuss briefly in the third chapter, I find most existing theories of causality in cultural history extremely unsatisfying and do not intend to propose one in these pages. This does not mean that events do not have efficient causes, or that elites do not profit from certain economic and social configurations and do their best to reproduce them. Indeed, I dedicate part of chapter 4 to discussing how the cultural institution of the baroque theater might have been harnessed for precisely such a purpose. I only resist the functionalist assumption that it was *created for* such a purpose.

Finally, this book is limited geographically, in that it deals primarily with the history of spectacle in France and Spain, as well as in Italy to the extent that Italian culture influenced so heavily those two cultures. The choice of France and Spain reflects my own interests and the fact that they were two of the three great powers of early modern Europe, powers whose cultural histories, particularly in regard to the theater, followed markedly diverse paths. The diversity of the respective histories of spectacle in these two cultures puts productive pressure on my desire to generalize, to synthesize, and to find explanations that might be valid for much of the world now known as the West.

I begin chapter 1, "Actors, Agents, and Avatars," in the present, pointing to the prevalence of psychoanalytic models of subjectivity in the interpretation of culture, and arguing that this prevalence is a function of the psychoanalytic vocabulary's implicit dependence on a *theatrical* model for describing modes of mediation between individuals and the social in the modern world. This mediation is performed by what one could call virtual selves, or human avatars. Beginning with the notion of the avatar as it has appeared in discussions of interaction in virtual spaces, I ask whether the current obsession with the possibilities of virtual interaction, and of the potential collapse of the boundaries separating this virtual world from the world of real bodies and real sensations, is evidence that our own, apparently physical selves are, in some way, already virtual beings. For insight into this question, I turn to the related notion of performativity (that usage of language that affects or even produces what it purports merely to describe), as developed most effectively in the work of Judith Butler, who argues that our selves are indeed like virtual selves in that aspects of them as deep as, say, one's sex are not an immediate truth of the physical body, but rather are susceptible to manipulation and even construction. I take issue, however, with the dominant semiotic connotations of performativity and return to its articulation by John Austin in order to argue for a reappropriation of the theatrical connotations of the verb "to perform." From this primarily theatrical understanding of the efficacy of performativity, I claim that the active ingredient in the performative imposition of bodily forms on an individual is the gaze of a disembodied audience, a gaze whose existence is described by Jean-Paul Sartre in *Being and Nothingness* and analyzed by Jacques Lacan in some of his earliest teachings.

If Lacan offers us a model of the process by which virtual selves are constructed, he also makes clear that this process is a historical one, in that the "subject" psychoanalysis describes is one whose birth was announced by the same phrase that ushered in the beginning of modern philosophy, Descartes' *cogito ergo sum*. This "subject" is the intellectual manifestation of a new way of experiencing the self in space, a way of experiencing that depends on the ability, for example, to distinguish actors from characters and the space of the one from that of the other. The psychoanalytic subject, in other words, is a product of a specifically theatrical spatiality, much like the other forms of subjectivity discussed in the final chapter. Because this spatiality is not always and everywhere the same, it behooves us to understand what existed before it and from what, therefore, it emerged.

In the second chapter, "Real Presence, Sympathetic Magic, and the Power of Gesture," I broach the topic of medieval conventions of spectacle, arguing that the efficacy of religious and political spectacles in the Middle Ages needs to be understood in the context of what nineteenth-century ethnographers called the magical worldview. Abjuring the notion of world view, I suggest that what is in fact at stake is a form of spatiality, *presence*, that allows for the direct interconnection of bodies with words, gestures, and meanings—allows for, in other words, the *substantial* transmission of meaning across what for modern sensibilities would be empty space. Mimesis, in its medieval manifestation, would be much like the definition Michael Taussig gives it on the basis of his ethnographic readings: the tendency of the copy to partake of the power of the original. In this sense, less of a distinction need be drawn between the liturgy and the performance of the miracle of transubstantiation (because in each case they are mimetic repetitions of original and powerful events) than between all medieval performance and the notion of theater itself, which only begins to take the shape that we recognize in the modern age. The chapter ends with a look at the work of a man many have called the father of the Spanish theater, Juan del Encina. I argue that, with the ability his characters show to navigate between different spatial and temporal dimensions, he has taken a small but decisive step in the direction of a theatrical mode of being.

The third chapter, "Saint Genesius on the Stage of the World," uses the myth of Saint Genesius and its various retellings in the Middle Ages and early modernity as a guide to the transformations in staging practices and theory between the two periods. Having outlined the basic parameters of theatricality, I argue that any spectacle taking place in that spatiality and according to its conventions—hence theater per se—is *metatheatrical*, in that the constitutive division between the real world and its reproduction is itself always potentially reproducible on the stage.

In the fourth chapter, "A Tale of Two Cities: The Evolution of Renaissance Stage Practices in Madrid and Paris," I trace the history of stagecraft and theory in those two cities through the sixteenth century, trying to show how and when the metatheatrical conventions became dominant. On the basis of this brief history, I return to one of the manifestations of the Genesius myth in seventeenth-century theater, Lope de Vega's *Lo fingido verdadero*, or *True Pretence*, reading the play as an extended map of what I call the four spaces of theatricality. Throughout this chapter I develop the notion that among the spaces of theatricality there is an insertion of the medieval experience of presence into modern spatiality, a remnant haunting modern spectacle that I call the *crypt*. The crypt, constrained and highly localized "pockets of presence," retains some of its power to invoke the miraculous—to physically impact the viewer—and does so by acting as the stopgap for the potentially endless relativization of frames characteristic of theatrical space. Because of this power, the crypt is also that which responds to and guides the visual desire to reveal that which remains concealed; it is the promise of *reality* in a world of endless illusion.

The last chapter, "Theatricality versus Subjectivity," presents the main theoretical argument that I announced at the outset of this introduction: that the vocabulary I present in these pages should replace the vocabulary of subjectivity as a tool for describing historical change. I proceed by reviewing the subjectivity thesis in three disciplines—philosophy, political theory, and literature—demonstrating that in each case the term should be understood to have only a limited, highly determined applicability, pertinent only to that field. The use of the same word in several fields of study in the human sciences has created the illusion that there really was such a thing as "the subject" that "emerged" in the sixteenth century to change the course of modern history. Furthermore, to the extent that historicists want to talk about "the subject" as a result of subjectification, I suggest that they are in fact borrowing a model from psychoanalysis, a model which, while itself obviously historical, refers not to the result or product of historical change, but to the *that* which changes, in the sense of "a new form of subjectivity develops." Theatricality avoids many of these confusions, doing much of the intellectual work that the subjectivity thesis aims to do while retaining an extremely specific scope: the experience of space.

CHAPTER 1

Actors, Agents, and Avatars

Sporadic and triumphant reports of its death to the contrary, the language of psychoanalysis has, at the end of the century whose birth coincided with its own, achieved the stature of a full-blown culture industry. The reasons for this are hardly mysterious. As a theory that purports to reveal the fundamental structure of the human psyche, psychoanalysis stakes a claim to a knowledge that is inherent to every human endeavor. Where its claims have been most powerfully felt, however, is in the realm of the analysis, explication, and criticism of literature, art, and cultural production in general. Early manifestations of psychoanalytic cultural and literary criticism were concerned with the analysis of the author's or artist's psychology via the text or work he or she produced, treating that text or work as if it were the speech of a patient in analysis. Another practice that began early on—which was evident, in fact, in Freud's own writings—but that, unlike the former tendency, has not fallen into disrepute, is the use of artistic or literary works to confirm, explicate, or demonstrate the validity of psychoanalytic models and theories.[1] Finally, a third general manifestation of the analytic attitude toward culture has become dominant in the last twenty years: the recourse to a psychoanalytic model of the human subject as a basis for demonstrating how texts—taken in the broadest possible sense—are able to affect human agency, and how power reproduces itself via this manipulation of agency.

The aim of this chapter is to show how both the contemporary tendencies in cultural criticism and the psychoanalytic model of agency they either explicitly or implicitly entail invite another, more fundamental level of analysis—an analysis of the subject's spatiality, its organization of the space it inhabits. What such an analysis shows is that this organization of space is, first, specifically theatrical and, furthermore, that its theatricality is a historical phenomenon, one whose contours are best delineated via a historical investigation of the material conditions of the medium from which it gets its name: the theater. By describing how theatricality is expressed in contemporary theoretical discourse, I hope to set the stage for this historical analysis in the chapters that follow, an analysis that will reveal the theatrical experience of space as it emerges against the background of its nemesis and sibling, presence. On the basis of this historical analysis, I will finally, in the last chapter, present these two terms as the pivotal poles of a new analytic vocabulary, a tool for explaining what is unique about the modern world. This new vocabulary is not meant to replace that of psychoanalysis, nor is it dependent on psychoanalytic theory for its claims. Rather, what I intend to show in this chapter is how the discourse of subjectivity that currently abounds as an instrument for *theoretical* analysis is as beholden to theatrical spatiality as are the *historical* notions of subjectivity I analyze in the last chapter. Nevertheless, these theoretical instances of the subjectivity discourse do not share the weakness of those historical usages—namely that they confound disparate notions under one category—and hence my analysis does not, as it does in the latter case, constitute a criticism against these instances, but rather a dialogue with them.

AVATARS

Using a technology called Virtual Reality Markup Language (VRML), cyberspace enthusiasts may now construct more or less realistic representations of themselves to be their full-time representatives in the virtual community. These "avatars," as they are referred to by the advocates of the Universal Avatar Project, a group dedicated to formulating one of the first manifestations of a social contract for this virtual world, are designed by their "masters" to play whatever role the master wishes them to play. But the understanding seems to be that their masters, for the most part, are not looking for mere passing toys, ephemeral masks to be changed at whim. Rather, if the group's white paper is any indication, those who are seeking to set down the conventions of avatar interaction conceive of these entities quite seriously as second selves, entailing a certain "persistence of identity," and perhaps deserving of the same respect owed to the masters in conventional, real-world interaction.[2]

In one scenario from the white paper in question,

> Moses is at home in his VRML living space. His house was designed by a famous virtual architect, his avatar was created using the Avatars 'R Us construction kit. He was able to easily purchase both products online, because his Universal Avatar had embedded financial transaction capabilities.

What is immediately striking about the language of the scenario is the tendency toward confusion between master and avatar. Which of these is Moses? He is said to be in his virtual living space, which would seem to indicate that the avatar is the referent, and yet his (Moses's) avatar is also referred to as having been created with a kit, as having been purchased, etc., leading one to believe that Moses is the master. The confusion in this passage is not unique, and in fact the blurring is probably quite deliberate. One's avatar *is* one's self in interactive virtual reality. By means of it, one may lounge about one's virtual house (with one's intelligent, virtual pet), go shopping in a virtual mall, entertain virtual friends (who are the avatars of other real people), and go on virtual dates.

It is important to the authors that interactivity be experienced by an avatar much as a master might experience it in real life:

> Moses shakes hands with Dan. To create compelling immersive virtual experiences, users and their avatars should be able to interact and have an impact on each other. They should be able to shake hands; one user should be able to tickle the other and see an automatic giggle; one user should be able to kick the other, and see the other begin to limp.

When a child plays a video game, he or she is often no more invested in his character than a chess player is in any individual piece on the board. The characters serve as means to the end of winning the game, but one could not be said to be overly identified with them. In contrast, the relation between an avatar and its master seems to be extraordinarily tight. Unlike the video game character, the avatar appears to carry a piece of the master with it in cyberspace; it reflects his or her individuality, his or her human uniqueness. Like any personal creation, a master feels protective of it, and feels emotional pain if it is criticized. But more than that, an avatar experiences *for* a master; it is that prosthesis through which the master feels his or her way through a world he or she cannot physically enter, and feels emotionally the presence of others, a presence entirely mediated through, and therefore entirely dependent upon, the identity of his or her avatar.

The Universal Avatar Project wishes to respect the sensitivity of this bond between avatars and their masters:

> A intelligent virtual conversation ensues. Since the system allows for a variety of delay-mitigation strategies, a delay-mitigated virtual conversation between the three could be performed. When Nina talks, even though Dan and Moses won't hear the digitized voice for half a second and be able to respond for three seconds, both of their avatars can lean forward and provide visual backchannel encouragement for Nina's communication, to provide a seamless virtual conversation.

Why should it be important that this intelligent virtual conversation appear seamless? A failure to respond gesturally by an avatar could trigger an unpleasant association with a situation in real life, in which a misplaced gesture or a faux pas creates a misunderstanding, causing feelings to be hurt, or a pall of discomfort to fall over the group. If something similar happens in a virtual conversation, do the participants feel shame?

One last situation: Maclen and Kate have gone on a virtual date to a virtual amusement park. After a fun-filled day in which they fight the Borg in a Star

Trek immersive game, "Maclen runs his custom Java applet for a kissing animation, and Kate responds with stars spinning, fireworks and bells." That's how Kate responds, but how does *Kate* respond?

The question, put most generally, is: what do masters feel when avatars kiss, or are tickled, or are put down while engaging in intelligent conversation? What is at stake when we talk of rights, rules, and conventions for avatars? And finally, does it undermine the apparent immediacy of the body to discover that one could feel viscerally a slight to one's avatar—a racial slur, for instance—that one could have a sexual experience on-line, or that one could feel the touch of another being through an avatar's virtual skin?

The body of an avatar is produced through programming, which is in turn informed by cultural values and expectations, institutional regulations, the limits of certain languages, images and sensations, and all the desires involved in and invoked by all the above. The human body, on the other hand, is endowed with a real physicality that ostensibly transcends such influences. It can be opposed to the ideality of the avatar's body, a body that can be shaped and even composed by desire. A human body, a real body, is what is given.

It is against the certainty of this distinction between the real and the virtual that Slavoj Žižek cautions in *The Indivisible Remainder*:

> One must be careful, however, to avoid various traps that lurk here. The first among them is the notion that, prior to the computer generated virtualization of reality, we were dealing with direct, 'real' reality: the experience of virtual reality should, rather, make us sensitive to how the reality with which we were dealing *always-already was* virtualized. The most elementary procedure of symbolic identification, identification with an Ego Ideal, involves—as Lacan had already put it in the 1950s, apropos of his famous schema of the 'inverted vase'—an identification with a 'virtual image [*l'image virtuelle*]': the place in the big Other from which I see myself in the form in which I find myself likeable (the definition of Ego Ideal) is by definition virtual.[3]

If normal, physical, nonvirtual reality was somehow always-already virtualized, this could explain how a human body could feel the pain of an insult, or even that of a "physical" attack, to its avatar: harsh words in real life can hurt one physically; one does feel viscerally a racial slur, or the words "I don't love you any more." But if these words do not in fact impact the body in a material way, they must be affecting it through some mediated form, a sense of self that is both "virtual"—in this case, made of meaning, susceptible to language—and physical.[4] This sense of self, or image of self, which has the capacity to represent the individual's body in the world of meaning, is what Lacan and Freud called an "ideal ego," that "virtual image" described by Žižek as depending for its construction on the identification with an "ego ideal." I will come back to the nature of this relation in the third section of this chapter. For the moment, I merely stipulate that there is such a thing as a virtual self that pre-exists its creation in cyberspace, or at least something like it. The next question, then, is: How is this virtual self, this human avatar, constructed? And by whom? I suggest that the current enthusiasm over the philosophical concept of *performativity*, particularly in the politically charged gender epistemology of Judith Butler, is provoked precisely by its insight into the construction of human avatars.

PERFORMATIVITY

The term performativity, in Judith Butler's articulation of it, describes a process by which a body is endowed with a certain form. Perhaps the most fundamental form the human body assumes is the distinction between male and female. Common sense dictates that a human body is either a male body or a female body (with the various other genetic possibilities, such as the numerous types of hermaphroditism that have been identified, usually discarded as anomalies). This distinction is taken to be fundamental, unalterable (notwithstanding the "perverse" use of medical technology to surgically alter the body), and in many senses determinant of what kind of human being one is, in that men and women may be said to be different in ways that are thought to be statistically verifiable (men are, on average, stronger than women, etc.). Butler's claim is that such thinking, recognizable in traditional as well as not-so-traditional thinkers, depends on a series of demonstrable errors. Even feminist thought has often left alone the ontological distinction of sex, seeking instead to problematize the culturally inflected, non-value-neutral categories of gender. According to this doxa, gender exists in the cultural realm, where it is subject to the vagaries of time and cultural difference; men's and women's bodies may have certain constant physical attributes that are always associated with them, but the roles men and women play, the skills and responsibilities expected of them, anything that enters into their social being, are all to be seen as aspects of gender, which is not essential to the human being but is constructed or imposed by society.

Rather than "deconstructing" the binary opposition of *gender* roles, revealing them to be mutually dependent, and disrupting the supposedly natural distinctions between the two, Butler's basic trope in *Gender Troubles* was to deconstruct the perhaps now more fundamental, and mostly unquestioned, binary of *gender and sex*. Humans, according to her argument, do not have immediate access to things in the world, but rather approach that world and everything in it via a host of filters, webs of meaning, cascades of images and expectations, none of which are innocent at any point in one's life. One's assigned sex is only *meaningful* as gleaned through this multiplicity of filters, and therefore, by the time one encounters "sex," or tries to say anything about it, that encounter is already the result of gender. Gender, in a logical if not chronological sense, *precedes* sex.

If gender can be said to precede sex, that is because, in fact, the language bearing the cultural categories of gender is never purely *constative*, a sort of language that merely describes an object or a situation; rather, that language is *performative*, in that it produces the reality it claims to describe (much as a priest's words "I hereby pronounce you man and wife" do not, as they would appear to grammatically, merely describe the priest's own act of pronouncing, but rather actually perform the work of creating a married couple out of two single individuals, to use one of Austin's famous examples). If the language of gender is performative, then it does not describe the neutral, physical reality of sexual difference; it produces it.[5]

Butler is clear, however, that the concept of performativity she is developing depends for its functioning on far more than the use of language. Humans *actively* become their sex by *enacting* gender:

> In other words, acts, gestures, and desire produce the effect of an internal core or substance, but produce this on the surface of the body, through the play of signifying absences that suggest, but never reveal, the organizing principle of identity as a cause. Such acts, gestures, enactments, generally construed, are performative in the sense that the essence or identity that they otherwise purport to express are fabrications manufactured and sustained through corporeal signs and other discursive means. That the gendered body is performative suggests that it has no ontological status apart from the various acts which constitute its reality.[6]

The gendered actions that are performed are performed within the social and cultural realm of meaning; they are intended to "express" a sense of "masculinity" or "femininity" to the real world, an expression by which the performer tries to prove he is a "real man" or she is a "real woman." But the "reality" of the sexual identity that the performer is trying to establish beyond a doubt is actually created by the innumerable performances of others who, like him or her, are trying to establish the same proof. If this is the case, then the gendered body, the real physical sex of the body, has no ontological status—or, to put it in stronger terms, the body, as a sexed thing, as a real support for the cultural veneer of gender roles, cannot be said properly to exist, because the object we call sex is "always already" presented or revealed by the categories of gender.

Apparently, even in some circles from which Butler might have expected more support, this claim did not go over too well. As she recounts in the preface to her next book, *Bodies that Matter*, after the publication of *Gender Trouble* she was continually beset by colleagues expressing concern over her failure to take into account the "materiality of the body."[7] Here we are again confronted with the "commonsensical" opposition to the idea that selves can be, in some sense, virtual: that is all fine and well, goes the normal response, but what about the materiality of the body? Well, the body is material, and that material is still there. To claim that gender performs sex and that therefore sex has no ontological status prior to gender, is definitely not the same as to say that there is no body, or that the body has no materiality. To conflate these two positions is already to assume the certainty that *Gender Trouble* was all about disrupting: the certainty that sexual difference was purely a question of ontological, pre-linguistic, physical materiality.

Bodies that Matter, then, set about to deconstruct another binarism, that between the materiality of bodies and the ideality of cultural norms and values. From the fact that the human body is a material entity it does not follow that its materiality cannot be subject to powers assumed to be ideal, or in some sense nonmaterial, such as discursive power. Butler had shown that sexual difference was subject to the performative power of gender categories, but now her critics were suggesting that there was something in the materiality of the body itself that could perhaps resist this performativity. So she responded with the notion of materialization, claiming, in effect, that if one wanted to argue that the material body had some say in sex, that was fine, but in so doing one would also have to admit that even that materiality itself was not unaffected by the performative power of gender.

The idea is that, in order for human bodies to be received as just that—human—they must, in a material way, conform to certain, often unspoken, social expectations that govern their appearance, their behavior, and the appearance and behavior of the other bodies they desire. These social expectations, or "regulatory ideals," are "materialized" insofar as bodies conform to or adopt them. "Thus, 'sex' is a regulatory ideal whose materialization is compelled, and this materialization takes place (or fails to take place) through certain highly regulated practices."[8] These regulated practices are not to be understood as occupying a superstructure outside of the absolute confines of the body, but as actually altering the body, acting materially to determine its surfaces and its being: "In this sense, what constitutes the fixity of the body, its contours, its movements, will be fully material, but materiality will be rethought as the effect of power, as power's most productive effect."[9] This power, in the form of regulatory practices, does not just perform one's sex as a category of knowledge, having to do with what one understands as one's sex, but further, and more profoundly, it performs (aspects of) the very materiality of the body as that body strives desperately to *materialize* (become existent, occupy space) before its fellows, to take a place among the living, the desirable, the human.

It should be clear from this that Butler's performativity cannot be thought of as a singular performance, even if her earlier work put a lot of stock in the subversive potential of certain *theatrical* acts (by which she means enactments prone to hyperbole[10]) or parodies, such as, most pertinently, the performance of drag. Drag is potentially subversive for Butler because, "in imitating gender, drag implicitly reveals the imitative structure of gender itself—as well as its contingency."[11] While it is often these singular acts that Butler's readers have interpreted as being the most powerful, or politically interesting, instantiations of performativity, this is precisely where one runs the risk of misunderstanding the crux of her contribution. Performativity, as a mode of imposition of bodily forms—or, as I have termed it, the process of construction of a human avatar—does not, for the most part, describe an agency-rich method of creating one's self and body to one's own specifications. Rather, performativity is a description of how bodies and selves are controlled and compelled to conform to social standards:

> Performativity is thus not a singular "act," for it is always a reiteration of a norm or a set of norms, and to the extent that it acquires an act-like status in the present, it conceals or dissimulates the conventions of which it is a repetition. Moreover, this act is not primarily theatrical; indeed, its apparent theatricality is produced to the extent that its historicity remains dissimulated (and, conversely, its theatricality gains a certain inevitability given the impossibility of a full disclosure of its historicity).[12]

If "normal" performativity appears theatrical, played out in a hyperbolic way, it is so only to the extent that we, the observers, are unaware of the history of performances that this performance repeats. And it is from this repetition of a history of performances that performativity derives its power to shape and fix bodies and selves. Each time the body in question repeats its performance, it simultaneously reiterates and reinscribes the norms dictating that performance. But what is it that compels the individual to enact those norms, and to perform and hence materialize its body in conformity with those norms?

At times Butler refers to the potential of punishment for those who fail to comply,[13] but mostly her argument rests on the claim that regulatory practices materialize bodies, such that bodies come to exist, to be recognized as human, within the horizons of a certain set of practices. Resistance, if not futile, is always circumscribed by these regulatory practices, and must ground itself from within their confines; hence the importance of such destabilizing techniques as drag. Power is defined not as the imposition of one subject's will upon that of another, but as what enables the will to arise and defines its horizons of possibility: "If power is not reduced to volition, however, and the classical liberal and existential model of freedom is refused, then power-relations can be understood, as I think they ought to be, as constraining and constituting the very possibilities of volition."[14] It is this statement which most clearly differentiates Butler's Foucauldian from her psychoanalytic tendencies: for a Foucauldian, power precedes will; for a Freudian or a Lacanian, will, or desire, can be coöpted by power, but never entirely produced.[15] It is by understanding how the individual's desires are brought into play within social interaction that we can best explain how it is that (and to what extent) our virtual selves are constructed, imposed upon us, and to what extent we may be free to define and create them ourselves.

For Butler, the particular power of performativity lies in its rehearsal or reiteration of a set of norms, or previously performed contexts. Interestingly enough, this take on performativity is derived not from the work of John Austin, who coined the term in his 1962 book, *How to Do Things with Words*, but rather from a critique and appropriation of Austin's work by Jacques Derrida. Derrida did not intend by his critique to invent a new concept of performativity, but rather to say something in general about language, namely, that it depends for its comprehensibility on what he calls iterability. He bases his claim on a series of exclusions Austin makes from his inquiry into what makes a performative utterance *felicitous*; that is, what makes it perform. I hope to be forgiven if I quote here my candidate for the most overquoted passage in contemporary philosophy, that same passage which, in Derrida's estimable hands, sparked one of the most virulent anglo-continental philosophical debates to date:

> a performative utterance will, for example, be *in a peculiar way* hollow or void if said by an actor on the stage, or if introduced in a poem, or spoken in soliloquy. This applies in a similar manner to any and every utterance—a sea change in special circumstances. Language in such circumstances is in special ways—intelligibly—used not seriously, but in ways *parasitic* upon its normal use—ways which fall under the *etiolations* of language. All of this we are *excluding* from consideration.[16]

Derrida's critical appropriation of this passage is familiar enough: namely, that in excluding these parasitic etiolations (weakenings of natural vigor) of language that are those uses considered not-serious, Austin is in fact trying to exclude from his inquiry the very instantiations in language of what is essential to its functioning. These etiolations of language—the actor's speech, the poet's verse—model the essence of language for Derrida because they demonstrate its property of iterability, or citationality. "Could a performative utterance succeed if its formulation did not repeat a 'coded' or iterable utterance, in other words if the expressions I use to open a meeting, launch a ship or a marriage were not identifiable as *conforming* to an iterable model, and therefore if they were not identifiable in some way as 'citation'?"[17] Language is always parasitic, always not-serious, because it depends on the citation of previous uses and contexts for its comprehensibility. Therefore, it appears that Butler's performativity is a hybrid of the classic definition—a usage of language that produces what it purports to describe or express—and of a separate but related concept, iterability. In Butler's reading, however, the performativity of a social construct like gender is empowered by its quality of citationality, that very quality whose presence in a linguistic situation was reason enough for Austin to exclude it (wrongly, according to Derrida) from consideration, because a performative utterance in that situation (one in which it was not taken seriously) could never work.

Derrida's reading, while in some ways quite productive, was most likely (as has been pointed out by Searle and his sympathizers ad infinitum during the course of the subsequent debate mentioned above) not a "correct" interpretation, in that it (deliberately) reads Austin's statement at a different level than it was probably intended. There is, for example, another way to understand the "peculiar way" in which these utterances become "hollow or void." Derrida's critique aims at the heart of language understood as the transmission of some autonomously *intended* message; if meaning is radically dependent on the citation of previous usage, the transmission of this pure intention appears undermined, since one must always be saying something other than what one means, and since one's listener will most always be referring to different contexts and different usages in order to make sense of one's utterance. The actor's lines, however, are also in a peculiar way hollow or void of intentional content if one removes oneself from the frame established by the stage; for certainly, Austin would admit, the actor's words would not be hollow or void to the other *character* to whom they are addressed. They would, on the contrary, be overflowing with meaning, a meaning that makes sense within the context fixed by the limits of the theatrical frame. The actor's words are only hollow and void, lacking in seriousness, if one posits that they have an ulterior purpose beyond the transmission of a certain intended meaning to that character's interlocutor. They are words and actions, that is, presented to the ears and eyes of an audience, an audience that cannot be said properly to exist within the world of the stage. And not only is the actor's *speech* undermined by this "being-for-another," the actor's *being*, or more accurately the being of his or her character, is one that exists for another, an Other, again, of whom he or she can have no knowledge.

Just as Derrida used his reading to question Austin's move to exclude such a context as an etiolation of language and to argue that such usage is, in fact, an essential aspect of spoken communication, so I would claim that this second peculiar way in which language is staged is no less essential to normal usage and, in fact, that this *theatricality* is constitutive of a particular historical form of interpersonal relations and of self-consciousness itself.

To repeat: if the actor's speech, action, and presentation of self are in some way not serious, and hence not worthy of being included in an analysis of real language, of how language works in an everyday situation, it is not merely because these words and actions are those of another; more pertinently, they are not serious because they are not directed at the character with whom his or her character is interacting, at least not exclusively. The actor's presentation of his or her character is dedicated to a gaze that is, from the perspective of the characters, disembodied. For my claim to be true—namely, that what is true of the stage is true of everyday speech and action—then speech and action in everyday life, like that on the stage, are also dedicated to, or played out for the benefit of, a disembodied gaze. When a person speaks, acts, becomes the person he or she is becoming in everyday life, he or she is guided in his or her speech and actions, in his or her gestures and clothes, in his or her likes and dislikes, by the desires he or she attributes to this gaze, a desire he or she wishes to embody. This gaze, then, and the desire it engenders, is the mechanism by which performativity in its extra-semiotic sense functions to produce, to materialize certain bodies, and, as Butler insists, to reject or make abject certain others.

To say that an individual becomes or adopts certain modes of speech and action and, eventually, even forms of being, is not the same as to say that the individual chooses these forms because they suit him or her, as in the naive idea of performativity discussed before. On the contrary, the gaze captures the individual's desire, motivates him or her to play those roles and become those selves that are most pleasing to it. The individual, in turn, learns how to play different parts at different times—learns to manipulate his or her performance within the confines of desirability as delimited by the gaze. Often he or she fails to meet its expectations, developing feelings of inadequacy, depression, worthlessness; in other cases, he or she manages to escape from its tyranny. But most of us, most of the time, become who we become under the auspices of the gaze, negotiating its demands, failing at times, succeeding at others. But almost always we are acting, playing our lives out before an audience we cannot see.

Andrew Parker and Eve Kosofsky Sedgwick, in their excellent introduction to a volume of articles dealing with the cross-pollinations existing between performance studies and the philosophical notion of performativity, draw attention to the essentially public nature of performative language, implying that it depends for its efficacy on an audience of sorts. What they emphasize, however, is the effect of this relation on the audience itself, in its role as witness to a performative statement:

> Austin's rather bland invocation of "the proper context" (in which a person's saying something is to count as doing something) has opened, under pressure of recent theory, onto a populous and contested scene in which the role of silent or implied witnesses, for example, or the quality and structuration of the bonds that unite auditors or link them to speakers, bears as much explanatory weight as do the particular speech acts of supposed individual speech agents.[18]

The idea here is that the power of the performative context runs both ways. Not only does the presence of an audience of "implied or silent witnesses" function to activate the performative function, the audience itself is imperceptibly changed. Having participated in one more repetition of a particular ritual, they engage in a subtle but ever deeper reinscription of that practice into the domain of the normal, the rational, and the natural.[19] While I accept fully the implications of this notion of reciprocal interactivity between performers and witnesses, what this notion fails to address is the extent to which the role of the gaze in the formation of the individual's avatar, bodily ego, or virtual self, functions irrespective of the actual presence of others at a performance. The gaze has become a central aspect of the psyche, and it continues to watch us even when we are completely alone.

THEATRICALITY

Given the long tradition in the West of comparing life to theater, to say that humans behave as if they were acting on a stage might not seem particularly surprising.[20] In the twentieth century, this intuition has, for example, been canonized in the sociological methodology of Erving Goffman's 1956 book *The Presentation of Self in Everyday Life*. For Goffman, when an individual enters the presence of others, he or she immediately sets about reading the situation in terms of what roles are being played and what sort of role will be expected of him or her, as well as gauging the possibilities he or she has of controlling the set of conventions that will be accepted by the group, such that it might include conventions amenable to his or her own spectrum of self presentation. Consequently, "when an individual projects a definition of the situation and thereby makes an implicit or explicit claim to be a person of a particular kind, he automatically exerts a moral demand upon the others, obliging them to value and treat him in the manner that persons of his kind have a right to expect."[21] The implication in terms of the agency of social actors is that their roles are, up to a certain point, consciously or deliberately assumed, because they take the form of a demand—more or less compelling, depending on the personality of the performers—to be acknowledged as truly being the person they present.[22]

Goffman identifies a different demand, one he calls a "moral standard," in the extent to which "the cultural values of an establishment will determine in detail how the participants are to feel about many matters and at the same time establish a framework of appearances that must be maintained, whether or not there is feeling behind the appearances."[23] The potential lack of feeling behind the performances is an instance of what he refers to as the "amoral" character of the attitude of individuals as performers—in contrast to the "moral" standards guiding the frame of appearances to be maintained—who generally

> are concerned not with the moral issues of realizing these standards, but with the amoral issue of engineering a convincing impression that these standards are being realized. . . . To use a different imagery, the very obligation and profitability of appearing always in a steady moral light, of being a socialized

character, forces us to be the sort of person who is practiced in the ways of the stage.[24]

Therefore, while Goffman describes the actors in terms that, at first glance, grant them a great deal of agency, he also recognizes an element of compulsion in the assumption of their roles, a compulsion that is not to be confused with a moral obligation to respect community standards, but rather is one that seems in contrast empty and self contained: the compulsion to maintain the illusion of the performance at all costs.

Goffman identifies at least one mechanism of this compulsion in what we might call a fear of being shamed. When a group establishes the implicit conventions of a social performance—the register the actors are meant to assume, the gestures they are permitted to make, the subjects that are acceptable for discussion—a great deal of energy is invested into maintaining a smooth and natural flow to the performance. This flow is directly dependent on the investment of each of the individuals involved in her own self-definition, which has become an integral part of the group. As Goffman says,

> [g]iven the fact that the individual effectively projects a definition of the situation when he enters the presence of others, we can assume that events may occur within the interaction which contradict, discredit, or otherwise throw doubt upon this projection. When these disruptive events occur, the interaction itself may come to a confused and embarrassed halt.[25]

A misplaced word or gesture, a glance narrowly directed but apprehended by the wrong player—any such gaffe or faux pas can bring down the opprobrium of the group on the guilty party, while the group suffers palpably from the rift caused in the fabric of its social fiction. For, in effect, the performance is all about the establishment of this fiction as a truth, the truth of the group's natural bond, its mutual and transparent comprehension.

As closely as this model fits to the idea of theatricality I am advancing, Goffman does endeavor to place distance between the terms of his analysis and a performance on an actual stage. The principal difference he stresses is, perhaps surprisingly, the lack of an audience in real life. That is to say, an audience constitutes a "third party to the interaction—one that is essential and yet, if the stage performance were real, one that would not be there. In real life, the three parties are compressed into two; the part one individual plays is tailored to the parts played by the others present, and yet these others also constitute the audience."[26] Certainly this caveat has a great deal of truth to it, and yet I have continued to insist on the presence of an audience when none is, in actual fact, present.

This aspect of being-looked-at—that it is a form of experience independent of the actual presence of others in one's vicinity—is also central for Jean-

Paul Sartre in his discussion of the problem concerning the existence of others in *Being and Nothingness*. The main concern of this book is the insurmountable chasm separating the "in-itself" [*en-soi*] of inert, objective existence, and the "for-itself" [*pour-soi*] of self-consciousness. In the course of an inquiry concerning the existence of others, Sartre raises the possibility of another mode of being as a point of mediation between these two extremes, a mode he calls "being-for-others." In this mode of being, the subject's realization of the ever-present possibility of other consciousnesses in the world makes it aware that, while existing for itself, as a being in its own world, and as the central being at that, it must also exist-for-others, as an object in another's organization of the world. The other, therefore, has access to some aspect of the subject's own being to which the subject does not, since the subject cannot know itself purely as an object, and since it has no access to the other's experience of the world and, specifically, to the other's perception of the subject. The presence of the other as subject is experienced as a gaze, or a feeling of being-looked-at, but in his account Sartre makes it clear that while the gaze is only made manifest in other individuals; it is the force of the Other as such. As he puts it, "In a word, what is certain is that I am looked-at; what is only probable is that the look is bound to this or that intra-mundane presence. Moreover there is nothing here to surprise us since as we have seen, it is never eyes which look at us; it is the Other-as-subject."[27] The fact of inhabiting a world we assume to be inhabited by other subjects, others who perceive objects and organize the space of their perception around themselves, makes us constantly aware of the possibility that we are being watched, an awareness that is all the more acute when we cannot perceive any evidence of an observer (an idea that was central to Jeremy Bentham's plans for the perfect prison, as Foucault has discussed in *Discipline and Punish*).

More than merely destabilizing what could otherwise be a solipsistic world view, however, this experience of the gaze is seen by Sartre (just as being-for-others was seen by Hegel before him) as a necessary and constitutive element in the emergence of self-consciousness.

> The problem of the Other should not be posited in terms of the cogito; on the contrary, the existence of the Other renders the cogito possible as the abstract moment when the self is apprehended as an object. Thus the "moment" which Hegel calls being for the Other is a necessary stage of the development of self-consciousness; the road of interiority passes through the Other.[28]

In other words, self-consciousness, that mode of being in which one apprehends oneself as an object, as a *res cogitans*, is not a state to which a being who is alone in the world can aspire. Rather, the being must experience the possibility that it is apprehended in the world of objects as experienced by others in order for it to be able to be conscious *of* its self as opposed to being merely a point of consciousness, apprehending the world but not itself in the world.[29] A problem arises, however, since the existence of the Other in my world, while making possible my own apprehension of myself in self-consciousness, also opens up the existence of a world, and in particular an organization of space, alien to the world I perceive, but which nevertheless is the same world as the one I perceive (if I am not to lapse into solipsism) and, to make matters worse, a world in which I am included.

When I encounter another (person) in my universe of objects, it is not only as an object but as "an element of disintegration in that universe," a disintegration of my space, a space defined by my grouping of the objects in my universe. When an other appears in that space, "there is a regrouping in which I take part but which escapes me, a regrouping of all the objects which people my universe."[30] The Other, that is, the existence of others in general, is therefore not merely experienced as "the absence of a consciousness in relation to the body which I see" but as "the absence of the world which I perceive, an absence discovered at the very heart of my perception of the world."[31] The gaze, then, not only intervenes in a formative way in my relation to my self, in my self-consciousness, it actively disengages me from the space I inhabit as *my* space, an ordering of things *for* me; it forces upon this space an intermediary role, an abstractness foreign to things that exist only for me. I and the objects around me, including other people with whom I interact, are always interacting in a space that exceeds us and precedes us, in that its organizational unity derives from the Other's gaze.

This Other, whose gaze organizes the space I inhabit, does not exist within this space; it is necessarily excluded in order for that space to attain its own, apparently objective, coherence. To the extent the Other is shown to exist, this can only take place at the expense of "reality" itself, just as the recognition of the audience as real (and not just another character written into the play) must perforce disrupt the fantasy world of the play being enacted for its pleasure. Like the audience is for a character on a stage, the Other is, for Sartre,

> the being toward whom I do not turn my attention. He is the one who looks at me and at whom I am not yet looking, the one who delivers me to myself as unrevealed but without revealing himself, the one who is present to me as directing at me but never as the object of my direction; he is the concrete pole (though out of reach) of my flight, of the alienation of my possibilities, and of the flow of the world toward another world which is the same world and yet lacks all communication with it. But he can not be distinct from this same alienation and flow; he is the meaning and direction of them; he haunts the flow not as a real or categorical element but as a presence which is fixed and made part of the world if I attempt to "make-it-present" and which is never more present, more urgent than when I am not aware of it.[32]

The last few words are the most telling: the Other is the meaning and direction of my alienation as a character, and of the flow of the story I am living out; he is neither real nor categorical, yet he haunts the flow of my existence; and while I can fix him and make him a part of the world (as God, an icon to be worshipped, a leader), his presence is most powerfully invoked precisely when I am not aware of it. The point of emphasizing this homology between the Other and the audience's meaning for a character on the stage is not merely to find another way of explaining a complex philosophical concept, but rather to claim for this relation a very real, very historical connection, a connection that becomes clear in Lacan's rearticulation of the gaze in psychoanalytic terms.

It is important that Sartre's analysis of the phenomenon of being-for-others is predominantly scopic, having to do with the "gaze" of the Other (in general) as manifested in the eyes of others. Lacan, teaching his seminar during the same time period that Sartre is working on *Being and Nothingness*, develops a schema of subjectivity in which a similar notion of the gaze plays a central role, and it is in his teaching that the most deliberate connection is made between the gaze and the object or cause of desire.

Lacan's schema involves the appropriation of several Freudian concepts concerning the relation of the human self to the social, particularly those of the *ideal ego* and the *ego-ideal*. Central to Freudian thought is the notion that the ego, that sense of self we refer to when we say I, is not a primordial, simple, immanent point of experience of the word, but rather is to be understood as an object, if one of the first and most privileged objects.[33] At the beginning of its existence, as it begins to distinguish its body from its environment and from the body of its mother, the child invests (cathects) the sensory "image" of its body with libidinal energy, it enjoys its own body, revels in it. Upon entering the world of meaning and suffering the first prohibitions that come from interaction with other subjects and their desires, the infant develops an ego-ideal, whose function is to serve as a model of identification for the infant, in accordance with the desires and expectations of the others with whom it must live.[34] This ego-ideal is, as we have already seen with Žižek, defined by Lacan in optical language as that perspective from which subject sees itself as lovable. The ideal ego is then produced as a third moment, an image mediated by the ego-ideal, representing for the infant the possibility (unattainable except in extreme cases of megalomania) of an enjoyment-in-self of the kind it now imagines it once had.[35]

It is certainly commonplace to notice the affinity between this model of selfhood and a theatrical stage; indeed, this and the fact that Freud often derives central tenets from great works of drama in the western tradition has led some commentators to criticize Freud's theories as generalizing from not only a historically and culturally specific series of observations, but from a specific form of cultural expression as well.[36] My claim does not contradict this tack, but rather locates in this specificity the great strength of Freud's contribution. Freud's model of the self issues from a moment of crisis of a certain historical mode of subjectivity, one whose principal element is precisely its *theatricality*. Lacan's radicalization of Freud's thought does nothing if it does not make even more explicit the theatrical nature of the Freudian subject.

The core of Lacan's theory is the dictum that the subject is split, and that this split is what constitutes the subject in the most radical sense. The subject is the site of the split between being and meaning, between seeing and being looked at, between the act of enunciation and the statement uttered, etc. The founding metaphor of this split is the difference between actor and character. Just as the actor becomes a character for the gaze of a certain audience, an audience that cannot be said to exist from the perspective of the character itself, so does the subject become an ego, a self, for an audience that cannot be said to exist at the level of the articulation of that self. The subject builds its ego under the auspices of the Other's gaze, in that very space that Sartre described as alienated from the subject, and that Lacan calls, in fact, the "space of the Other" and has been referred to as "the other stage" (*l'autre scène*), but that we might name as well "the space of the stage":

> You will then see that it is in the Other that the subject is constituted as ideal, that he has to regulate the completion of what comes as ego, or ideal ego—which is not the ego-ideal—that is to say, to constitute himself in his imaginary reality. This schema makes clear . . . that where the subject sees himself, namely, where the real, inverted image of his own body that is given in the schema of the ego is forged, it is not from there that he looks at himself.
>
> But, certainly, it is in the space of the Other that he sees himself and the point from which he looks at himself is also in that space. Now, this is also the point from which he speaks, since in so far as he speaks, it is in the locus of the Other that he begins to constitute that truthful lie by which is initiated that which participates in desire at the level of the unconscious.[37]

The schema to which Lacan refers is the famous, and famously obscure, "diagram of the inverted vase" familiar to most from its inclusion in Seminar XI. This diagram, which appears on one page of the eleventh seminar and even there is barely explained, was the subject of some one hundred pages of analysis in the seminar of ten years earlier, Seminar I, on *Freud's Papers on Technique*.[38]

The point of the diagram and this lengthy, detailed, and exceedingly clear exposition was to develop a way of thinking about the ego as a scopic phenomenon, an elaboration of Lacan's famous mirror-stage theory developed in the late 1940s. In the diagram, Lacan reproduces a parlor trick cum experiment in optics in which an observer can be made to see a vase with some flowers in a mirror where such an object, at least so arranged, does not in fact exist. What exists, on the side of the observer's body, is something else: a box, with the back side open, and a vase suspended upside down inside it. On top of the box, rightside up, are the flowers, but without a vase. Behind the box, about where the observer should be standing, there is a concave mirror. In front of the vase, and in the observer's line of sight, a flat mirror. If the observer is correctly positioned within the cone of light emanating from the concave mirror and converging on his or her visual cortex, he or she will see, reflected in the flat mirror, a virtual vase containing an equally virtual bouquet. The scenario is Lacan's metaphor for the constitution of the ideal ego. This image (the vase) attains its coherence in a virtual world, what Lacan calls the space of the Other. It is where the Other sees us, and where we see ourselves as seen by the Other. It is, as Žižek notes in the passage with which I began this chapter, a virtual space.

But it is not only a space where we are seen and where we see ourselves as seen, it is also the space in which and from which we speak, since, as Lacan says, "it is in the locus of the Other that [the subject] begins to constitute that truthful lie by which is initiated that which participates in desire at the level of the unconscious." The truthful lie is the utterance that the analysand speaks to the analyst, somewhere off behind him or her, an utterance that has the structure of a liar's paradox, an *I am lying*. How is it that a subject can, in fact, utter the words *I am lying*, without balking at the paradox that emerges from a too intensely logical analysis? Well, think of an actor saying the lines. The same logic that allows us to separate the I of the character from the I of the actor releases us from the obligatory absurdity of such a phrase. The same logic, according to Lacan, lies at the heart of the Cartesian subject, that form of subjectivity, as he says again and again, that forms the basis of Freud's discovery. The *I* of the statement *I think* seeks in vain to establish, to permanently fix the *I* of its enunciation, the *I* of its being; one of the ways it tries to convince itself that this being has been attained is through the fantasy it plays out in the space of the other.[39]

It is also truthful, this statement, this lie, in that it is in this very act of enunciation that the actor reveals the fundamental discrepancies between the *I* of the statement that is the *I* of the story being told to the audience, and the *I* of the enunciation, the *I* whom the character's I is trying to establish as its own, as the certainty of its own truth. This level of truth, the truth that the character wishes to establish (just like the performer in Goffman's social situations) exists at the level of the actions and words that are exchanged on the stage of the Other, scripted actions and scripted words. This script is another word for what psychoanalysis calls fantasy, the mechanism with which a subject structures its reality in such a way as to cover over the incommensurability between the ego-ideal and the ideal ego, between the models it learns to identify with and the imaginary self it tries to construct. This fantasy is what the subject plays out for the benefit of the gaze of the Other, a gaze that holds the promise of the subject's true being, if only the subject could have access to it.

The tensions that develop between the various scriptings, between the ideals adopted and the possibilities of enacting those ideals, are the core of the problems clinical psychoanalysis seeks to treat. However, how it goes about treating them is more complicated. The analytic situation is intended to bring about a state known as transference, in preparation for the intervention, or interpretation, of the analyst. Lacan calls the transference the moment of closure of the unconscious, an unconscious that should not be thought of as a thing, or a place, but rather as an event: any of the slips, gaffes (mistakes in staging) that reveal the tensions underlying the subject's presentation of self. The transference is an enactment, Lacan says, of the reality of the unconscious, of its ephemeral eventness, of its pulsation. It is a repetition, which could also be understood in the French sense of a rehearsal, of that fundamental fantasy that makes the subject's performance believable to itself, that covers up the distance between the speaker and the words spoken, the body and the image it strives to represent. The gaze of the Other becomes the object and origin of the subject's desire when it is posited as that unattainable perspective from which the ultimate truth of my fantasy, of my performance, will be verified, and in that sense it fills in, shuts down the apertures, the disruptive events of the unconscious. The transference is only an enactment of the truth of the unconscious insofar as it is an enactment of its opposite, an enactment or repetition of that fantasy connecting what I am for others with what I am for myself, what Sartre refers to as bad faith and Žižek as the function of ideology. From the character's viewpoint, however, the analysis is the wrong moment to go into this mode, because just as the character/analysand gets into the telling of its story for the benefit of the disembodied gaze, that gaze suddenly becomes embodied; the analyst speaks, or coughs, or makes some apparently significant sound that disrupts the flow of the fantasy scenario and makes the analysand (suddenly stripped of her character) aware of the analyst's *presence*.

In his seminar (I) of 1953–54, Lacan describes this experience in the following terms:[40]

> In extracting it from my experience, I told you just now that at the most sensitive and, it seems to me, significant point of the phenomenon (the transference), the subject experiences it as an abrupt perception of something which isn't very easy to define—presence.
>
> It isn't a feeling we have all the time. To be sure, we are influenced by all sorts of presences, and our world only possesses its consistency, its density, its lived stability, because, in some way, we take account of these presences, but we do not realize them as such. You really can sense that it is a feeling which I'd say we are always trying to efface from life. It wouldn't be easy to live if, at every moment, we had the feeling of presence, with all the mystery that that implies. It is a mystery from which we distance ourselves, and to which we are, in a word, inured.[41]

In his later teachings and writing, Lacan will connect (if perhaps only implicitly) this element from his own analytic experience with a concept from Freud's teaching, that of *Trieb*, which Lacan translates not as instinct, but as *pulsion*, or drive. In this later work, drive is always opposed to desire, always on the side of the body and the real, as opposed to that of meaning, the Law, language, the Other.[42] The end of analysis is at this time described as a traversal or piercing of the fantasy through to the realm of pure drive.

I am not going to suggest at this point any explicit definition of what the experience of pure drive may in fact be (it is definitely not some sort of pre-cultural, animal engagement with the physical world, uncorrupted by contact with meaning). Rather, I am interested in the notion of drive or the experience of presence as it is articulated in opposition to the theatrical schema I have described as the normative, modern mode of being, a mode of being with which psychoanalysis tries to contend by endeavoring to repair its inconsistencies (in pre-Lacanian practice), or by shooting the whole thing to hell (to put it in terms appropriate to the violence of Lacanian practice). In this sense, drive and presence are related analogically, in that the experience of drive is to the experience of desire as the spatiality I call presence is related to that of theatricality. While the latter terms are mediations that incorporate and build on the former terms, this does not imply that the former terms refer to *immediate* realities, but rather to prior forms of mediation. Nevertheless, drive and presence retain a performative power for the realms of desire and theatricality, in that their relative atavism *vis à vis* these later forms of mediation tends to disrupt the experience of normalcy the later forms support: just as drive is positioned at the dis-rupture of desire in the analytic relation, presence is concealed everywhere in theatrical spatiality, and retains therein some of the mystical, religious, and magical power that was the norm of the world organized according to its mandates. To the same extent, the normal workings of both desire and theatricality depend on their incorporation of drive and presence: with desire we seek the directness of a contact with the world that we believe we have lost with the primary repression of our drives; in theatricality we search endlessly for the little pieces of the real that constitute our only experience of presence.

The implication of the last quote from Lacan's early writing is that in our existence as characters on the stage of the Other, in addition to being attracted to the promise of presence, there is a sense in which we are also constantly trying to efface it from life, and in which it presents to us a mystery to which we are, to a greater or lesser extent, inured. When the analyst helps to produce a situation in which the theatricality of the analysand's being is disrupted, this other form of being, this other mode of experience, is attested to, whether as something that helped cause the rupture, or as the state that temporarily results from it. One contention of this book is that this other mode of being, called by Lacan the experience of presence, exists in opposition to the theatrical mode of being still dominant in the West. Most of the ways in which individuals interact with one another and with the institutions forming the basic structures of our societies are dependent on this theatricality, from our systems of political representation and social control to our experiences of aesthetic enjoyment to our interpersonal relations. My other contention, however, is that this has not always been (nor is it everywhere) the case. The theatricality of being is a historical mode of being, and like all things historical, it had a beginning and it may have an end.

One of the great innovations of Lacan's work was to recognize the historical nature of the subjectivity he was describing (which is not to engage in the usual universalist/historicist debate, since to say that something is historical is not to deny that one or any aspect of it may also be universally, or generally, valid). In fact, it is surprising how often this fact is overlooked by both intellectual allies (seeking in Lacan's work a weapon in the battle against historicism) and foes (trying to scuttle Lacanian thought as yet another example of the unexamined imposition of western ideas on Other times and Other people). In her book *The Threshold of the Visible World*, for example, we have the case of an ostensible disciple of Lacan, Kaja Silverman, claiming that Lacan fails to historicize his concept of the gaze, and making that claim by way of a reading of his most historically conscious text, Seminar XI, *The Four Fundamental Concepts of Psychoanalysis*.

In her book, Silverman advances a perfectly acceptable argument about the historically specific nature of Lacan's description of the gaze in terms of the history of the camera, pointing out that Lacan's own language in his discussion of optics is steeped in the imagery of photography. She adds, however, despite some clues to the contrary—for instance, his emphasis on the etymology of "photo-graphed," to be drawn with light—that he fails utterly to place the concept in its proper historical context:

> He associates the gaze not with values specific to the last century and a half, but rather with illumination and 'the presence of others as such' (91, 84). Within the context of *Four Fundamental Concepts*, the gaze would thus seem to be as old as sociality itself. Even in his deployment of the photographic metaphor, Lacan resists historical periodization.[43]

Perhaps most surprising in this passage is Silverman's expectation that Lacan, in describing a phenomenon from his clinical experience, *should* make an effort to historicize it, and that further he should choose to historicize it in the method and period that she has chosen to focus on. Indeed, exceeding the terms of a purely academic squabble, Silverman goes on to claim that this oversight actually renders "untenable" his "elaboration of the field of vision."[44] As a cultural historian working in a different period than she is, I find her choice of the mid-nineteenth century as the appropriate starting point for the period of the gaze somewhat puzzling. However illuminating it might be to link Lacan's description of this phenomenon with the discovery and popularization of the camera, it is a logical fallacy to thereby draw the conclusion that the entire theory is invalid (and consequently ready to be replaced by one's own).

Furthermore, the claim that Lacan fails to historicize his model is patently false; he merely fails to place it within the same historical parameters that Silverman describes (which might suggest that he is not describing the same thing). Lacan speaks about the "privilege of the gaze in the function of desire," and says that we can apprehend it

> by pouring ourselves, as it were, along the veins through which the domain of vision has been integrated into the field of desire.
> It is not for nothing that it was at the very period when the Cartesian meditation inaugurated in all its purity the function of the subject that the dimension of optics that I shall distinguish here by calling 'geometral' or 'flat' (as opposed to perspective) optics was developed.[45]

This privilege of the gaze in the field of desire, then, far from being "as old as sociality itself," appeared at a very specific moment in *intellectual* history for Lacan. The Cartesian subject, the form of subjectivity on which Freud's innovations are based and for which they are valid, was inaugurated at the same time as the development in science and painting of "geometral" optics. This period—which spans the century previous to that of Descartes—saw the development of techniques of pictorial representation that Lacan adduces as evidence of a new and different form of subject, a subject who is concerned with, even entranced by, the relation of itself to the world it sees represented on a canvas: "For us, the geometral dimension enables us to glimpse how the subject who concerns us is caught, manipulated, captured, in the field of vision."[46] In this passage and others, he explicitly associates the gaze with a kind of representation that precedes the invention of the camera and even of the camera obscura, a form of representation that suggests to the looker, even as she looks, that she is being looked at.

It should be clear, then, that the subject of psychoanalysis is for Lacan a historically specific subject, one described in the intellectual tradition by Descartes and manifested in cultural history by the development of new methods of visual representation. Understanding this historically specific formation is important to psychoanalysis because it aids the psychoanalyst's primary purpose: to understand, and hence to be better able to intervene in, the organization of individual subjective experience in the here and now. As I argue in chapter 4, however, the vocabulary of subjectivity, while useful in the highly focused discipline of psychoanalysis, suffers from a debilitating vagueness when an attempt is made to appropriate it for the explanation of wide-ranging historical and cultural change. If Lacan was attuned to traces in cultural and intellectual history of the development of a new kind of subjective formation, a formation of particular relevance to the practice he was developing in the wake of Freud, this does not necessarily imply that the vocabulary used to describe this formation is adequate or appropriate to describe changes—even changes occurring at approximately the same time—in philosophy, political organization, and aesthetic practice. Rather, the change in the coordinates of a psychoanalytic subjectivity are indicative of a change of another kind, a change I have described as phenomenological.

This chapter has been concerned with describing a model of self—indebted to psychoanalysis and practically ubiquitous in contemporary critical discourses—a self that is simultaneously virtual and corporeal: virtual in that it exists in a virtual space completely separate from the space occupied by the human body; and corporeal because the images and representations portrayed in this virtual space are so tightly wired to the feelings, desires, and motivations that emanate from and affect the human body. The analysis of human ego and of how this ego functions socially, aesthetically, politically, and philosophically is, therefore, ultimately dependent on the analysis of the virtual space it inhabits. The remainder of this book is dedicated to describing the historical emergence of this space, the space of theatricality, from the perspective of a particular cultural formation—the modern theater. However, in order to understand the space of theatricality, it is necessary to begin with a description of the space from which it emerged and against which it can be understood: the space typical of medieval practices of spectacle, the space of presence. This is the task of the next chapter.

CHAPTER 2

Real Presence, Sympathetic Magic, and the Power of Gesture

The European Middle Ages did not know theater. They knew something else, other forms of spectacle, of ritual, of games, of ceremony, and of entertainment; but the tendency to call these phenomena *theater* responds to a genealogical desire, a desire to know the origins of that modern form of spectacle whose organization of space has so dominated western visual practices from the moment of its flourishing in the sixteenth century to the present.[1] The result of this desire has been to elide differences, to impose on the past an alien figure and, in so doing, to neglect the opportunity to explore another mode of being, a different way of inhabiting the world.[2]

I am aware that, with these statements, it may appear I am continuing the—for some—perfidious tradition of the myth of medieval exceptionalism. That myth and the reactions it has provoked are perhaps best expressed in a deservedly famous essay from 1990 by the medievalist Lee Patterson, in which he attacked the "*grand récit*" endemic to western cultural history that idolizes the Renaissance as the vital source of the present's self-knowledge because it perceives that era as the historical moment marking the birth of the modern, while summarily rejecting everything medieval as premodern:

> According to this universal scheme, the Renaissance is the point at which the modern world begins: humanism, nationalism, the proliferation of competing value systems, the secure grasp of historical consciousness, aesthetic production as an end in itself, the conception of the natural world as a site of scientific investigation and colonial exploitation, the secularization of politics, the idea of the state, and, perhaps above all, the emergence of the idea of the individual—all of these characteristics and many others are thought both to set the Renaissance apart from the Middle Ages and to align it definitively with the modern world.[3]

In support of this claim, Patterson argues convincingly that even those recent methods and practitioners of cultural and intellectual history that purport to return to history and allow the past to speak for itself—for example, Foucault, Stephen Greenblatt and the "new historicism"—are guilty of reducing the

Middle Ages to a caricature in order to prove some point, a point inevitably having to do with the newness of the sixteenth or seventeenth century and its pertinence to modern life.

Indeed, such an attitude toward the Middle Ages did color scholarly conceptions of the history of the theater, particularly scholarship in the twentieth century, which had been working more or less complacently under the shadow of E. K. Chambers' monumental *Mediaeval Stage* ever since its publication in 1903.[4] In fact, Chambers states explicitly at the outset that the principal motivation for his *chef d'oeuvre* was to prepare the ground for a "little book" about Shakespeare,[5] the magnificent novelty of whose "magic stage" could not be fully grasped without this introductory work: "It is the object of the present book briefly to record the rise, also in the fifteenth century, of new dramatic conditions, which, after existing side by side with those of medievalism, were destined ultimately to become a substitute for them and to lead up to the magic stage of Shakespeare."[6] Nevertheless, Chambers' sin in this instance would seem to have been not so much that he posits a rupture between the medieval and the Renaissance forms of theater, but that he so completely subsumes the importance of the former into explicating and even advancing the further glory of the latter. This, of course, is precisely the attitude to which Patterson so strongly objects. No one, he says, "wants to deny that change of a major order took place in Europe between 1300 and 1600. . . . But what needs to be challenged is the crude binarism that locates modernity ('us') on the one side and premodernity ('them') on the other, thus condemning the Middle Ages to the role of all-purpose alternative."[7] However, while Patterson claims to value the notion that the Middle Ages and the Renaissance do indeed differ in some fundamental way, in his enthusiasm to identify any and all cases of the "crude binarism" he so rightly deplores, he seems ready to discard any distinction one might posit by means of the "we have that too" ploy, a game of intellectual one-upmanship that smacks of *ressentiment*. For example, with regard to the principal common denominator of most contemporary attempts to define this difference, the notion of modern "subjectivity," Patterson claims that, had they bothered to look, historians "could have found plenty of relevant medieval material. After all, the dialectic between an inward subjectivity and an external world that alienates it from both itself and its divine source provides the fundamental economy of the medieval idea of selfhood."[8] In other words, just as evidence can be presented in a way that over-emphasizes the difference between two cultures or periods, almost the same evidence can be presented so as to overemphasize their similarity—depending, of course, on the historian's agenda in the matter.[9] In either case, one is left facing two equally unsavory options: either the medieval drama is continuous with the Renaissance, and therefore merely a predecessor of its aesthetic achievements, or it is different, and the Middle Ages are reaffirmed in their marginality.

Nevertheless, most scholars still hold to the notion that, as Patterson concedes, a great change did take place between 1300 and 1600, and whereas this change has been problematized and nuanced in many areas, it remains almost completely unchallenged with regard to the history of theater.[10] It is not at all clear, however, that all those upholding this difference relate toward the artifacts of medieval culture in the way that Chambers did. Medievalists such as Hans Ulrich Gumbrecht and Paul Zumthor would seem, in fact, to have reversed the binarism of medieval exceptionalism, finding in medieval culture phenomena of enormous complexity and beguiling fascination.[11] In the pages that follow, I too will be arguing in favor of a difference, in that my descriptions of spectacles during the medieval period are organized around the pivot of what I call *presence*, a concept whose nature will emerge gradually from these descriptions. The various forms of spectacle that are organized according to this principle of presence also gradually, but especially in the sixteenth century, start to exhibit another organizing principle, theatricality, in affinity with altered conceptions of knowledge and ways of exercising political power; presence is not replaced in the modern period, but its effects are transfigured, displaced, and reincorporated in different but equally powerful forms.

If most scholars of the medieval stage have agreed on the uniqueness of their object of study from other and specifically later forms of spectacle, they have not achieved any consensus concerning the origins and ultimate nature of medieval spectacle itself. Broadly speaking, the history of medieval scholarship in the twentieth century has bifurcated into two opposing camps: those who propose a single origin for the European stage in the liturgical and semi-liturgical drama of the Middle Ages; and those who posit some complexification of that story, such as Chambers' hypothesis of a fundamental conflict between the Church and the "dramatic instinct" of the folk, or Wyckham's hypothesis of two separate religious origins, the theater of Christ's divinity and that of his humanity, or Enders' thesis of the origins of drama in legal rhetoric.[12] But in many respects, even these views are not so opposed as they would seem. While Chambers argues fervently that the Church waged a constant war against dramatic representation, even he admits that despite this antagonism, the canonical dramatic form emerged principally from religious productions. More recent work, such as that of Hardison, revises that view only to insist on the primordial position of the vernacular religious drama in relation to the Latin liturgical drama.[13] Gustave Cohen argues in favor of a "dramatic instinct" à la Chambers, but insists that all drama has its origin in religious sentiment and that all religion expresses itself spontaneously in dramatic form.[14] What all these theses have in common is the assumption that whatever the exact origins of the loose agglomeration of types of spectacle emerging in the late Middle Ages, it is not the slightest bit problematic to refer to them as dramatic, if by that term one means having something essential to do with theater as it is understood in its modern sense. As we have seen, even those who posit a qualitative break between medieval and Renaissance theater still believe they are telling a story of the origins of the latter; as Gustave Cohen puts it, "*Natura humana no facit saltus*,"[15] there is no such thing as discontinuity in human nature. While I would agree with such a statement in my conviction (against Foucault's earlier work) that most epistemic change occurs gradually rather than by sudden rupture, my intuition is that to approach medieval theater with the tools of aesthetic criticism bequeathed by the Renaissance and its subsequent history of theater is to risk misunderstanding the phenomenon of medieval spectacle completely; spectacle in the Middle Ages, whether religious or secular, relates to a different organizing principle from the theater that has become the model of the modern stage. The logic of religious and secular spectacle in the Middle Ages is essentially the same, that of a performative repetition intended to invoke, conjure, or make present some event.[16] The mode of being that generates and depends upon this relation between bodies and what they encounter carries with it a distinct experience of space and of causality, and to grasp the nature of this experience we need to examine phenomena that, at first glance, may have no obvious relation to the theater: sympathetic magic and the doctrine of the Real Presence. The present chapter seeks to clarify this relation by describing what can be called a "magical worldview" in terms of a specific experience of space and causality, and by positing that the various phenomena grouped together under the category of medieval theater—principally religious drama and courtly and street spectacle—need to be understood in light of this worldview.[17]

MAGIC

As Hardison points out in his review of the scholarship of medieval theater, the great histories—Chambers', and consequently Young's—were written in the heyday of evolutionary ethnography, as exemplified in the work of Sir James Frazer, whose *Golden Bough, a Study in Magic and Religion* had been published in 1890.[18] In fact, Frazer's thesis of the common roots of magic and religion in a "mimetic instinct" natural to humans formed the basis of Chambers' own theory of the origins of medieval theater in the mimetic or "dramatic" instinct of folk drama, which he associates with pagan rituals constantly under threat of expurgation by the Church.[19] In his exposition and explanation of certain folk rituals, Chambers refers explicitly to Frazer's notion of the "expulsion of death," describing how an effigy of death is constructed of straw or wood, "treated with marks of fear, hatred or contempt, and is finally carried in procession, and thrust over the boundary of the village."[20] This and similar forms of ritual, such as the seasonal miming of the clash between winter and summer,[21] are examples of the sort of ritual from which Frazer derived his notions of mimetic instinct and sympathetic magic.[22]

In *The Golden Bough*, Frazer described a mode of interaction with the natural world that he called magical. In analyzing the principles on which this magical relation is based, he posited that there existed two: "first, that like produces like, or that an effect resembles its cause; and second, that things which have once been in contact with each other continue to act on each other at a distance after the physical contact has been severed."[23] Calling the former principle the homeopathic, or the law of similarity, and the latter the law of contact or contagion, he combined both under the general rubric of sympathetic magic,

> since both assume that things act on each other at a distance through a secret sympathy, the impulse being transmitted from one to the other by means of what we may conceive of as a kind of invisible ether, not unlike that which is postulated by modern science for a precisely similar purpose, namely, to explain how things can physically affect each other through a space which appears to be empty.[24]

Two elements I wish to stress in his definition are the notion of mimesis implicit in homeopathic magic, or like acting upon like, and the concept of space underlying both the homeopathic and the contagious. The latter, although we will return to it in much greater detail, is worth mentioning now, because of his obviously powerful impulse to interpret as a single problem a series of relations that might have been otherwise incomprehensible, namely, the problem of how objects can be understood to act on other objects across distances. If, as science since the seventeenth century had insisted, space were infinitely extended dimensionality with no substance, the idea of action at a distance would necessarily involve a medium to fill that "apparently" empty space.[25] The "ether" was one such substance, posited by nineteenth-century scientists as a means of explaining, for example, the observation that light behaved as a wave moving at a finite speed, or that large objects such as planets could affect each other gravitationally at a distance. What I am suggesting, and will elaborate below, is that the Middle Ages experienced space in a fundamentally different way: as full, impressionable and substantial, whose dimensions existed relative to observers and, more specifically, participants, as opposed to being empty and independent of them—an experience that, for instance, would not necessitate a notion of "ether" in order to explain action at a distance.[26]

The other element to underscore, which is the central theme of this section, is the notion of mimesis inherent in Frazer's description of homeopathic magic, a notion that, rather than in the sense of imitation or representation that has become dominant ever since the Renaissance commentaries on Aristotle's *Poetics*,[27] conceives of the mimetic action as somehow participating in the reality it mimics, either affecting it directly or appropriating in some way qualities associated with it. The power of the copy to draw "on the character and power of the original, to the point whereby the representation may even assume that character and that power," is a notion of mimesis that Michael Taussig has cultivated in his *Mimesis and Alterity*, as an alternative to the representational model of imitation dominant in Western culture,[28] and is, I believe, one of the keys to understanding the nature of spectacle in the Middle Ages.

If this notion of mimesis is important to an understanding of medieval spectacle, it is because its corresponding notion of spectacle needs to be grasped in the context of a magical "worldview."[29] The first to characterize the working of magic as a function of worldview was the Scandinavian scholar Sigmund Mowinckel.[30] One principal aspect of such a worldview is a notion of causality completely foreign to the "scientific" worldview characteristic of the modern era. Whereas the latter worldview accepts the logic of pure chance, of random causality, for those who inhabit the magical world, events are not "accidental" or "random" but rather function according to a causal logic determined by a specific agency of power.[31] Additionally, this power to affect causality in a way advantageous to one's own position is accessible to individuals, to differing degrees, and almost always takes the form of a mimetic repetition of "the exact pattern of words, music, or dance that once proved efficacious."[32] If an individual's actions can affect the natural order of things in such a way, it is because the individual is conceived not as a separate observer of the objective world, but as an intrinsic participant, a "microcosm reflecting the macrocosm, so that the macrocosm is in turn a projection of man.... Each natural object and natural phenomenon has a direct influence upon some aspect of man's body or psyche, and man's actions can in turn affect the elements."[33] Such a description is also reminiscent of Foucault's pre-classical "episteme" from *Les mots et les choses*, in which he characterizes European culture prior to the end of the sixteenth century as being guided by the notion of resemblance, or similitude.[34] In his description, the medieval universe is stitched together by the threads of similitude and contagion, "holding the extremes apart (God and matter), yet bringing them together in such a way that the will of the almighty may penetrate into the most unawakened corners."[35]

Perhaps the most evocative practice associated with the magical worldview is what has come to be known popularly as "voodoo death," the practice of killing or causing pain to someone by means of torturing a likeness of that person.[36] Instances of such practice were widely recorded throughout medieval Europe and, although certainly with less frequency, were reported by Frazer to have continued among certain peasant communities up to the present. A sorcerer in fourteenth-century Coventry, for example, is said to have made a wax figure of a neighbor and driven a needle into its forehead, causing intense pain in the head of his neighbor. Later he removed the needle and drove it through the figure's heart, at which point the neighbor immediately died.[37] Such a practice, while considered a perversion of science because of its evil effects, was nevertheless not considered supernatural but rather an intrinsic capacity of nature, just as plants whose leaves were shaped like livers were believed to promote the health of the liver, or a talisman made of a vulture's eye could promote improved vision.[38]

Just as the modern distinction between science and magic is not applicable to everyday common beliefs and behavior in the Middle Ages, so too the common distinction between magic and religion becomes problematic. In one view, magic is held to be distinct from religion in that the former coerces higher and/or natural powers and the latter supplicates them. But the attitude of common people toward the sacred and toward prayer was seldom so well-defined.[39] From the bodies of saints to the recitation of prayers to the paper and ink with which holy words were written, the objective presence of the sacred was held to have a special and, indeed, quite practical power. The cult of the saints, for instance, led not only or even principally to the pious *imitatio* of their deeds, but rather to the obsessive adoration of their preserved bodies. As Huizinga writes, "[t]he physical presence that the saints possessed by virtue of their depictions was unusually intensified by the fact that the church permitted and even favored the veneration of their relics.... Before St. Elizabeth of Thuringia was buried, a crowd of devotees cut or tore strips from the winding sheets of her face and cut off her hair and nails, pieces of her ears and even her nipples."[40] These relics appear at times to have served as amulets, imparting "peace, fertility and good weather" everywhere they were carried.[41]

Likewise, the words of prayers could also function as charms that could either work alone or be used to intensify the effects of a particular ritual. Indeed, sometimes the words did not even need to be recited, as if the very substance of the paper and ink that bore them had become imbued with their magical power. One manuscript on exorcising demons, for example, recommends drawing the sign of the cross and writing the beginning lines of the Gospel according to John on a sheet of parchment and then scraping the words into holy water for the afflicted person to drink.[42]

Finally, the experience of sacred objects and words as practically effective cures, talismans, and charms extended even to the holy Eucharist. During the twelfth and thirteenth centuries, as the doctrine of the Eucharist was being redefined and Christ's body was explicitly claimed to become present in its substance at the moment of the blessing, people increasingly "demanded to *see* this miraculously transubstantiated host, and the custom spread of having the priest elevate it over his head after the consecration so that people at mass could behold it."[43] This gesture, which had traditionally been an imitation of Christ's gesture of slightly raising the bread while blessing it at the Last Supper, became highly exaggerated by the second half of the twelfth century in response to the people's desire to see and adore the body of Christ.[44] For those who came flocking to witness the elevation, the motivation tended to be straightforward: many believed, for example, that having seen the elevated host in the morning one was safe from suffering a stroke or going blind that day and that, in addition, one did not age during the time spent in church.[45] Nevertheless, this practice provoked serious concern on the part of the ecclesiastical authorities, who endeavored to determine the exact moment of the transformation in order to assure that at no time would the masses be adoring a simple piece of bread. In order to prevent such idolatry, the Bishop of Paris ordered the clergy to keep the bread under the altar and out of sight until they had finished pronouncing the words "This is my body," at which point they could raise the bread for the people to see.[46]

The debate concerning the exact moment at which, and indeed the mechanism by which, the priest brings about the miracle of transubstantiation delves into a set of assumptions about the power of gesture that Jean-Claude Schmitt has dubbed "symbolic efficacy." According to this notion, which Schmitt specifically associated with medieval culture, certain gestures or choreographies are capable of effecting a transformation on matter or on people by virtue of a power intrinsic to their form.[47] Schmitt includes within the purview of symbolic efficacy examples of what, with Frazer, I have been calling sympathetic magic—such as attempts at *envoûtement* (the use of wax images to harm an enemy) a practice Schmitt notes became prevalent even among the clergy in the early fourteenth century, suggesting that what these have in common is a notion of the potential for material force present in forms or actions that, for the modern observer, should have none. In other words, it is not that words, gestures, similarities, and proximities—whose power Frazer explained away by means of the association of ideas—become effective in a symbolic way; rather, such purely formal interaction as we would take to be "merely symbolic" is experienced in the Middle Ages as physically, materially effective.

The problem with this notion for the ecclesiastical authorities was, of course, that in the case of the transubstantiation of the host, the priest would have to be understood as wielding some sort of power over Christ, as opposed to the opposite. Therefore, rather than as efficient cause, the priest's gesture was to be understood as a sign accompanying the miracle taking place.[48] Clearly the authorities were at odds in this matter with both common practice and popular perception of the administering of the sacraments. Already in 1215 the Lateran council tried to institute a more rigorous observance of the mass, one that would limit what was perceived by certain monastic orders as an increased "theatricalization of the mass":[49]

> le cistercien Aelred de Rielvaux dénonce avec vigueur la transformation de l'église en un "théâtre" plein du son des instruments de musique *(organa, cym-*

bala), où les "gestes d'histrions *(histrionicis gestibus)*, l'agitation du corps, la torsion des lèvres, le jeu des épaules"... font penser qu'on est "venu à un spectacle et non à la prière."

[the Cistercian Aelred de Rielvaux vigorously denounces the transformation of the church into a "theater" full of the sound of musical instruments, where the "gestures of actors, the agitation of the body, the twisting of the lips, the play of shoulders"... make one believe one has "come to a spectacle and not to prayer."][50]

What this shows quite clearly is that, at least among the church authorities, there was a definite distinction to be made between spectacle and the business of the church and its clergy: prayer. This reaction was incorporated into ecclesiastical attempts to theorize the moment of the miracle, such as those of Hugues de Saint-Victor. According to him, there were three necessary elements for the effectuation of the sacrament: the *res*, or substance of the bread and wine; the *verba*, or words of the celebrant; and the *facta*, or actions he performs.[51] In Thomas de Chobham's revision of this position, the *verba* takes complete predominance, such that the miracle would take place even if the celebrant were to muddle the preparation and the other formalities of the sacrament, as long as he pronounced correctly the words, because, as he says, "*dans ces paroles* consiste *toute la substance* de la consecration du pain et du sang du Christ"[52] [*in these words* consists *the whole substance* of the consecration of the bread and of the blood of Christ]. In other words, while the hyperbole of gesture that had become common practice is condemned because of its association with the "theater"—jongleurs, dancers, court fools, troubadours?—the words of the prayer are still understood in terms of their *substantiality* and their ability to provoke or evoke a *substantial* transformation.

Nevertheless, Schmitt asks, even had he been taught this by his superiors, would a celebrant consciously avoid making the sign of the cross at the appropriate moment? Would he even ask himself what would happen? Gestures, even while serving only an ancillary function according to the authorities, nevertheless "commemorated" Christ's sacrifice by "imitating" his actions at the last supper. If the words carried more weight, it was because they not only "expressed" the essence of the sacrament, they "signified" it as well.[53] Now, this "signify" should definitely not be understood in the contemporary, semiotics-inflected sense of the word, as referring back to an infinite regress of equally unstable signifiers; rather, to signify in this context means to share in the essence of a thing: "Dans le cas du Verbe, il y a non seulement adéquation du 'signe' et de la 'chose' invisible qu'il signifie, mais véritable participation de l'un à l'autre"[54] [In the case of the Word, not only is there the adequation of the 'sign' and the invisible 'thing' it signifies, but true participation of the one with the other]. It is this notion—of a sign, of symbolic efficacy, and of bodily motion not as replacing things but as participating in their essence—that characterizes mimesis and the magical worldview of the Middle Ages;[55] and it is this notion that needs to be taken into account in any analysis of the spectacle of those cultures.[56]

PRESENCE

In *The Golden Bough*, Frazer describes one of the advantages of homeopathic magic when used for medical purposes as enabling the medicine man to perform all of his curative actions on his own body, which in turn serves as a mimetic sign for the body of the sick man, who can thereby be treated without exposing his own body to too much risk or inconvenience.[57] Although he does not bring it up at this point, this clearly becomes the basis of the logic of sacrifice that he eventually uses to contextualize Christianity.[58] What he never explains directly, however, is the link between the "symbolic efficacy" of a scenario like the one above and the mythology of sacrifice and martyrdom that he associates with Christianity. For Frazer, the logic of the scapegoat has to do with the transferability of evil from one being to another, which in turn arises from the "confusion between the physical and the mental, between the material and the immaterial."[59] But while there appears to be a more or less direct genealogy between the practices he calls sympathetic magic and the beliefs of organized religions, nowhere does he suggest that the logic of the scapegoat or of the sacrificed god and that of the homeopathic cure are the same.

As an example of a homeopathic cure, Frazer recounts how

> a Dyak medicine-man, who has been fetched in a case of illness, will lie down and pretend to be dead. He is accordingly treated like a corpse, is bound up in mats, taken out of the house, and deposited on the ground. After about an hour the other medicine-men loose the pretended dead man and bring him to life; and as he recovers, the sick person is supposed to recover too.[60]

When one thinks of this scenario in light of the *Visitatio sepulchri* that has been described by most scholars as the origin of the medieval drama, it is difficult to say very clearly where the difference lies. Of course, the Christian ritual self-consciously refers to a figure both historical and universal (both a man and God), whereas the Dyak ritual takes place only in the here and now. Still, one could argue that the basic dramatic structure—a repetition of a scenario in which a man dies, his corpse is disposed of for some time, and then he rises again, bringing life to those (or the one) in whose name he had died—is fundamentally the same. Nevertheless, while it has become commonplace to refer to the sacrificial victim or the scapegoat as that being who *symbolically* bears the weight of a community's guilt and in dying expiates that guilt, what is not so common is to question the nature of that symbolic function: that is, does it work in some profound, psychological sense, in which a community's collective unconscious is relieved of the burden of its unacknowledged desires to transgress the very laws that hold it together; or does it rather function in a more direct way, in which the enactment of the rituals commemorating the slain God are actually perceived to effect a cure of some sort upon the community?

What I am suggesting is that, at its core, Catholic doctrine, and particularly those aspects of it that will become the heart of the liturgical drama in the Middle Ages, operates according to the logic of sympathetic magic. Certainly anthropologists and sociologists of magic and religion since Frazer have remarked upon the magical elements of the sacrament of the Eucharist. As Gregory Dix points out, the sacrament is, practically speaking, a magical ceremony whose performance is "neither a memorial nor a representation, but an actual re*presentation* of the sacrifice of Christ."[61] In other words, the sacrament of the Eucharist is the prototypical instance of that motion of mimesis as production of presence that characterizes both the magical worldview and the medieval experience of spectacle.

During the early Middle Ages, the exact nature of the miracle of God's presence was not an all-consuming preoccupation. In fact, it was not until the ninth century that the topic was addressed by Ratramnus (d. 868), who became the first to suggest that God appeared only figuratively in the sacrament as opposed to materially.[62] His suggestions were rebuffed by Paschasius, whose literalist version became the received view—weathering only a few attacks in the eleventh century—until the official sanction of Peter Lombardi's *Sententiae* in the twelfth century.[63] The concept of transubstantiation first appears in 1140 in a work by Rolando Bandinelli, later to become Pope Alexander III, and was to be confirmed by the fourth Lateran council of 1215 and eventually elaborated by Aquinas.[64] It was also during the thirteenth century that the doctrine started to achieve a true popular appeal, which culminated when the vision of Saint Julia of Liège led to the creation of a special feast day for the celebration of the Eucharist, Corpus Christi.[65] Celebrated first in Liège in 1246, it was finally institutionalized by Urban IV in 1264 and its liturgy composed by Aquinas.[66] As I discuss below, it was via the feast of Corpus Christi and its elaborate pageants that the liturgical dramas first began to leave the physical cover of the Church and explore different staging possibilities.

But what exactly is transubstantiation, and why did it exert such appeal on the common populace? As a young Catholic sent by my parents to Sunday school, I can certainly submit that the sacrament of the Eucharist was among the most confusing of the doctrines we were taught. I remember an instance one Sunday morning when the class was being taught by Father John, one of the parish priests, instead of by the nuns who were usually our instructors. The occasion was a lesson about the Eucharist. At one point during the discussion, Father John, in what I suppose was intended as a moment of disarming sincerity, suggested that it was perfectly understandable if we found it difficult to believe that the communion wafer, when blessed, actually became the body of God.[67] Now, the point of this reminiscence is that even then, as the recipient of a long and uninterrupted Catholic upbringing, not only could I not believe in the Real Presence of God in the Eucharist, I truly could not imagine what it could even mean to believe such a thing.[68] And while I would never be so bold as to question the belief of other Catholics, those who do or might claim to actually believe (although, as Father John put it, this was a matter of faith that even he had to struggle with from time to time), it seems more than likely to me that no one today believes in the same way the crowds who rushed to witness the elevation of the host in the fourteenth century believed; for them it was not a question of an existential leap of faith (Kierkegaard's prototypical statement of faith in a world that has lost contact with God would most certainly be a source of perplexity for the medieval experience), it was a question of reality.[69] As Huizinga puts it, "[f]or the daily understanding of the mass of people, the existence of a visible image made intellectual proof of faith entirely superfluous. There was no room between what was depicted, and which one met in color and form—that is, depictions of the Trinity, the flames of hell, the catalogues of saints—and faith in all this. There was no room for the question, Is this all true?"[70]

Indeed, it was against this notion of the reality, of the substantial Real Presence, of the body of Christ in the Eucharistic host, that sixteenth-century Protestants such as Luther, Zwingli, and Calvin preached, all the while upholding the notion of the sacrament as a representation of Christ's sacrifice, a reaffirmation of his symbolic body in the community of the Church, or even the virtual or spiritual co-presence of his body with the substance of the bread. What they all agreed upon was, in Calvin's words, "that the very substance of his body or the true and natural body of Christ is not given there; but [rather are given] all those benefits which Christ has supplied us with in his body."[71] It is probable that a fundamental conflict exists not merely between the doctrine of Real Presence and Protestant revisions of it, but between it and some or most of the major tenets of modern thought. For example, in 1663 Descartes' books were placed on the Church's *Index liborum prohibitorum*, and in 1671 both the King and the University of Paris issued decrees against the teaching of his thought.[72] It is more than likely that the principal reason for this lay in the incompatibility between his metaphysics and the doctrine of Real Presence.

The problem concerned Descartes' theory of matter, in which the physical world was deprived of all sensible qualities, such as color, taste and smell— which he conceived of as secondary qualities existing only as perceived by the senses—and was left with only the primary qualities of "shape, extension, and mobility."[73] In the view of such a metaphysics, "the sensible appearances (*species*) of the bread are just that—appearances. They are not real properties of the external object but rather mental phenomena caused by matter in motion."[74] However, it is central to the doctrine of Real Presence that the "entire substance of the bread and wine is changed into the whole substance of the body and blood of Christ, while the appearance of bread and wine remain."[75] In other words, without some notion of substance as substantially unique, and of appearance or species as belonging to the substance, the miracle of transubstantiation threatens to dissolve into pure semantics: the featureless dimensions of what we once called bread we now call God, but has anything really changed? What would be the difference between such a doctrine and that of a virtual or spiritual presence? As Gumbrecht puts it,

> [b]read as a substance is transformed into the substance of Christ's body (whereby, according to the predominant theological opinion, the substance of Christ's body replaces the substance of the bread). But without the primary givenness of bread as substance (or of some other substance) such a transformation could not take place. Christ's body could not become substantially present without another substance offering itself as a point of departure for this becoming.[76]

The point of this distinction is that, to put it glibly, substance really matters; in the Catholic doctrine and in medieval experience, the bread and wine of the Eucharistic celebration can in no way be construed as "signifiers" of God's presence on earth, which is, perhaps, the only way they can be construed today.[77] Rather, the transformation of the substance below the species of bread and wine takes place at the level of real, lived experience, an experience of magical, salutary impact, and one that inspired awe and excitement among the masses who came to bear witness.

This analysis of magic and of the doctrine of Real Presence was intended to provide the coordinates for a different mode of being from the one or ones we have come to inhabit in modern society. Such a description can certainly be corroborated in numerous ways by medieval historians dealing with other aspects of medieval life, although the histories they tell might appear to be tainted by evolutionary prejudices or a curious nostalgia for a different (simpler?) relation with the world. This is certainly the case of Johann Huizinga's classic *The Autumn of the Middle Ages*, whose text opens with the now famous lines:

> When the world was half a thousand years younger all events had much sharper outlines than now. The distance between sadness and joy, between good and bad fortune, seemed to be much greater than for us; every experience had that degree of directness and absoluteness that joy and sadness still have in the mind of a child.[78]

What strikes us as a blend of infantilizing compassion and a patronizing ethnographic instinct can also serve to remind us that one's being-in-the-world might well have been different then, and that this difference might well have had to do with the impact of substance—that the experience of spectacle might have been rooted more in the encounter with things' presence than in the interpretation of intention or the rooting out of the truth behind phenomena. This is not to say that interpretation was not prevalent; far from it: the science of interpretation, in particular Biblical exegesis, was highly esteemed by the Scholastics. Rather, it is to say that the meaning of phenomena was present in the phenomena themselves, ready to be extracted by those well-versed in the craft of reading what Foucault, following Merleau-Ponty, called the prose of the world.[79] Perhaps it is precisely the substantial impact of forms and spectacles that accounts for what Huizinga describes as the overt stylization of medieval life, the desperate attention paid to ritual formality, as when, out of his attention to the formal obligations of hospitality, Philip of Burgundy refused to allow his guest, the wife of Louis XI, to return home, despite the pleas of her servants and the threat of her husband's rage.[80] In fact, Huizinga finds this "prevailing formalism" also to be the base of the medieval faith in the power of spoken words, such as blessings, magic, and condemnations.[81] And so we are faced with a continuum of sorts, between faith in doctrine and the experiences of everyday life, a continuum Paul Zumthor finds at work in the performance of the liturgy:

> spectaculaire en ses moindres parties, elle signifiait les vérités de foi par un jeu complexe offert aux perceptions auditives (musique, chants, lecture) et visuelles (par la splendeur des bâtiments; par ses acteurs, leur costume, leurs gestes, leur danse; par ses décors), tactiles mème: on touche le mur saint, on pose un baiser sur le pied de la statue, le reliquaire, l'anneau épiscopal; on respire le parfum de l'encens, de la cire des cierges.[82]
>
> [spectacular in the least of its aspects, it signifies the truths of faith by way of a complex play offered to the auditory (music, chants, reading) and visual (by way of the splendor of the buildings; by the actors, their costumes, their gestures, their dance; by the decor), and even tactile perceptions: one touches the holy wall, one poses a kiss on the foot of the statue, the reliquary, the bishopric ring; one breathes the perfume of incense, of the candles' wax.]

And it is to the liturgy that we now return, as a centerpiece of medieval drama, a drama that should be understood in the context of the mode of being we have just explored. In other words, a world that experiences space and causality in the ways I have described necessarily has a different experience of spectacle, and it is this experience that I will attempt to describe next.

PERFORMANCES

Karl Young suggested three criteria for differentiating true theater from non-theatrical performances in the Middle Ages: he called these *action* (movement on the stage), *dialogue*, and *impersonation*. Of these three, impersonation has been considered the most important, or at least the most viable distinguishing feature. Young defines the concept as follows:

> In some external and recognizable manner the actor must pretend to be the person whose words he is speaking, and whose action he is imitating. The performer must do more than merely *represent* the chosen personage; he must also *resemble* him, or at least show his intention of doing so. It follows, then, that the dialogue and physical movements of those who participate in the liturgy will be transformed from the *dramatic* into *drama* whenever these persons convey a story and pretend to be the characters in this story.[83]

The distinction, of course, is based on the modern notion of a character: a figure, whether of historical, mythical, or purely fictional origin, who, by means of the portrayal by an actor, comes to life on the stage and in the imagination of an audience, an audience that, nevertheless, still maintains an awareness of the separation between that character and the actor portraying him or her. Because Young's purpose is to determine at what point theater *per se* detaches itself from its liturgical moorings, the concept serves for him as a means of distinguishing dramatic representation from the actions performed by a priest during the mass. This moment comes, for Young—as for the majority of theater historians—in the tenth century, with the first performances of the *Quem quaeritis* sequences of the *Visitatio sepulchri*,[84] a dramatization of that section of the liturgy recounting the visit of the Marys to Christ's tomb. Until this point, the mass had been, in Young's view, a "true sacrifice" as opposed to "an aesthetic picture of a happening in the past"—not a "representation of an action, but an actual re-creation of it."[85]

I think it's worth questioning Young's distinction, not because I believe that the canon "playing the role" of one of the Marys in a *Visitatio* is performing the same function as the priest conducting the mass, but rather because I think that the criterion on which he bases the distinction is problematic when applied to the medieval context.[86] This is also Hardison's criticism, although he takes it in a different direction, arguing that distinctions between liturgy and drama are misplaced because the liturgy already was drama.[87] In contrast, my claim is that, whereas both the liturgy and the liturgical drama function according to the same logic, that logic is fundamentally different from the logic of the theater, if we take the word "theater" (as we do) to mean that form of performance that has become canonical since the seventeenth century. William

Tydeman, defending Young's thesis of the distinction between the liturgy and the liturgical drama (and implicitly coming out in favor of the likeness of liturgical drama and theater), argues that, unlike an actor, a priest "does not expect us to accept that he himself has become Christ."[88] However, it is quite an interpretive jump to claim, without support, that a medieval "actor" would have this expectation of his audience. Tydeman himself makes the point elsewhere that medieval performance did not require individual characterization; rather "[w]hat was required was doubtless an iconographic representation of the scriptural figure, not a naturalistic portrayal of a human being. The acting of liturgical drama was conceived of in formal, stylised terms and governed by considerations of liturgical propriety."[89]

Hardison, making his argument for the unity of drama and the liturgy, draws upon the writings of what he calls the allegorical tradition, a tradition spanning from Amalarius and continuing through Aquinas and Innocent III that held that allegorical interpretation of the liturgy could be useful for illustrating the liturgy for the *simpliciores*, or common people.[90] According to Hardison, these writers describe the liturgy in unmistakably dramatic terms, like those of Honorius in his *Gemma animae* (c.1100):

> It is known that those who recited tragedies in theaters presented the actions of opponents by gestures before the people. In the same way our tragic author (i.e., the celebrant) represents by his gestures in the theater of the Church before the Christian people the struggle of Christ and teaches them the victory of His redemption. Thus when the celebrant says the Orate he expresses Christ placed for us in the agony, when he commanded his people to pray.[91]

However, for there to be drama as opposed to merely dramatic elements, according to Young, the performer must do more than represent, he must resemble; and Hardison obliges, by quoting the father of the allegorical tradition, Amalarius, who in his *Praefatio altera* also puts forward a notion of resemblance, insisting that "[s]acraments should have likeness to the things for which they are sacraments. Therefore the celebrant should be like Christ, just as the bread, wine and water are similar to the body of Christ."[92] Hardison's argument, then, is that the liturgy was always about impersonation, and that, as a result, Young's distinction does not hold.

Nevertheless, if Young is mistaken in assuming that impersonation is an adequate criterion for distinguishing liturgy from drama, Hardison is equally mistaken in implying that because a celebrant or a liturgical performer "resembles" Christ or one of the Marys, he is thus the functional equivalent of an actor. A (modern) actor does not "resemble" his or her character; his or her character is an effect of the actor on the audience members, on their imaginations. The character exists suspended in an imaginary world created by the interrelation of all the elements on the stage, including the relation of the actor's gestures and words to those of his or her fellow actors, and to the imaginary world of the set.[93] When the priest repeats the gestures of the breaking of the bread and the words of the blessing of the sacraments, or when a canon displays in wonder the empty funereal veil that he has picked up from the steps of a church's sepulcher, they are, in part, performing different functions, the canon's being one of clarification or illustration; but they are also engaging in the same function, one for the most part alien to the modern stage: reenacting a timeless truth by means of an imitation of it, thereby making that truth present to a community of participants.

It is telling in this respect that commentaries on the quality of actors' performances only begin to appear in the mid-sixteenth century, such as a savage criticism of the *Confrères de la Passion* in 1542, claiming that on account of their ineptitude "derision and public clamour often arise in the theatre itself";[94] or the complement paid to the Bourges production of 1536 of *Les Actes des Apôtres* that "the majority of the onlookers considered the business to be the truth and not pretence."[95] This emphasis on the illusion that what is happening on the stage is somehow real is foreign to the medieval imagination, for which a performance requires no illusion to be real.

If the notion of impersonation is problematic for the discussion of medieval spectacle, dramatization strikes me as more acceptable. The idiosyncratic nature of medieval conceptions of classical staging techniques has been widely acknowledged. Isidor of Seville wrote the following description of a Latin stage, which remained perhaps the most influential source of knowledge on the subject for centuries to come, at least until the revival of the plays of Plautus and Seneca in the late fifteenth century in Italy:

> The "scene" was the place below the theatre built in the form of a house, with a platform which was called the orchestra. On it the comic and tragic actors sang, and the *histriones* and *mimi* danced. There the comic and tragic poets ascended for their contests, while the others (the *histriones*) provided suitable gestures for the words they chanted.[96]

What were called the *comediae elegiacae*, an early form of comic drama inspired by the plays of Terence, were never composed of pure dialogue, but rather of a mixture of narrative and dialogue, a fact that may be explained by the widely held assumption that Terentian comedies were recited by the author or an author figure, and only dramatized by mime-like *histriones*.[97] Even if one accepts, as I do, that this depiction of Latin stage practice does not mean that the Middle Ages did not have their own, and different, dramatic practices, the fact that this interpretation should be so readily acceptable suggests that the logic of dramatization was a familiar one.

Dramatization, I want to suggest, marks a different relation to reality than does the modern term "acting." Whereas an actor takes part in the production of an imaginary reality that coexists or momentarily replaces social reality, dramatization makes present, adds a bodily dimension to, a narration that is already in some sense real. This is as adequate a description of the dramatization of the *Visitatio sepulchri* as it is of the medieval conception of Latin stage productions: whether the words are spoken for the performers or by the performers, they are real in a sense that transcends their repetition at each particular moment, and that belies the sense of transcendence we give a theatrical work by an author of genius.[98] Shakespeare's characters represent the work of an individual author of genius, so capable with language and the depiction of human emotions and desires that his characters may be represented in almost infinite contexts, each time to a different effect and each time emphasizing the renewed "reality" of the story told at the present moment on the present stage—a reality that emerges from the particular relevance of the representation to that context. A dramatization creates the effect of an instantiation, a momentary entry into our senses of a timeless, immobile, and substantial truth. It would be hard to imagine the success (at least in traditional theatrical terms) of a production of Shakespeare, Lope, or Racine wherein the performers mimed actions and held placards over their heads with the words of speeches on them, a practice that was prevalent in the Middle Ages, as Kernodle describes in the context of medieval street theater.[99]

One common medieval manifestation of the relationship between a performance and the atemporal reality it invokes has been called allegory. As Roy Mackenzie wrote in 1914 concerning a class of performances known as morality plays, "[a] Morality is a play, allegorical in structure, which has for its main object the teaching of some lesson for the guidance of life, and in which the principal characters are personified abstractions or highly universalized types."[100] These personified abstractions (such as Love, Envy, Gluttony) and universal types (the old man, the fool), may not be instantiations of a historical, religious, or mythical eternal reality, but they are instantiations of a moral reality. As Hardison puts it, while the morality play is fictional as opposed to historical, it is still conceived on the basis of fidelity, but fidelity to doctrine as opposed to history.[101] Or, in Gustave Cohen's words, stage figures are allegorical when they incarnate the "secret of human destiny, grace, health, redemption, worldliness or saintliness."[102] Hardison explains the prevalence of allegorical forms in the medieval drama by virtue of their usefulness as tools for the instruction of doctrinal truths. These truths are best expressed in simple, stylized forms, because more complex forms (and by this he means a type of characterization more consonant with the modern stage) will tend to obscure symbolic meanings behind the allure of the forms themselves, encouraging the spectator to ask "What happens next?" as opposed to the proper pedagogical question, "What does it mean?"[103] Again, the notion of interpretation behind this question is not one of positing a kind of intentionality behind the facade of a text or a performance; this impulse involves the isolation of an intentional and particular author figure as the ultimate bestower of meaning, whereas in medieval interpretive practices, meaning was immanent in the text or performance, and indeed in the world in general.[104] The question "What happens next?" on the other hand precisely requires a projection of the spectator into the world of a performance, a running-ahead of oneself propelled by a desire to know the author's, another character's, or an interlocutor's intention towards the spectator's person.

Finally, as modern spectators accustomed to modern theatrical conventions, we tend to find allegorical performance bizarre; it strikes us as somehow "unnatural." In a medieval context, however, this was probably not the case. In light of the importance of ritual formalism in everyday life that Huizinga has described, it is probable that the designation of "natural" to describe some behavior in everyday life would have been quite meaningless. Because courtly engagements involved such advanced degrees of stylized behavior, the abstract, stylized nature of morality plays and courtly masks would have been exceedingly familiar, to the point, even, of requiring some additional external demarcations and internal structurations (masks, assigned seating?) to distinguish them as performances.[105] It is this extremely complex relation of performance to reality that we should keep in mind as we trace the development of religious and political spectacles up to the sixteenth century.

RELIGIOUS SPECTACLE

The most accepted theory regarding the emergence of drama in the Middle Ages, whether one believes the Church was ultimately hostile to the "dramatic instinct" or supportive of it, is that the *Quem quaeritis* dialogue from the tenth century Saint-Gall manuscript marks the "first definite appearance of a dramatic form."[106] This dialogue, which persisted more or less unaltered for four centuries, consists of a brief dialogue dramatizing the moment the followers of Christ come to seek out his body at the tomb, only to discover that he has been resurrected:

> Quem queritis in sepulchro, o Christocole?
> Ihesum Nazarenum crucifixum, o celicole.
> Non est hic, surrexit sicut ipse dixit; ite nunciate quia surrexit.
>
> [Whom seek you in the tomb, O followers of Christ?
> Jesus of Nazareth who was crucified, O Heaven-Dwellers.
> He is not here, he has risen as he said; go announce that he has risen.][107]

A slightly elaborated version appears in a Spanish manuscript from the twelfth century, and again in the fifteenth century, copied verbatim, but this time with the addition of quite precise stage directions:

> Hic tres pueri in similitudine mulierum induti uestimentis candadis peragant de choro usque ad altare unus post unum blande cantantes hanc antiphonam:
> Ubi est Christus meus, Dominus, et filius excelsi? Eamus uidere sepulchrum.
> Alius puer stans retro altare in similitudine angeli indutus uestimentis candadis, dicat hanc antiphonam:
> Quem queritis in sepulchro, O Cristocole?
> Et mulieres respondeant blande antiphonam:
> Jhesum Nazarenum crucifixum, o celicole.[108]
>
> [Now three boys in the guise of women dressed in bright garments pass from the choir to the altar, one after the other, singing charmingly this antiphony:
> Where is my Christ, God and son of Heaven? We are here to see his tomb.
> Another boy standing behind the altar in the guise of an angel dressed in bright garments, speaks this antiphony:
> Whom do you seek in the tomb, O followers of Christ?
> And the women respond charmingly with this antiphony:
> Jesus of Nazareth who was crucified, O heavenly ones.]

In addition to these dialogues, there is evidence that the performance of the *Visitatio* normally included scripted physical actions as well, such as the displaying of the crucifix and the funereal veil, genuflecting, and censing the altar or sepulcher.[109]

The consensus among theater historians is that this dialogue and its repeated performance throughout the Middle Ages constitutes what Hardison calls "the bridge whereby medieval culture made the transition from ritual to representational drama."[110] But if the new performance is representation, in what way is this representation different from the representations involved in the mass? If the blessing of the bread was a repetition of Christ's actions at the last supper, intended and perhaps experienced as a production of Christ's presence at the mass, then it is no stretch to imagine that the ritual enactment of the *Visitatio*, if not loaded with the same significance by the ecclesiastical authorities, was in fact experienced in much the same vein, as the powerful presencing of the moment of Christ's resurrection and of the effects this resurrection promised for mankind. Perhaps this can explain why, in 1316 at Worms, a crowd rushed into a church, creating an enormous tumult and shoving aside the clergy in an attempt to witness a representation of the resurrection, believing that in this way they too might avoid death.[111] Such a conclusion is reinforced by the fact that the *Visitatio*, like the sacrament of the Eucharist, was performed at the altar, which had been, since the days of the early Christians, associated with the tomb in which Christ had been buried, and was also, in many or even most churches, the crypt wherein had been placed the remains of some saint or holy man whose relics were believed to have great protective powers.[112]

It has been suggested by Chambers and those following him that the basic model for staging drama in the Middle Ages developed out of the liturgical drama and hence out of the practice of the mass itself. Therefore, when the *Visitatio* finally moved to the front of the church and then to the town square, as the story goes, the basic organization of the performance space retained its original associations with the symbolic architecture of the church's interior.[113] But it cannot simply be maintained that wherever the drama went it imprinted this symbolic architecture onto a passive and malleable space. Medieval theatrical space was also largely dependent on whatever architectural framework characterized the locale in which a drama was performed, and it was not until the end of the fifteenth century that what could be called autonomous theatrical spaces became truly autonomous.[114] Instead of mounting productions in a prefabricated space designated for that purpose, organizers would take advantage of some pre-existing location, "preferably an enclosed or at least a well-defined area."[115] For example, a *mystère* entitled *L'Incarnation et la Nativité de Jésus-Christ* was performed at Rouen in 1474, in which heaven was located on one side of the village square in front of the "Crowned Axe" and Hell was across the square from it, in front of the inn "where the sign of the Angel hangs."[116] From this it can be gathered that outdoor production could be very large, often taking up entire sections of a town. This playing space, in turn, would be divided into a periphery composed of "pieces of localized scenery" arranged around a *platea* or "unlocalized acting space." The pieces of scenery, little tents or houses often referred to as mansions, would either be facing spectators, arranged in a circle, or detached and scattered around town.[117] Actual places mentioned in the dramatic script (Bethlehem and Herod's palace in a nativity play, for example) would be represented by the mansions, while the platea would be used whenever the characters were to be seen traveling from place to place or time was to have elapsed.[118] In contrast, in the theater after the sixteenth century, it is precisely the empty space in the middle of the stage where the action takes place, while movement between places and the passage of time between events occur off-stage.

One peculiarity of medieval staging that emerged from this spatial arrangement was the simultaneous appearance of different scenic locations. Rather than the space of the play shifting to represent wherever the action might be taking place, the players, along with the audience's attention, would move from one scene to another, eventually covering the entire space of the performance. At times, different locations, represented by different mansions, would be in use concurrently.[119] In contrast, the dominant form of theatrical spectatorship in modern times, a rectangular box within which the audience views the action of the play from one side—a paradigm that has, of course, become the norm for much contemporary viewing, most notably for television and film—was practically unknown in the Middle Ages, first being used for the express production of a play in Paris in 1540.[120]

Toward the end of the thirteenth century, following the institutionalization of the feast of Corpus Christi, the day officially assigned for the commemoration and adoration of the Eucharistic Host, the religious procession, starting in Spain, began to incorporate some of the dramatic elements associated with the Easter and Christmas celebrations. At first, beginning around 1320, the procession accompanying the Host through the town was embellished with what were known as *invenciones*, sculptures of animals or human figures intended to delight and astonish the populace, and these were accompanied by song and dance.[121] Eventually the inanimate figures were replaced by humans, who at first remained immobile, what in the Italian context was known as *corpi di carne*, and only later, probably by the end of the fifteenth century, began to act out certain sequences in the style of the English Corpus Christi cycles.[122]

Finally, many of the dramas, particularly those dealing with the lives of saints, had as their central concern the depiction of the saint's martyrdom. Often these scenes of torture would be performed in gross detail. In order to be able to represent faithfully the ordeals of the saint, dummies would be used, such as in the French saint play depicting the martyrdom of St. Denis, in which Denis was "whipped, racked, tormented on a red-hot grill, assaulted by wild animals, steeped in a furnace, crucified, and beheaded, his bones broken and his bowels exposed through his split belly." In a representation of the martyrdom of St. Barbara, her naked body was "bound to a stake, beaten, burnt, and deprived of her breasts, rolled in a nail-studded barrel, and dragged over a mountain by the hair before final execution."[123]

What these different examples of staging practices show is that, from its inception, religious spectacle in the Middle Ages occurred in what I call a "full space," in contradistinction to the popular notion of "the empty space" associated with the modern theater. A religious production was, to begin with, an already-allegorized space, its arrangement intended to reproduce the symbolic architecture of the interior of a church. In addition, the production space tended to adapt itself to the place in which it was mounted, adopting the contours of its limits and matching its symbolic geography to that of its containing landscape. One reason for this might have been that, as I argued earlier, medieval drama had a different relationship to reality than does modern theater. Rather than taking place in an empty, geometrically determined space in which stories can be played out in relative independence of the reality of the audience's world, the hyperbolic solidity of the space of medieval drama reflected the instability of the distinction between the reality being represented and the reality of the representation. As Hardison says, "the stage of the Resurrection is not the Protean stage of the Elizabethans, which can be a palace one moment, a tavern the next, and the rebel camp a few moments later. Rather, it is the bounded container of all that exists."[124] Just as its time is "cosmic,"[125] representing immutable, eternal truths, so its space is that of an ever-present reality, that must by nature overlap with and include the space of the production. While he claims that the early vernacular religious plays, such as the *Seinte resurreccion* and the *Jeu d'Adam*, are "relatively free of liturgical influence,"[126] it is not likely that they are free of this relationship between represented space and space of representation.

In the Latin prologue to the *Jeu d'Adam*, the author presents a series of instructions to the players in which, after describing how the paradise is to be constructed and decorated and how Adam and Eve are to be attired, he writes:

> And the Adam must be well trained when to reply and to be neither too quick nor too slow in his replies. And not only he, but all the personages must be trained to speak composedly, and to fit convenient gesture to the matter of their speech.... Whosoever names Paradise is to look and point towards it.[127]

After the prologue, a "*lectio*," and a chant by a choir, a Figure (*figura*) begins the dialogue by instructing Adam and Eve on their obligations, at which point the text continues:

> Then the Figure must depart to the Church and Adam and Eve walk about Paradise in honest delight. Meanwhile the demons are to run about the stage (*per plateas*), with suitable gestures, approaching the Paradise from time to time and pointing out the forbidden fruit to Eve, as though persuading her to eat it.

Two elements leap out from these directions: first, that the actual presence of Paradise (whose construction is described in detail) is deictically emphasized and reemphasized; and second, that the text continues to describe the *Figura* as leaving and entering the Church, whose presence we can thereby conclude is of some symbolic importance. For a contemporary Anglo-Norman resurrection play, Chambers maps out the placement of the various mansions and finds that they do, in fact, replicate the architecture of a church.[128] So it is quite likely that regardless of a play's dependence on the specific ritual inscribed in the liturgy, the space of the representation was, at least in part, both a space already allegorized according to the reality of Christian doctrine and a full space whose plenitude constituted an indispensable aspect of its experience. Likewise, the medieval obsession with keeping a performance space full of bodies, whether real or artificial, speaks to the notion of theatrical space as being precisely that which is constituted by the presence of bodies in it, as opposed to that place in which bodies may be shown. When, in the Spanish Corpus Christi procession, human bodies replace motionless figures, their purpose is most likely to contribute to the constitution of the space in which the procession is taking place, and in which the Host is being adored. When dummies were substituted for actors in order to better depict the horrors of saintly martyrdom, they were certainly serving the cause of a perverse pleasure that is no stranger to our own time and culture; more than that, though, they testify to the incapacity of a culture to evacuate space, and to its need and enjoyment of the constant impact of presence.[129]

POLITICAL SPECTACLE

Let us call political that spectacle which is consciously and explicitly associated with the propagation or display of power, thereby bracketing the unconscious and implicit relations to power that all forms of spectacle might, in some way, entail. Gumbrecht has hypothesized that one way of describing power against the predominant "Foucauldian" vein (in which power is seen as all-pervasive, discursive and multivalent, likened to a grid determining one's subject position, etc.[130]), is to understand it simply as the potential of occupying a space with one's body, a potential that need not ever be fulfilled in order to be effective.[131] While any definition has its limits, this strikes me as a particularly basic one, at the very least a necessary if not sufficient condition for all situations of power given that, in any aspect of a situation or struggle in which one could not assert that potential, one would have to concede to being powerless in regard to that aspect. That said, I would suggest the following caveat in the case of medieval spectacles of power: rather than depending on the potential of occupying a pre-existent space, they involve the constitution of a space as already potentially occupied, the creation of the political space *per se*.

In 1434, a Spanish knight by the name of Suero de Quiñones, bound by his oath to the service of a lady who did not return his affections, devised the following ordeal in order to free himself from his self-imposed bondage: in the company of a group of nine other knights of his choosing, he would occupy a bridge and deny anyone passage unless they would submit to breaking a lance with him or one of his knights. If a Lady were passing unattended, she would be allowed to pass only if a knight broke a lance in her name. They would stand their guard for 30 days or until 300 lances had been broken.[132] Certainly the frequent and onerous travails that knights are known to have undertaken for purely honorific purposes are well documented. What is bizarre for modern readers is that the connection between the ordeal and the goal it is meant to attain is often far from clear, as in the present case. The pertinence of

Suero's ordeal, however, is that it explicitly deals with the occupation of a place central to the daily travels of many people, a place converted into a highly determined space of power, a threshold whose crossing will automatically trigger a trial of arms. Furthermore, by occupying that space, a space he has created by virtue of his oath ("a speech-act," in current jargon), Suero empowers himself to escape the space of obligation to his beloved in which he is trapped. The distinction we are tempted to make, between the real nature of the space occupied on the bridge and the purely imaginary bondage to the beloved, is both the result of our historical distance and the reason for our difficulty in grasping the logic of the ordeal; for a Spanish knight of the fifteenth century, both spaces are equally real.

Unlike the kings who ruled over the fixed courts of the centralized absolute monarchies characteristic of seventeenth century Europe, medieval kings tended to move from town to town. At first, their entry into a town would be a simple affair, mainly consisting of the townspeople bringing out provisions for the king and his entourage as a sign of welcome.[133] It is not until the beginning of the fourteenth century that the elaborate processions associated with the royal entry into a city began to take place. This is because the notion of a procession was relatively new to the fourteenth century, having first appeared in Europe, specifically in Barcelona, in or around 1320 in conjunction with the Feast of Corpus Christi.[134] As Guenée and Lehoux have argued, the processions marking royal entries follow to a remarkable degree the conventions of the Corpus Christi processions, down to the addition of a decorative dais over the king's carriage only shortly after a similar decoration began to be used to cover the carriage of the Holy Sacrament in processions around Europe.[135] The procession would generally proceed from the gates of the city, where the city's administrators and important citizens had gathered in full regalia to greet the entourage, to the church, where the king would pray and preach a sermon and, finally, be presented the keys of the city *"in signum majoris obedientie et subjectionis"*[136] [in a sign of great obedience and subjection].

An anonymous chronicle describes in some detail the entry of Henry into Paris in 1431, beginning with the arrival of the king and his entourage at the chapel of St. Denis, where they are met by the Bishop of Paris and by a group of merchants, officials, and citizens of Paris, each wearing the appropriate regalia for their station.[137] From the chapel, the king and his somewhat enlarged retinue now continue toward Paris, on the way to which they are met by a different sort of spectacle:

> Et tantost aprés, en deça de la dicte Chappelle, en approchant la dicte bonne ville de Paris, vint au devant dudit seigneur une deesse nommee Fama, moult richement aourné, monté sur une coursier couvert des armes de la dicte ville de Paris.

[And a while later, on this side of the said chapel, approaching the said city of Paris, came in front of the said lord a goddess named Fame, most richly adorned, mounted on a charger covered with the arms of the said city of Paris.]

Following the goddess are eighteen warriors (*preux*) from classical history and mythology, nine male and nine female, all ceremoniously armed and mounted on chargers. Finally,

audevant d'icelle deesse et preux chevauchoit un herault vestu de robe vermeille et chapperon d'azur, at par dessus une tunique des armes de la dicte ville de Paris, lequel menoit et conduisoit le dit mistere.[138] Et si tost qu'il apperceust le dit roy, mist pee a terre et lui fist la reverence par troiz foiz; et ce fait lui presenta icelle deesse et preux en disant ce qui s'ensuit:

[ahead of this goddess and these warriors trotted a herald dressed in a vermilion robe and blue vestment, over which he wore a tunic displaying the arms of the city of Paris, and he guided and led the said mystery play. And as soon as he saw the king, he jumped to the ground and did him reverence three times; and this done he presented to him the goddess and the warriors saying as follows:]

> Les Preux jadis et renommee
> Tendoient qui est figuré
> Ci en dame et vous represente
> Paris, qui en toute s'entente,
> Sire, vous reçoit humblement.
> Gardez-la amoureusement,
> Car dele ville ainsi famee
> Est digne d'estre bien gouverné.[139]

> [The warriors of old and much fame
> Extend to you, figured here as a woman,
> She who represents Paris,
> Who in all things will strive,
> Sire, to receive you humbly.
> Guard her lovingly,
> Since such a city so famed
> Is worthy of being well governed.]

The point of this display is not merely that it makes certain associations between the king's possession of the city and a complex play of ideas, although this is certainly also the case (Paris, in the garb of Fame, but also reputation, is presented to Henry for her protection by an august line of biblical and mythical rulers, from Hector of Troy to Charlemagne).[140] More important, the king's symbolic space of governance, his rights as well as his obligations to the city,[141] are enacted in full view of all and, crucially, right in front of the gates of the city immediately before the king enters it, such that the symbolic space of the performance and the real space of the city are effectively fused. This space of governance is constituted by a dramatic performance with all the trappings of theater, but which nevertheless includes the participation of real officials with real roles in the governance of the city and in which the actions played out, no matter how apparently fanciful, had utterly real implications for the city, its inhabitants, and the king.

The permeability of the boundary between what we would distinguish as symbolic and real performances was a constant aspect of courtly life in fifteenth century Castille, particularly as concerns one of the most popular forms of courtly entertainment, the *masques*.[142] As Gumbrecht observes, "when [we] concentrate on the chronicles from the time of the first two Castilian kings in the 15th century, Juan II and Enrique IV, we realize that their lives were consumed by a practically unbroken sequence of masques, so that *the boundary between the play and daily life* couldn't have actually been visible."[143] This opinion is seconded by Pellerito, who describes courtly life as one in which daily life and literature or fantasy were fused in an array of *momos*[144] (masques) and *invenciones* (special effects).[145] In 1399, for example, at the coronation of Martin I, documented by Gerónimo de Blancas, there emerged, from a cloud that descended near the king, a boy dressed as an angel, "cantando maravillosamente; y subiendo y baxando diversas vezes dexávase caer por todas partes muchas letrillas, y coplas escritas, unas en papel colorado, otras en amarillo, y otras en papel azul, con tintas diferentes, todas al propósito de la solemnidad, y fiesta, que allí se hazía"[146] [singing marvelously; and rising and falling several times, let fall all over verses and couplets written, some on colored, others on yellow and still others on blue paper, with different inks, all about the solemnity and celebration at hand]. On another occasion, in 1460, after a dinner attended by the count Miguel Lucas de Iranzo, courtier of Enrique IV, a group of the count's gentlemen, dressed as foreigners with masks on, approached the table where he was seated with the countess and reported to have just been released from a brutal captivity on the condition that they would come immediately to the count's house to serve and honor him.[147]

What is astonishing about such scenarios is that no fixed boundary seems to be established between courtly entertainment and courtly reality: a flying angel distributes leaflets with verses pertaining to the coronation at hand; servants dressed as wealthy foreigners tell a fictive story to a real count so as to honor him in his home. What joins these cases and others like them is that any absolute boundary between pretense and reality is overridden by the effect of defining a space whose reality is thereby established. As did Henry's entry into

Paris, the masques celebrated by the Spanish nobility served to bring into existence a space in which their authority could be established and their power experienced sensually, rather than merely at an intellectual or conceptual level.

Finally, there were instances in which dramatic representations were used to depict interrelations between powerful political figures. This was often the case in sixteenth century England, where the "interludes" began largely as political satire, such as in 1523, when, during a visit by Carlos V to London, a "disguising" depicted the French king as a wild horse to be tamed by "amitie," a metaphor for the alliance between Carlos and Henry.[148] In fifteenth-century Spain, we find reference to an explicitly political representation that apparently played a serious part in the beginning of a civil war. On 5 June 1465, a mock trial and execution by the noble league of King Enrique IV, what has come to be known as *la Farsa de Avila*, was performed against the walls of the city. An effigy of the king, dressed in black and seated on his throne, was placed on a platform against the wall. The opposing prince, Alfonso, was present in person in the crowd. After a period of time in which the nobles flung various accusations at the effigy, it was uncrowned by Alonso Carrillo, the archbishop of Toledo, the various other accoutrements of Enrique's reign removed by other attending nobles, and finally thrown to the ground, at which time prince Alfonso rose to take his place on the throne amidst shouts of "¡Castilla por el rey don Alfonso!"[149] This event marked the beginning of the civil war that would last until the reunification of the regime under Isabel. Perhaps the Farsa served as the first step in a concrete political action by creating the dramatic space in which Alfonso could make his challenge effective, a space already imprinted with his presence and with the violent decoronation of an extant king.

SEEDS OF THEATRICALITY

The way people experienced the space of spectacle did not change suddenly with the dawn of the first new year of the sixteenth century. Nor is one mode of spatiality necessarily exclusive of another: it is entirely conceivable, for instance, that one's experience of religious spectacle is founded on presence while one's experience of political spectacle is a theatrical one. What I am describing, then, is best termed a shift in dominance between the two modes of spatiality, such that, from the turn of the sixteenth century, theatricality begins to play an ever larger role in the mediation of experience while presence is confined into ever more specific and limited arenas of everyday life.

Although one must take a macroscopic view of the history of spectacle to witness this shift in dominance from start to finish, important aspects of it are also visible at precise moments. One such moment has been called the moment of the birth of modern theater in Spain, in the work of the poet Juan del Encina.

Without engaging in adulatory rhetoric, or taking a position in the debate as to whether Juan del Encina is truly "the father" of Spanish theater, I will nonetheless claim that in his work something happens that probably did not happen before him, and that this something marks one of the more decisive moments in the shift from presence to theatricality. This something is the invention of character, and by describing the specific contours of this invention, we lay the groundwork for a more detailed exposition of theatricality in the following chapter.[150]

To stake a claim for Encina as being either more medieval or more modern than others have described him is not new. But the tone this debate has taken has almost always been one of disparagement—that he is "still" medieval, with underdeveloped characters, shaky plots, and an indeterminate use of place and time, etc.—versus apology: that in many ways he really is "almost" modern, a true precursor to Lope de Vega; that his character development is quite advanced for the time, etc. In this light, when I refer to Encina's work as involving "the invention of character," I am consciously referring to such debates while at the same time eschewing them. For character is not some artistic essence of the modern period that the medievals failed to grasp; rather, it is a term that in the modern vocabulary designates an entity for which there was, literally, no *space* in medieval spectacle. This is so because a character inhabits not a full, impressionable space, but an abstract, empty space. Therefore, by agreeing that Juan del Encina participated in the invention of character, I am really only suggesting a clarification of what "character" really means.

Perhaps the most intelligent appraisal of Juan del Encina's position in the history of Spanish theater is Ronald Surtz's *Birth of a Theater*. Whereas Surtz does place Encina firmly on one side of the medieval/modern divide, his discussion of the divide is nuanced and his description of the different kinds of theater quite rich. The principal vocabulary he uses for characterizing the rift between the medieval and modern stages is that of dramatic ritual versus illusionistic theater. Whereas the former describes the form of spectacle common to both classical antiquity and the European Middle Ages, the latter was born in the Italian Renaissance and exported to the rest of Europe during the sixteenth century. In Spain, the entire dramatic tradition prior to Lope de Vega belongs in the former category.[151]

For Surtz, in order for a particular spectacle to count as illusionistic theater and hence be modern, it must require "the spectator to believe that the action he sees and hears taking place on the stage is happening in a time different from that of the moment and duration of the representation, and in a space different from that of the stage itself."[152] Encina's drama, which he argues originated from a fusion of liturgical drama and courtly entertainment,[153] never creates a distinction between the time and place of the performance of the spectacle and the time and place of the story being performed:

Rather than having to imagine themselves transported to biblical Judea, Encina's spectators see the sacred event happening right there in the room in the Duke of Alba's palace where they have gathered to hear Matins. There is no strict division between the play world and the world of the audience, for the shepherd Juan's direct address of the Duchess of Alba in the audience has incorporated the spectators into the reality of the play.[154]

In large part, I accept Surtz's distinction. The notion of a spectator "seeing him or herself transported" to another time is a modern phenomenon, because it relies on a theatrical experience of space. However, where Surtz sees "no strict division between the play world and the world of the audience," I see Juan del Encina as constantly playing with just such a distinction. And where Surtz sees only the participatory interaction between spectators and audience that precedes and precludes the separation of modern theatrical space, I see Encina creating and transgressing that boundary, a creation and transgression that is in many ways the focal point of his drama.

Surtz's argument relies on the fact that Encina's eclogues all take place in the present, even when "characters" from Biblical stories are involved. Since their time is the present and, indeed, their space is that of the ducal palace where they are being performed, they require no separation of the space and time of the audience from that of the story, and consequently allow the audience members, the Duke and Duchess whom Encina wishes to be his patrons,[155] to participate as themselves in the drama. But is the "present" portrayed in Encina's eclogues and the "present" of a *mystère*, a liturgical drama, or *El auto de los reyes magos* really the same? I have argued that these performances rely on a mimesis whose function is to invoke or participate in a timeless present, an event that, although also historical in some senses, attains its truth in its universality—that it is, in other words, as real now as it was when the event in question (say, the Resurrection) actually occurred. The present of Juan del Encina's eclogues is not this kind of present, at least not all the time. Rather, the presentation of his plays to the Duke and Duchess is framed by a present that is utterly concrete and far from universal, a present that he anchors by identifying himself, the author, within it.

Encina begins his first eclogue by describing how the first of two shepherds, the one called Juan, entered the hall where the Duke and Duchess were seated:[156]

> Y aquel que Juan se llamava entró primero en la sala adonde el Duque y Duquesa estavan oyendo maitines y, en nombre de Juan del Encina, llegó a presentar cien coplas de aquesta fiesta a la señora Duquesa.[157]

> [And the one called Juan entered first in the hall where the Duke and Duchess were gathered to hear Matins and, in the name of Juan del Enzina, came to present a hundred couplets concerning that feast to the Duchess.]

The shepherd named Juan, who was almost certainly Juan del Encina himself, presents the Duchess with a hundred couplets in the name of the author Juan del Encina. At this moment, then, the Duke and Duchess are asked to recognize both the presence of Encina in the room, and his absence, as he both is and is not the shepherd who is presenting the poems in his name.

Juan the shepherd's worth as a poet, in fact, becomes the focus of this eclogue, as he and his interlocutor, Mateo, engage in a war of words over the value of his verses:

> Mateo:
> Déxate dessas barajas,
> que poca ganancia cobras.
> Yo conoço bien tus obras:
> todas no valen dos pajas.[158]
>
> [Cut the crap,
> since you're not winning any points.
> I know your works well:
> none of them is worth two straws.]
>
> Juan:
> Y no dudo aver errada
> en algún mi viejo escrito,
> que cuando era zagalito
> no sabía casi nada.
> Mas agora va labrada
> tan por arte mi lavor
> que, aunque sea remirada,
> no avrá cosa mal trobada
> si no miente el escritor.[159]
>
> [I don't doubt that I've erred
> in some of my old writing,
> since when I was a boy
> I knew almost nothing.
> But now my labor, with art
> is so elaborated
> that even if it's looked at twice
> nothing badly worked will be found
> if the writer doesn't lie.]

The last line is the *coup de gràce* in Juan's exposition of his own self worth, as it involves the relativization and manipulation of the very genre of his exposition from the inside out. The structure of the trope is one of truth via pretense (which we will analyze in much greater detail in the following chapter), in that

Encina the poet demonstrates a truth—the artistry of his poetry, the cleverness of his play with theatrical spaces, etc.—by encasing that demonstration in a pretense in which the poet in question is a shepherd named Juan, arguing with another Shepherd, Mateo, etc. In order for this trope to be effective, in order for the noble audience to get the joke, they must grasp not merely the *unity* of the time and place and the *participation* of the characters with their own persons, but also the *distinction* between Juan the poet and Juan the character.

The complications multiply in the next eclogue, which was performed the same night. In this piece, the same Shepherds, Juan and Mateo, are joined by two others, Lucas and Marco, completing the square of the four evangelists, Mark, Luke, Mathew and John, who begin to speak about the Good News of the coming of the Lord, each capturing the style of his respective namesake. Both Henry Sullivan and Bruce Wardropper agree that the appearance of the evangelists lifts this eclogue to a level of striking complexity:

> By the time the second eclogue is under way, he argues, the aristocratic audience is required to suppose that the actors are—at one and the same time—their own sheep-herding employees, the Nativity shepherds, their court poet and his enemies, the four Evangelists, as well as real actors portraying fictional characters.[160]

In Surtz's view, the audience is prepared for the "ambiguity" created by the introduction of the four evangelists by the allegorical form of the liturgy, in which the priest is understood to be *both* himself and Christ.[161] However, there is nothing in the liturgical texts, or in any other of the descriptions of medieval spectacle we have discussed so far, to suggest that the viewers would perceive any dualism at all in such performances. In other words, the celebrant speaking Christ's words and repeating Christ's gestures conjures Christ's presence, but these events in no way occur in distinguishable realities. Juan del Encina's performance, on the other hand, draws attention precisely to the interplay of realities, by insisting on the paradoxical co-presence of Juan the poet, Juan the shepherd, and Juan the evangelist.

One last example of the splintering of space in Encina's eclogues comes from the last pair of the "Salamanca" series, *Égloga representada en requesta de unos amores*, and *Égloga de Mingo, Gil y Pascuala*. Although conceived of and published as a pair, Encina indicates in his preface to each that they were performed a year apart, and the action within the plays reflects this same passage of time. This correlation between actual time and represented time would seem to support Surtz's contention that no distinction yet exists between the two, in that "[t]he spectators are not required to imagine that what they see before them is occurring somewhere else or in a time different from the present."[162] But it is my contention that the opposite is true, that Encina and his actors are in fact forcing their noble audience to confront them on two different planes of existence, first creating distinct, theatrical realities, and then transgressing the frame in order to incorporate their audience into the new space.

The seventh eclogue tells the story of the shepherdess Pascuala, a shepherd Mingo who, although already married, is trying to win her for himself, and a squire who encounters them and decides to win her love as well. Encina's prologue describes "una pastorcica llamada Pascuala que, yendo cantando con su ganado, entró en la sala adonde el Duque y Duquesa estavan. Y luego después della entró un pastor, llamado Mingo, y comenzó a requerilla"[163] [a shepherdess named Pascuala who, walking along with her herd, singing, entered the hall where the Duke and Duchess were. And after her entered a shepherd named Mingo, and began to woo her]. This is the only time in the seventh eclogue that Encina mentions the presence of the Duke and Duchess, although we can clearly assume that they remained there for the duration of the performance. And although all the action would seem necessarily to take place not only in their presence but inside their hall, neither the two shepherds nor their noble companion the squire ever notice their presence.

When the squire agrees to become a shepherd in order to win her love, Pascuala agrees to have him, and the eclogue comes to an end with a traditional celebratory song and dance. The next eclogue, number eight, continues the story of Mingo, Pascuala, and the squire (now named Gil), a year later, and we learn that Gil has kept his promise and has become a shepherd. Now, however, their presence in the ducal hall becomes an explicit focus of the play, such that Mingo, who was blissfully unaware of the nobles' presence the year before, is terrified to enter the hall.

Mingo:
En me ver ante mis amos
me perturbo y me demudo.

[Seeing myself before my masters
I am getting upset and blushing.]

Gil:
¿De qué te perturbas, di?
¡Sí nunca medre tu greña!

[What are you so upset about?
Your disheveled looks won't get you ahead!]

Mingo:
Dígote que de vergüeña
estoy ageno de mí.

[I'm telling you
that I'm beside myself with shame.]

Gil:
¿Que estás ageno de ti?
Torna, torna en ti, Dios praga,
y pues espacio nos vaga,
desasnémonos aquí.[164]

[Beside yourself?
Get back inside yourself, God willing,
and since there's plenty of space
let's dismount here.]

The easiest assumption would be that, in a completely modern sense, the space of the hall is being used to represent two different places. But there is a problem with this reading as well. A little later in the eclogue, Mingo says that Pascuala left him for Gil "en aquesta mesma sala" [in this same room] the year before.[165] But if that is the case, then how are we to account for the fact that Mingo was then totally unaware of the masters who so completely terrify him now?

The most likely answer is that Encina is able to *either* separate the place of the action from the given space, as in the seventh eclogue, *or* make it identical to the place of the performance, as he does in the eighth, but is not fluent at maneuvering between these possibilities. Lacking a tradition of stage conventions allowing for such flexibility of space, Encina feels obliged to rewrite history, claiming the same reality for the space of the prior year that he now claims for the present one, even if that claim produces its own inconsistencies. But these inconsistencies are there, and they demonstrate that Encina and his audience were capable of distinguishing the space of the performance from that of the action. It is this distinction that accounts for Encina's invention of character.[166]

What should we conclude, then, from this evidence? Does the invention of character by Juan del Encina give us a definitive moment, the decisive turning point, in the shift between two radically different modes of being? In fact, what I hope to show is the opposite: that even if it is the most decisive single element of the shift from presence to theatricality, the invention of character is, in itself, a relatively trivial moment. In this sense it does not matter if, a few years earlier or a few decades later, one finds similar evidence in the work of another playwright. Nor is it an extraordinary cause for skepticism that some of the very examples of courtly entertainment I have used to exemplify the political functioning of presence are in fact quite close to the theater of Juan del Encina. No one change, no single innovation in itself, accounts for the transformation of spatiality in the early modern period. What this analysis of Juan del Encina does show, however, was that the seeds of theatricality were planted in distant and disparate gardens, and that it was only the conjunction of a multitude of such changes that brought about a situation new enough to require a new vocabulary to describe it. This new vocabulary is the subject of the next chapter.

CHAPTER 3

Saint Genesius on the Stage of the World

In John Schlesinger's 1976 film *Marathon Man*, the hero, played by Dustin Hoffman, is brutally tortured by a fugitive Nazi villain played by Laurence Olivier. In preparation for the role, Hoffman apparently experimented with a variety of mind-altering substances in an effort to "get into his character"—who was meant to be dazed, sleep deprived and in terrible pain—as intimately as possible. Needless to say, his efforts only led to the need to retake the scene more times than is normally necessary, an inconvenience that prompted the somewhat exasperated Olivier to exclaim, "Oh, gracious, why doesn't the dear boy just *act*?!"[1]

There can perhaps be no more striking (or one-sided) illustration than this story of the much discussed rivalry between the American and British schools of acting, the "method" developed by Konstantin Stanislavsky versus the "technique" deployed by the great actors of the English stage. The tension, succinctly put, is between the method's injunction to full identification with the character, mediated by the recollection of events in one's own life evoking a similar emotional state (not, however, by the ingestion of mind-altering substances)—in brief, an attempt to dissolve the boundaries separating oneself from the character one wishes to portray—and the technique's directive to *act* one's character, to master a series of, well, *techniques* for the manipulation of body, expression, and voice in order to deceive a spectator into believing in the truth of one's representation.

This apparent division, however, masks a more fundamental commonality. Both of these approaches to the portrayal of a character depend on the same theory of what an actor is and how he or she is related to this entity called character. This theory comprises two principal elements: first, that the space in which the action of the story being represented is what I call an alternate, but viable, imaginary space (in that it is a space simultaneous and coterminous with one's own that, while not *in fact* existing, exists nonetheless in the imagination of some group of people who, in turn, can imagine *themselves* existing and acting in that space); second, that the character is in some sense an autonomous entity inhabiting that imaginary space. In this context, a method of acting is a series of recommendations concerning how best to bring that character "to life" in such a way that the audience for whom one is performing may experience that imaginary space as believable—in such a way, in other words, that the imaginary space becomes *viable* for them, too, and the characters inhabiting that space become viable objects of identification. If "method" and "technique" differ, then, it is in how they approach this single goal: technique insisting on the need to distance oneself from the character, in order best to construct it by means of the actors' tools—their bodies and voices—and method advocating the (temporary) dissolution of the self and its replacement with the self or *persona* of the character.

What theorists and teachers of acting, be they partisans of technique or of method, do not often realize, is that this theory of actor and character they share is not itself a universal and self-evident truth. This "modern" theory of character is, rather, a historically specific phenomenon, the result of precisely that change in the practices of spectacle that I am describing in this book and, therefore, a central coordinate of that mode of being I call theatricality, whose ascendance characterizes so strongly the modern age. If chapter 2 was intended to describe, by way of an exposition of medieval techniques of spectacle, the mode of being called presence, the rest of this book will be dedicated to the notion of theatricality, although with some attention to the ways in which presence is incorporated by and supports the relations predominantly determined by theatricality. The present chapter, then, will introduce the notion of theatricality by contrasting it, as it always must be contrasted, to that of presence, and by defining it in relation to two of its principal manifestations: the experience of character and the experience of imaginary space. I begin in the eighteenth century with Diderot's provocative treatise on acting, *Le paradoxe sur le comédien*, and trace its notion of character back to the seventeenth century, to its appearance and thematization in two canonical plays, Lope de Vega's *Lo fingido verdadero* and Jean Rotrou's *Le véritable Saint Genest*. After arguing that these are explicit examples of the inherently metatheatrical structure of the modern drama that has establishes itself at this time in France and Spain, I retreat even further into the past to examine how the same theme that is treated in the plays of Lope and Rotrou, the martyrdom of the actor-saint Genesius—a theme that would appear logically to require a metatheatrical staging technique, that is, a play within a play—appears in a fifteenth century French *mystère*, *L'ystoire de la vie et glorieux corps de saint Genis*. On the basis of this comparison, I argue that it is precisely the notions of character and space that I associate with theatricality that determine the radical difference between the fifteenth and seventeenth century renditions of this story and that are, therefore, indispensable elements for defining the essence of the modern theater. At this point the ground will be laid to turn in the fourth chapter to the material and theoretical transformations in the form of spectacle in France and Spain—comprising, for example, changes in stage architecture in the contexts of Paris and Madrid—in order to describe the phenomenon of theatricality as it emerges in and throughout the sixteenth century. This phenomenological description of the material basis of theatricality finally serves as the background for a return to Lope's play, and a reading of it as an exploration of the new spatiality, and of its philosophical and aesthetic ramifications.

DIDEROT'S PARADOX

While Diderot's advice to actors might have seemed paradoxical in the eighteenth century, to our ears it is in perfect keeping with at least one side of the debate I have described. The gist of Diderot's paradox is that the great actor is not the one who feels the most—not, that is, what he calls the man of sentiment—but rather is the man of "sang-froid."[2] Granted, an actor's job is to portray a reality, usually a human reality, and often one brimming with emotions. But despite this obvious fact, a great actor must be emotionally cold or, more to the point, must possess the ability to distance him or herself entirely from the emotions being portrayed.[3] The principal reason for this preference is that the story represented on the stage, unlike the ongoing stories of our real lives, must be repeated with frequency, and actors who are in fact emotionally involved in the story they are presenting cannot hope to present that story in the same way every time. The great actor, on the other hand, is indiscriminate; he is like a mirror, coldly and consistently reflecting the vicissitudes of human existence: "Il ne sera pas journalier: c'est une glace toujours disposée à montrer les objets et à les montrer avec la même précision, la même force et la même vérité"[4] [He won't change from day to day: he is a mirror always disposed to showing objects and showing them with the same precision, the same force and same truth].

The key to this mechanical consistency is that actors are able to sharply distinguish between themselves and the characters they portray. Actors, in other words, have an ability to replicate themselves on the stage, to create a facsimile and then detach themselves entirely from its emotional situation, while simultaneously making the audience feel all the more potently those emotions. The simulacrum becomes like a shell, surrounding the actor's person but not touching it, a shell of which the actor is the soul, in that she[5] gives it life, but from which her own emotional life is completely independent. This character, this "phantom," he insists, is not she: "Ce n'est pas elle."[6]

This self-replicating ability, however, is not limited to actors. Rather, it is a quality shared by all who aspire to a public life and, to some degree, to all political subjects:

> L'homme sensible est trop abandonné à la merci de son diaphragme pour être un grand roi, un grand politique, un grand magistrat, un homme juste, un profond observateur, et conséquemment un sublime imitateur de la nature, à moines qu'il ne puisse s'oublier et se distraire de lui-même, et qu'à l'aide d'une imagination forte il ne sache se créer, et d'une mémoire tenace tenir

son attention fixée sur des fantômes qui lui servent de modèles; mais alors ce n'est plus lui qui agit, c'est l'esprit d'un autre qui le domine.[7]

[The sensitive man is too much at the mercy of his diaphragm to be a great king, a great politician, a great judge, a just man, a profound observer, and consequently a sublime imitator of nature, unless he can forget himself and distract himself from himself, and with the help of a strong imagination know to create himself, and with a tenacious memory keep his attention fixed on the phantoms that serve as his models; but then it is no longer he who acts, it is the spirit of another that dominates him.]

Thus Diderot himself gives us the first clue that not only is the actor's paradox probably not entirely paradoxical, it does not exclusively concern actors either, but rather human *interaction* in general. If actors and successful public figures have a special ability in common, it is not that of duplicating the self—an ability that would appear quite common, if not unavoidable—but is rather that of detaching their emotional reserves from that second self, their character. The logical correlate to this detachment is that one subordinates one's emotional responses to the domination of one's character, a character fashioned, Diderot insists, after a fixed ideal. Thus we already see in Diderot a formulation of what Freud will codify in his theory of the ego: namely, that the self or ego is a character one develops and portrays for the outside world, and in deference to which one sacrifices some portion of the desires that constitute one's inner self. In this sense, then, Freud's discovery is specific to a particular, historical mode of being, one whose model of selfhood is this relation between actor and character and whose space of interaction is the space of the stage. To say this, however, is in no way to disparage Freud's discovery. For to do so would be tantamount to claiming that this mode of being is no longer ours, that we are not determined by its norms, a claim, I hope to show, as naive as it is unwarranted.

Although Diderot's formulation might not strike the reader today as particularly paradoxical, the fact that it was intended to appear as such to his contemporaries suggests that in Diderot's time the received wisdom was that great, that is, convincing, acting involved the capacity to identify with one's character. Two plays from the seventeenth century that deal explicitly with actors and acting provide evidence that this view was, in fact, widely held. In Lope de Vega's *Lo fingido verdadero*, probably performed first in 1608, Ginés, an actor in Roman times, explains the secret of his success in the following terms:

El imitar es ser representante;
pero como el poeta no es posible
que escriba con afecto y con blandura
sentimientos de amor, si no le tiene,

y entonces se descubren en sus versos,
cuando el amor le enseña los que escriben,
así el representante, si no siente
las pasiones de amor, es imposible
que pueda, gran señor, representarlas . . .[8]

[To imitate is to be an actor;
but just as it's impossible for the poet
to write with affect and charm
the feelings of love, if he has it not,
which are then to be found in the verses,
of those whom love teaches to write them,
so for the actor, if he feels not
the passions of love, it is impossible
for him, great lord, to represent them . . .]

Ginés categorizes acting with other forms of artistic creation, such as poetry (a general term for all creative writing, theater included), as a form of mimesis, for which one depends on an actual lived experience as a model. Writing and acting are two variations of the same mimetic practice; the difference being that writing imitates with words, while the actor imitates with her body. In both cases, however, the artist must be privy to a firsthand knowledge, a subjective experience of great similarity to the object of imitation. Just as, one might reason, a painter—whose realm is the visual—must experience via her senses the reality she depicts on her canvas, so the poet and the actor must experience emotionally the reality they portray through their media of representation. Note that for neither the poet nor the actor is the object of representation present to the senses; the substance of the reality they represent is an emotional content, the content of character. When Diderot suggests a century later that one ought not endeavor to feel subjectively this emotional content but rather to portray it via an exact rendering of its outward signs in observed behavior, he is revitalizing the figure of the painter as the appropriate model of theatrical mimesis; but his purpose is identical to Lope's: to make a character, a figure defined by a particular emotional content, believable for an audience. Since most audiences neither do nor did accept the reality portrayed on the stage as actually occurring on the same plane of reality as their own, "believable" should be understood as viable, that is, as being perceived as a person with whom one could interact meaningfully were he or she a part of one's immediate reality.

Another instance of the seventeenth century's take on Stanislavsky's method can be found in Jean Rotrou's version of the story told in Lope's play, the legend of Saint Genesius. In Rotrou's *Le véritable Saint Genest*, the actor Genest councils his leading lady Marcelle to approach a difficult character via analogy:

Marcelle:
Et voilà l'embarras!
Ce que vous treuvez beau me semble ridicule.
Comment rendre touchante une femme crédule
Qui mieux qu'un bel époux préfère un sot trépas,
Et comprendre un esprit qui ne se comprend pas?
Comment juger, sentir . . .

Genest:
Mais par analogie.
Jamais aucun objet préférable à la vie
Ne s'est-il emparé de votre coeur?[9]

[*Marcelle:*
And there's the rub!
What you find beautiful seems ridiculous to me.
How do I render touching a gullible woman
Who to a handsome husband prefers a foolish corpse,
And understand a soul that doesn't even understand itself?
How do I judge, feel . . .

Genest:
Why, by analogy.
Has no object, more precious than life,
Ever taken control of your heart?]

Marcelle's complaint is that there is what might be called a subjective dissonance between her and the character whom she is to imitate. She cannot render touching, because she cannot make viable, portray in a believable manner, a character whose values she deplores; she cannot, in other words, *identify* with this character and consequently does not believe herself capable of adequately representing her for an audience. For Diderot this would be the complaint of an inferior, ill-prepared actor: there is no need to identify with such a person; one merely peruses the infinite variety of characters surrounding us in our quotidian existence, finds the appropriate model, and makes a copy. Genest, on the other hand, takes the complaint seriously, and answers that one can represent even those characters most anathema to one's own if one searches for an analogy for that character's incomprehensible motivation in a motivation that, while structurally similar to it, is nonetheless comprehensible. As a contemporary example, a straight and perhaps even homophobic actor, who claims to find his character's love for another man incomprehensible, might successfully come to portray, and perhaps even to comprehend, that character if he approaches his feelings in a way analogous to feelings he may have had for a woman.

Whether by analogy or direct subjective experience, the seventeenth century believed that an actor imitated the emotional state of a character, thereby rendering that character viable for an audience, by coming to identify with that character as a human being living out a given emotional situation.[10] As we shall see below, the development of theatrical practices in the sixteenth century was accompanied by the emergence of a body of theoretical work that increasingly emphasized the goal of verisimilitude, the "realistic" portrayal of human events and interactions on the stage. Such a notion of mimesis as essential to poiesis is hardly new. Nevertheless, there is a potentially infinite number of conventions and configurations for any given act of imitation: a verbal description, for example, does not imitate in the same way as does a photograph. The question that confronts us is whether the mode of mimesis I have described above—which becomes the dominant mode for using human bodies to tell a story well into the twentieth century—in fact depends, as I have been claiming, on a different mode of being and spatiality than the forms of bodily mimesis that preceded it.

To reiterate, the form of mimesis I am describing is one in which a body represents a character, instead of functioning as a narrative medium, as in the telling of a story; or as an object of contemplation, as in sculpture or painting; or as an allegorical sign, as in a morality play; or even as a stand-in or indicator of a theological truth, or a catalyst for a miracle, as in the mystery plays and the Mass. This body is able to represent this character because there is something structurally analogous between the two. Since the analogy cannot lie at the physical level—the character, after all, does not have its own body—it must exist elsewhere, at the level, for instance, of the imagination. The actor, in other words, can represent a character only insofar as he or she already has an imaginary conception of him or herself, as long as he or she already is, therefore, a character. What is more, the audience for whom the actor represents his or her character is capable of negotiating this complicated distinction between the actor's own character and the character he or she is temporarily representing. It can do this because its members are themselves actors, actors who, for a period of time coinciding with the time of the production, collectively and tacitly agree to step out of their own characters (the roles they are playing in their everyday lives) and take on the ethereal and abstract role of the spectator.

The spectator's highly conventionalized lack of corporeality allows it to enter and perceive as viable or "realistic" an imaginary configuration of interrupted space and time that would be otherwise incomprehensible. The spectators—actors in the place called the audience—see themselves represented by characters on the stage, avatars through whom they engage in another reality and experience its emotional pleasures and pains. Likewise, they experience the characters on the stage not as mere representations, but rather as representatives of complex and mostly concealed psychologies and desires, motivations that they, like the other characters up on the stage, must interpret and explain.

When any two people interact, they do so via the mediation of representatives, namely, the words or signifiers they use to represent their intentions and desires. This recalls Lacan's definition of a signifier as that which represents the subject who utters it. However, the signifier does not represent the subject for another subject, but rather represents him or her for another signifier, for the representative of another subject—that is, for the words the other represents him or herself with.[11] To describe the same dynamic, albeit with a different emphasis, one could say that as inter*acting* subjects we are represented by our characters, and that, as a result, *a character is what represents an actor for another character*.[12] Such a formulation is, I believe, central to the spatiality subtending the theatrical form of bodily mimesis characteristic of the modern theater: theatricality. If it is the case, however, that the theater as such takes place in a world in which people already interact as characters portrayed by actors, then the stage on which these people witness the interaction of characters must, in some sense be a *metastage*, in that the actors who appear on it are themselves already characters, that is, the representatives of other actors (the people they are in real life). In the same way, the imaginary space of the stage, the space inhabited by characters and governed by different spatial and temporal laws than those that govern the hard wooden flats whose space it occupies, must itself be subject to the same rupture that engendered it, must itself be always poised to subdivide into relatively real and imaginary spaces. It is not an accident, then, that the two plays to which I have come for a seventeenth-century perspective on acting are, in fact, metaplays, or plays within plays. For while all plays at this time did not have recourse to this trope, it was certainly, as we shall see, an innovation of the period. And while the actual device of the play within the play may have been rare relative to the enormous theatrical production of the seventeenth century, it can be stated nevertheless that all plays potentially were metaplays; in other words, the essence of the modern theater is metatheater.

METATHEATER

If, as I want to claim, what we mean by "theater" is the modern theater, and that to designate as theater a spectacle from before the sixteenth century is a problem of vocabulary, then the statement with which I ended the previous passage risks descending into paradox: the essence of theater is metatheater? To be more precise, I could formulate it as follows: there can be no theater that is not already a metatheater, in that in the instant a distinction is recognized between a real space and another, imaginary one that mirrors it, that very distinction becomes an element to be incorporated as another distinction in the imaginary space's work of mimesis. This second distinction becomes incorporated as a third, and so on, as a potentially infinite *mise en abime*. Therefore, while there are plenty of plays that do not refer explicitly to the theater, all plays that share in this representational structure are characterized by this potential. But it is more than a mere potential, because the space of the representation, no matter what the content of the performance, is structured as metatheatrical—hence, in my terminology, theatrical—space.

The term "metatheater" was coined in 1963 by the critic Lionel Abel, in his book by the same name.[13] His definition, while requiring some elaboration, is a good place to start. Metatheater, he says, consists of those "theatre pieces about life seen as already theatricalized." The characters of metaplays, "unlike figures in tragedy . . . are aware of their own theatricality." Finally, sounding a note of historical specificity, he adds that "from a certain modern point of view, only that life which has acknowledged its inherent theatricality can be made interesting on the stage."[14] From the perspective of the theory of theatricality I am forwarding, each of these is a remarkably accurate statement. What requires elaboration, however, is the concept of theatricality so central to all of these claims. Before passing to this problem, however, it behooves me to touch upon the distinction between metatheater and two other concepts with which it is often confused: the play within a play, and the world as stage.

According to Abel, the distinction between a play within a play and metatheater is that the former suggests only a device, one that metatheater need not even encompass.[15] Georges Forestier, the reigning expert in France on the play within the play, heartily agrees, complaining of a pernicious tendency in criticism to confuse such disparate and unrelated devices and concepts as disguisings, role playing, and theatricality with the specific technique (*procédé*) of *le théâtre dans le théâtre*.[16] It is, of course, my intention to engage in precisely this pernicious tendency because, in my view, metatheater, which would encompass all those other corrupting elements, is nothing other than a generalization of the specific practice of staging a play within a play; this specific device, on the other hand, is merely a literalization of a tendency inherent in all theater. But as such, its history and various manifestations are of great interest.

If the general opinion of critics is in favor of drawing a solid distinction between metatheater and the device of the play within the play, the consensus would appear to be that there exists a close relation between the latter and the theological metaphor of the world as stage.[17] The same critics, however, also note that at the thematic level, the world-as-theater metaphor is often invoked in two forms: one, the form made famous by Calderón, in which the world is a stage on which the human drama is played out before the eyes of the divine playwright; the second, immortalized by Jacques in Shakespeare's *As You Like It*:

> All the world's a stage
> And all the men and women merely players.
> They have their exits and their entrances,
> And one man in his time plays many parts. . . .[18]

The crucial point to recognize is that while the metaphors can be expressed in the same words, they are in fact two entirely distinct metaphors. As all recognize, the theological notion was not in any way an innovation of the baroque period, but appears in such historically and culturally varied sources as Plato, John of Salisbury (1159), and Dante.[19] The distinction between the two metaphors echoes the distinction I addressed in chapter 1 between two possible readings of John Austin's notion of etiolated speech. Recall that, whereas Derrida read Austin as rejecting the actor's speech because his or her words were written by another and hence could not be expressing an original intention, I suggested that the more appropriate reading was that the actor's speech represented an etiolation of language because of the uncertainty concerning the intended receiver of that speech: is an actor's speech directed at the audience or at another character? The contrast between the two meanings of the world as stage is structurally identical: in the theological reading, the world is uncertain because we are all playing temporary roles in a play written and directed by God—the meaning of our words and actions, in other words, is determined by the intentions of another: God; in the secular or "structural" reading, the world is uncertain because we are all the time playing different roles for different audiences—our characters, in other words, are unstable. Just as I rejected Derrida's "theological" reading of Austin as inappropriate for a discussion of the problem of a specifically modern form of subjectivity, so I feel it necessary to discard the theological version of the world-as-stage metaphor as inappropriate for an understanding of metatheater, and hence of theatricality. Metatheater is not a theme but a structure, and it is the structure of metatheater that is specific to the historical problem of the individual's modes of self-conception and self-representation. Unlike the theological stage metaphor, it is an innovation of the sixteenth century; and unlike that metaphor, it is intimately related to the device of the play within a play.

Whereas the topic has been treated many times in articles or as part of larger studies, the only two extended studies devoted exclusively to the phenomenon of the play within a play are Nelson's *The Play within a Play* and Forestier's *Le théâtre dans le théâtre*. According to Forestier's definition, as long as there is a character who appears to play a role consciously in the presence of other characters, there is theater in the theater.[20] The necessary condition, then, for the existence of the device is the appearance of what he calls interior spectators.[21] However, he distinguishes the interior spectator of a true play within a play from a character who might, say, witness a disguising or a dance by insisting on the need for a "change in levels" to occur between the outer piece and the enframed piece.[22] The two stories must, in other words, take place in separate and distinguishable realities, what we might call, with Goffman, the keying of frames.[23]

Luiz Costa Lima, in applying Goffman's notion specifically to the relation of mimesis and representation, defines keying in a particularly concise way as "a device by means of which an agent carries out a series of actions that, from the standpoint of the primary frame, would convey a specific meaning that in fact does not apply."[24] The fact that there is always a "change in levels" between the interior and exterior dramas of a play within a play indicates precisely this relationship of "nonperformativity" of a given action to a separately framed reality. Again, this failure of performativity is precisely the same one that Austin tried to exclude from his analysis of everyday language and that Derrida focused on as being exemplary of the endemic citationality of language. What I am positing, on the contrary, is that this failure of performativity (which is also constitutive of fiction) is, in the realm of human interacting, a function of the keying of frames that are themselves sustained by the gazes of different audiences.

There is no disagreement over the fact that the device of the play within the play seems to have been an invention of the early modern period, and while each of the two critics tells a slightly different creation story, it is clear that use of the device achieved its apogee during the seventeenth century.[25] The story they agree on is that the influence of the rediscovery in Italy of plays and works of theory from the classical period, as well as the development of perspective in scene design and its eventual replacement of medieval, multiple location staging, were vital for the technique, which had been present in embryonic form in the Middle Ages, to finally come into its own.[26] They also both agree that this process necessitated the replacement of the ritual, communal, participatory theater of the mysteries with a new sort of spectacle that separated more strictly the gazers from the gazed. However, Forestier adds, this evolution would not have sufficed on its own; rather, the prevalence of the structure during the Baroque is the result of its affinity with the mentality of an epoque, a mentality that saw the world as a play and that expressed itself in terms of a redoubling of reality.[27] I would like to insist, however, that there is no evidence for a pre-existing aesthetic or mentality whose convergence with certain embryonic practices inherited from classical antiquity and the Middle Ages brought about the sudden appearance of this innovation in theatrical style. Rather, this innovation in the practices of spectacle is an integral element in a complex process of change that is not merely linked to an aesthetic or mentality, but is rather constitutive of it. This aesthetic, this mentality, is a result of the theatrical organization of space, and the play within a play is merely the most visible manifestation of its metatheatrical structure.

Forestier suggests that the epoch's mentality was in some sense an *efficient* cause of the device's sudden appearance at the end of the sixteenth century. In my view, the efficient causes are perforce multiple, highly contingent, and perhaps even too complex to trace accurately. Moreover, to assign a great deal of theoretical importance to the discovery of a historical phenomenon's efficient causes seems to me to be the signature of an unacknowledged teleological impulse, as if the myriad events converging to bring about a new norm or practice contained the knowledge of that outcome hardwired into some noumenal circuitry. The existence of a mentality I call theatricality did not cause the appearance of metatheatrical staging techniques in an *efficient* sense, in the sense that Forestier implies with his convergence theory. However, from another perspective, it *can* be argued that theatricality caused the appearance of these phenomena in a *teleological*[28] sense: namely, it can be argued, as I am arguing, *in retrospect*, that the techniques of the stage developed out of their innumerable efficient causes "in order that" theatricality could emerge.[29] And, as I will develop later, theatricality can be said to have emerged "in order that" a new political order, that of the modern nation state, could impose itself on western Europe.

That said, it still remains perfectly valid to claim that metatheatrical staging techniques form part, albeit an important part, of a broader array of cultural phenomena. The Spanish cultural historian Emilio Orozco Díaz, for example, considers such phenomena as metatheatrical staging techniques to be an instance of what he refers to as the theatricalization of all aspects of life in the Baroque, including the theater itself.[30] Like Forestier, Orozco Díaz attributes the enormous popularity of the theater to its coincidence with a certain worldview best expressed in the metaphor of the world as stage, but he also describes the phenomena he incorporates within the theatrical as involving a spatial dynamic that has fundamental similarities to the notion of metatheatrical space I am advancing.

According to Orozco Díaz, the Baroque is best characterized by a generalized and pervasive sense of the theater's pertinence to everyday life: "Todos actúan como actores, con la conciencia de su vestir, de sus movimientos y de sus gestos; sienténdose contemplados"[31] [All act like actors, conscious of their dress, of their movements and gestures; feeling themselves watched]; or, as he states at another point, "Se trata en todos los casos, según hemos visto antes, de una general participación, de un actuar en la vida como personaje de teatro representando un papel"[32] [In all cases it concerns, as we have already seen, a general participation, an acting in life as if one were a stage character playing a role]. It would appear, therefore, that Orozco Díaz's thesis concerns the perception of norms of interpersonal behavior at the time—behavior, as he points out, which, far from being reserved for instances of ceremony, extended to the most banal and quotidian practices.[33] However, his definition of theatricality (*teatralidad*) would appear to imply a more structural, spatial dimension as well. It concerns, he says, movement and the overflowing of borders, and if its ultimate explanation is a spiritual one (he links it explicitly with a Christian view of the universe) its principal manifestations are stylistic.[34]

What, then, is the relation between his stylistic and his sociological explanations of theatricality? While he never makes explicit this connection, it is precisely here that I locate the notion of theatricality I am trying to advance. Orozco Díaz describes baroque space as involving a dynamic of profundity and the tendency of the spectacle to penetrate into the space reserved for the audience—he sees it, in other words, as the increased fluidity between spaces, the overflow of theatrical into real space.[35]

> Responde a una concepción y visión de continuidad espacial que considera la obra inmensa en un espacio continuo, como situada en plano o término intermedio en relación con los otros planos que quedan detrás y los que existen delante, y dentro de los cuales estamos nosotros, los espectadores. . . . Esta interpenetración expresiva y espacial es esencial de la concepción artística barroca; lleva a la auténtica incorporación del espectador a la obra de arte.[36]

> [It responds to a conception and vision of spatial continuity that views the immense work as occupying a continuous space, as if situated on an intermediate plane in relation to the other planes that exist in front of and behind it, within which we the spectators can be found. . . . This expressive, spatial interpenetration is essential to the artistic conception of the Baroque; it produces the authentic incorporation of the spectator into the work of art.]

This tendency is observable, of course, in the theater, in practices such as asides and soliloquies as well as in the more explicitly metatheatrical devices we have discussed.[37] But it is also markedly present in other artistic practices, such as in painting.[38]

If Orozco Díaz describes the baroque innovation as the subversion of the borders between real and fictive space, the implication is that the distinction between these spatial dimensions pre-existed its subversion. My contention is the opposite: the very practices that Orozco Díaz sees as blurring the boundaries between illusion and reality are, in fact, constitutive of that distinction, at least in the domain of the visual arts. The constitution of a frame separating realities that are nevertheless susceptible to interpenetration and mise en abîme, *precisely because the spaces that comprise them are mimetically related*, is an essential characteristic of theatricality and therefore a technique most typical of the period defined by its ascendance, the Baroque.[39] However, as I will show in the following chapters, these practices accompanied the development of modern theater throughout the sixteenth century as well.

Now, what is radically new about the space behind the frame is the fact that it is a viable space, one inhabitable by the spectator via his or her representatives.[40] The fact that the space beyond the frame is itself partitioned into relative subdivisions of reality and illusion, themselves only determined by the positionality of spectators, makes of the entire ensemble, including reality ground zero (but who could be sure where that is?), a spectator-dependent system. In other words, the experience of space as being structured by a series of frames distinguishing the real from the imaginary, actors from characters, and spectators from those being watched invokes the ineradicable suspicion that one's own lived reality might, at any time, be the object of, and therefore exist for, the gazes of others. It conjures the disorienting sensation that one's own-most self might perhaps be no more than a character manufactured for the benefit of others. It is this epistemic condition, I believe, that accounts for the theatricalization that Orozco Díaz describes as characteristic of baroque life, and that explains the relation between this social phenomenon and the aesthetic innovations of baroque artistic practices.

ACTORS AND MARTYRS

According to legend, Saint Genesius was an actor living in Rome during the fourth century rule of the emperor Diocletian. Called to the court one day to portray the martyrdom of Christians for the Emperor, he was seized by the holy spirit and converted to Christianity on the spot, enraging Diocletian and bringing on his own head the very tortures he had, only hours before, been representing for the court. The story is a gold mine for thinking about the nature and potential paradoxes of theatrical representation and was, in the seventeenth century, the subject of a number of adaptations, of which Lope de Vega's and Jean Rotrou's are only the best known. Most relevant to my purposes is that the story's structure would seem to demand an explicitly metatheatrical rendering on the stage; how else to portray the conversion of a saintly actor at the moment of his enactment of another saint's martyrdom? But if this is the case, it would follow that this story could not have been the subject of a theatrical representation before the period in question. Nevertheless, a fifteenth century French mystery play has as its subject this very myth.[41] But, if what I have been claiming about metatheater is true—that it depends upon a certain epistemic condition specific to the modern period—then a fifteenth century mystery play could not be expected to tell the story of Saint Genesius, at least not to portray it.

As it happens, portraying the story of Genesius is exactly what this mystery play does do; it does so, however, without the slightest suggestion of a metatheatrical structure. The manuscript in question is approximately 100 pages in length, requiring 43 actors and, I estimate, about four hours to perform. The character Genesius (Genis) is barely ever referred to as an actor, although he is introduced surrounded by a troupe of what the Latin stage directions refer to as *mimi*,[42] who serve as a sort of comic relief, clowning around and breaking their musical instruments. They and the fact of Genesius's supposed profession, rather than serving any directly dramatic purpose, seem to function primarily as an indicator of how sinful his life was. After a discussion between Lucifer and Satan about their desire to acquire more souls, we encounter Genesius praying to his pagan idol and bemoaning the sacrilege of the Christians. Less than a fourth of the way into the script, after only two confrontations with Christians and one with the emperor Diocletian, he already begins to express his doubts about his own faith:

> Vraymant j'auray grant envye/ De savoir tout secretemant/ Se les crestiens communelmant/ Tyennent mellieur foy que nous autres. . . .[43]
>
> [Truly, I have a great desire to know, secretly, if the Christians, on the whole, have better faith than we. . . .]

Driven by his curiosity, he returns immediately to the Christians, who direct him to their priest, who in turn tells Genesius the history of the Christian faith from Genesis to the Redemption, a story he interrupts only in order to proselytize about the sacrament of the Eucharist:

> Tu dois croire sans rien doubter/ Que quant tu vois les chapellains/ Qui tiennent l'ouste en leurs mains/ Et la monstrent devotemant/ Que dieu est tout propremant/ Ainsi en cher et en corps et en ame/ Comme il naisquit de nostre dame. . . .[44]
>
> [You must believe without doubt that when you see the celebrants raise the host in their hands and display it with devotion, that God is there completely, in flesh, in body, and in soul, as he was born to our Lady. . . .]

This miracle is assured of occurring, the priest goes on to say, as long as the words are said in the same manner said by Christ at the last supper—as long as, in other words, the celebrant *repeats* Christ's words and gestures. This revelation concerning the mystery of the Eucharist is apparently most convincing, because immediately after hearing it Genis converts to the faith, all the while expressing profound contrition for his sins. The baptism that will seal his conversion is prepared and performed with great attention to ceremony, with the presbyter pouring the water over Genesius's head and an angel reading his sins from the pages of an enormous book.[45] (When Satan tries to claim Genesius's soul at the end of the play, he will look in vain for his sins in the pages of this book, but they will have been washed away.)

After his conversion, Genesius taunts and argues with the Emperor, engaging him in a theological debate in which the Emperor ridicules the paradox of the Trinity, asking how one person can simultaneously be three. Genesius defends the doctrine with a scholastic argument concerning the relationship of species to substance:

> Pour la pome cy mememant/ Et toy dis tout premieremant/ Qu'en ceste pomme a trois choses/ Qui sont dedans elle incloses/ La premiere c'est la colleur/ La secunde si est l'oudeur/ La tierce c'est la saveur bonne/ Et ses trois chouses sont in une. . . .[46]
>
> [The same for this apple here, and I tell you at first that in this apple are three things enclosed, the first is its color, the second is its odor, the third is its good flavor. And these three things are in one. . . .]

Recall that this theory of matter subtends precisely that experience of presence entailed in the doctrine of the Real Presence and that, as I discussed in chapter 2, this is precisely the theory of matter that will come into direct conflict with Cartesian epistemology.[47]

Finally, about the last fourth of the play depicts Genesius's martyrdom in horrific detail, as he is whipped naked until he bleeds from every part of his body, tied to a wooden horse with his finger and toe nails pierced by needles, and finally beheaded. At the moment of his death, Christ gives a speech from heaven, and his angels descend with swords to chase off the pagans. The play ends with Satan and Lucifer claiming Diocletian as their prize and carrying him into a hellmouth.

The space of this *mystère*, like that of medieval spectacle in general, is full, opaque, two dimensional, a picture *in* this world, even when it is otherworldy. For Genesius to be an actor as well as a martyr would require that he be a character in the sense that I developed above. It would require, in other words, that the space he inhabits be a viable space, a space constructed around a redoubling of the spectator's space; it would require a space one could enter into, whose expanding depths one could explore via a potential infinity of nesting frames. The space of the fifteenth century, however, was not such a space, and it could not hold such a character; so Genesius the martyr could not, at that time, also be an actor. When Lope de Vega, in 1608, became the first modern playwright to tell the story, it was natural that the structure he should choose would be a metaplay, just as it was natural for all those who followed, regardless of what aspects of the story each wished to emphasize. In Jean Rotrou's version, for example, Genest portrays for the emperor the story of Adrien the Christian. Whereas Genesius of the *mystère* never played any role as such for Diocletian, Rotrou's Genest succumbs to conversion precisely through his identification with the character Adrien, an identification necessitated by his acting method. In Rotrou's play, the story of Adrien the Christian dominates three out of the five acts—excepting the comments coming from the interior audience at the beginning and end of each act—and it is only at the end of the fourth act that the two stories become one, as Adrien's name is suppressed but his character is assumed in full by Genest:

> Ce n'est plus Adrien, c'est Genest qui s'exprime;
> Ce jeu n'est plus un jeu, mais une vérité
> Où par mon action je suis représenté,
> Où moi-même l'objet et l'acteur de moi-même,
> Purgé de mes forfaits par l'eau du saint baptême.[48]
>
> [It is no longer Adrien, but Genest who speaks;
> This play is not a play, but a truth
> Wherein by my actions I am represented,

> Myself the object and actor of my self,
> Purged of my faults by the water of holy baptism.]

While reading these lines, it is worth recalling that Genesius is the name of a character, also played by an actor, who is precisely not claiming for himself the same relation to his character that Genesius is claiming for his. For the audience to even understand the effect of collapsing the distance between Genesius and Adrien it must, at the very same time as it experiences this collapse as the "truth" of the play, maintain perfectly clear the distinction between Genesius and the actor portraying him. Likewise, for the line claiming that the play is not a play but the truth to make any sense for an audience, that audience must remain unshakably convinced that the play they are watching is, in fact, a play, because the very distance between play and reality Genesius is claiming to have superseded depends for its coherence on the distance separating the real audience from the interior one.

The interior audience, the one standing in for the real audience in the world of the play, also experiences this bifurcation into actor and spectator, as when Maximin, when he realizes that his real, historical self will appear as a character in the play, says,

> Oui, crois qu'avec plaisir je serai spectateur
> En la même action dont je serai l'acteur.[49]
>
> [Yes, believe that with pleasure I will be a spectator
> of the same performance of which I will be the actor.]

It is the audience's ability to engage the play from the perspective of its own divided selves that guarantees the coherence of what would otherwise be an untenable paradox. This ability, and how it relates to the spatial organization of the theater, becomes even more clear in Lope's *Lo fingido verdadero*. But before returning to this play, let us first examine in greater detail the changes in the theory and practice of stagecraft that accompanied the emergence of theatricality in the sixteenth century.

CHAPTER 4

A Tale of Two Cities: The Evolution of Renaissance Stage Practices in Madrid and Paris

One way of thinking about the difference between theatricality and presence is to analyze the experience of reading a book. One could say that, broadly speaking, this experience has two modes. On the one hand, one's hands feel the cover and pages of the book, while one's eyes flow over the shape of the letters, absorb the color of the ink and the texture of the paper. On the other, one experiences the meaning of the words, either the story being told or the ideas being discussed. In the theater a similar distinction can be made. On the one hand, one experiences a series of images, shapes, colors, sounds and bodily movements, all of which one can enjoy much in the way one enjoys the abstract movements and images of some modern dance. On the other hand, one also experiences, in representational theater, the story being enacted by those moving bodies. In a certain sense, the modern experience of theater is predicated on a subordination of the former to the latter, an erasure of one's own presence as a sentient body in the presence of the elements that are conceived of almost exclusively as vehicles for the conveyance of the story.

That's the easy part of the metaphor to explain; unfortunately, the medieval experience of presence is not simply the correlate to the experience of the materiality of the words on the page as opposed to the meaning they convey. This is because medieval spectacle still conveys meaning; it does so, however, in way that is patently less "semiotic" than modern theater, by which I mean that the status of signs in a medieval spectacle is different from that in a modern one. Modern theatrical signs—principally the actors, their words and their gestures—*signify*, in that they produce meaning predominantly via reference to other signs that have the same status, that exist in the same space, as themselves; medieval signs, however, *refer*, stand in directly for some real, recognizable object, figure or idea. To complete the image above, the medieval experience of that book would not solely be of the materiality of the words, but rather would be the experience of words as hieroglyphs, ideograms, signs whose meaning would be far less distinguishable from their sensual experience than signifiers are from theirs. Presence, then, names the capacity to experience the meaning of spectacle as occupying the same dimension, the same space of perception as the material of which the spectacle is formed; theatricality refers to the capacity to experience meaning as separable from the substantial dimension of spectacle, as occupying another spatial realm existing in a mimetic relationship to the real, substantial one.

Consider the words of the Abbé d'Aubignac as he ridicules what those of his time referred to as the *théâtre libre*, the theater free of the constraints of the unities of time, place, and action that became the principal rules of composition in France from 1630 through the Classical period:

> Il ne fallait point demander combien de temps durait une action que l'on représentait, en quel lieu se passaient toutes les choses que l'on voyait, ni combien la comédie avait d'actes. Car on répondait hardiment qu'elle avait duré trois heures, que tout s'était fait sur le théâtre, et que les violons en avaient marqué les intervalles des actes. Enfin, c'était assez pour plaire qu'un grand nombre de vers récités sur un théâtre portât le nom de comédie.[1]

> [One could not ask how long an action that was being represented lasted, or in what place occurred all the things that one saw, nor how many acts the comedy had. For one would be answered hardily that the action had lasted three hours, that everything had taken place on the stage, and that the violins had marked the intervals of the acts. In the end, it was enough to please that a great number of verses recited on the stage carry the name comedy.]

The Abbé is criticizing what he takes to be a defect of the pre-classical theater, its inability to distinguish between what we call now the time (or space) of action from that of performance. And, indeed, I am claiming that such a distinction was phenomenologically inaccessible prior to the modern age. But this inability is at the same time an ability, an ability to experience as a unity a distinction that for the modern age has been fundamental, perhaps even foundational. For not just modern theater, but the very experience of space that modern theater—as well as most other forms of modern spectacle, most all of which, I would argue, take their form from the template of the theater—presupposes, is predicated upon the separation of the dimension of meaning from that of being, and the subordination of the latter to the former.

Whereas medieval mimesis partakes of and affects the reality it imitates, theatrical mimesis reproduces it in an alternate realm. Because, as the theorists insisted, this theatrical mimesis potentially imitates the entire world and everything in it;[2] it necessarily imitates the very material of which its imitation is made, namely, the theater. Furthermore, in imitating the theater it imitates the very distinction upon which its mimetic power is founded, the distinction between the space (or time) of performance and that of action; and in imitating, or reproducing, that distinction in the space of action, it reinitiates the same process at another level of removal—it initiates, in other words, the permanent potential of infinite mise en abîme. This quality of potential mise en abîme is the ultimate signature of the modern experience of spatiality, and that signature is identifiable in at least two ways: the space on the stage can always become the place of another stage; and the character on the stage can always portray another character.

Clearly these claims have an aspect of generality to them. Whereas my specific examples, my case studies, come mainly from Spain and France, it is implicit in my treatment of these themes that what I am saying of the theater in Spain or in France is *generally* true of European theater, and that, consequently, what I am saying about the phenomenology of space and spectacle is also *generally* true of western mentalities. But by assuming a general validity to my specific observations and theories concerning particular theatrical practices in particular cultures, am I not risking contradiction by the simple observance of certain historical facts? Have I not chosen to study two cultures whose own histories of theater from medieval to modern times are, in fact, wildly divergent? The development of theatrical practice and theory in Spain and France from the fifteenth to the seventeenth centuries is indeed radically different. And if I believe I have found a formula that expresses, in a way that is generally valid, the differences between spectacle of the fifteenth and of the seventeenth centuries, I do not base this belief on existence of hidden commonalities between these two very different developmental histories. Rather I want to argue for the general validity of this formula *despite* the vast differences of the particular histories of each of these two cultures.

In order to do this, I will address, if only briefly, the history of the development of theatrical practice and theory in both Spain and France, paying attention both to the evolution of dramatic theory and to the changes in theater architecture, or *mise en scène*. Again, my point will not be to obscure the obvious differences in these stories, but rather to show that via such different paths both cultures nevertheless arrived at the same experience of theatricality: a stage that can become the space for another stage, a character who can portray another character.

ITALIAN INNOVATIONS

As Jean Jacquot points out, if the medieval practice of theater was largely decentralized, in that it would be hard to trace the influences of one culture over another, this is not the case for the development of theater during the Renaissance, when innovations in theory and practice in Italy were adopted in varying forms throughout the rest of Europe.[3] The fact that Italy was the origin of many of the changes that constitute the form of theater that we recognize today does not mean that all of the changes were adopted uniformly or simultaneously by its European neighbors. Rather, as we will see in some detail below, different aspects of Italian innovation were adopted in Spain and France at different times and were combined with different indigenous practices. But nevertheless, Italy was an enormous influence, so it is there that we must begin.

The form of Italian Renaissance theater traces its origin in large measure to two influences: the development of perspective in the early part of the fifteenth century and the rediscovery of Vitruvius' *Architecture*, written from 16 to 13 B.C., toward the end of the century.[4] Realizing that Latin comedies and tragedies—which were attracting renewed interest with Italy's turn toward its classical past—could not be adequately represented with current staging practices, scholars began an exegesis of Vitruvius' works toward the end of reconstructing an ancient theater.[5] Their reconstructions, however, because of the influence of perspective, were significantly different, adopting the techniques developed by Alberti to create scenes that were so realistic that, when viewed from the correct, central point in the auditorium, they could appear to be windows opening onto a piece of reality. This form of illusionistic mise en scène became a virtual requirement by the middle of the sixteenth century, substituting the traditional, compartmentalized facade in illustrations of the works of Terence and collections of Italian comedies[6] and—with Serlio's rendition of Vitruvius' three basic stage settings toward the end of the century—becoming the primary model for theater architecture in Italy, and eventually abroad. Along with the perspective stage were developed techniques for rapidly changing the scene design, allowing temporal succession to replace the previously dominant mode of representing different places, a mode in which all the places would be represented simultaneously on the stage. Together, these elements constitute the innovation of the Italian stage; whereas medieval theater had for a long time employed special effects,

> [l]'innovation de la Renaissance italienne fut, après avoir crée une scène capable de représenter par la perspective et le trompe-l'oeil un lieu unique, s'arriver à concevoir cette scène comme un espace abstrait permettant, à l'aide d'un matériel entièrement mobile, de représenter successivement n'importe quel lieu, bref de substituer la succession temporelle à la juxtaposition (voire à la dispersion) spatiale.[7]

> [the innovation of the Italian Renaissance was, after having created a scene capable of representing, via perspective and *trompe l'oeil*, a unique place, that it came to conceive of this place as abstract, permitting, by means of entirely mobile equipment, the successive representation of any place—in short, that it substituted for spatial juxtaposition (or dispersion), temporal succession.]

The abstract, interchangeable nature of this space is one of the most essential elements of theatricality; and whereas not all the elements of Italian perspective scenery survived the migration to France and Spain intact, this characteristic was among the most widely retained.

If the Italian Renaissance was highly influential to the development of modern theater in the domain of theater architecture and mise en scène, just as important were its contributions to the theory of theater. The principal sources of this contribution were a series of scholarly commentaries on the *Poetics* of Aristotle, which had been translated into Latin by Giorgio Valla in 1498, and then published in the original Greek for the first time in Europe in 1508.[8] It was on the basis of these texts that the theories of verisimilitude and decorum were developed, theories that would remain at the center of debates and controversies for centuries to come. Despite their eventual influence, the new texts were slow to catch on, many scholars still preferring the familiar commentary of Averroës, which failed to treat Aristotle's conception of tragedy as a dramatic form.[9] It was not until 1548 that the first commentary to explicitly treat the dramatic aspects of the *Poetics* was published. Robortello's commentary, *Librum Aristotelis de arte poetica explicationes*, reintroduced the notion of performance by deriving from the *Poetics* two kinds of mimesis, one involving the action of bodies, the other the description of words.[10] His purpose was to combine the traditional Horatian injunction to instruct while delighting with the Aristotelian notion of mimesis, which he did by arguing that if what audiences perceive appears relevant to their everyday life, then they may be persuaded to moral improvement. This appearance of relevance depended on the extent to which the mimesis was verisimilar, that is, the extent to which it would be received as true: "in general, to the extent that the verisimilar partakes of truth, it has the power to move and to persuade."[11] The verisimilitude of mimesis also provided the other half of Horace's credo, in that the poetic faculty had the inherent capacity to provoke delight: "What other end, therefore, can we say that the poetic faculty has than to delight through the representation, description, and imitation of every human action, every emotion, every thing animate as well as inanimate?"[12] With Robortello's commentary, then, the key element of Aristotle's mimesis became verisimilitude, the expectation that the representation be as close to its object as possible, an expectation that reached often absurd extremes in the interpretations of Scaliger and Castelvetro.

Julius Caesar Scaliger's *Poetice* appeared in 1561, and was the first to argue for a correspondence between reality and representation so tight that an audience would not be aware of the difference:

> For Scaliger, drama created a reality in which ideally the audience is unconscious of any artifice. Although Scaliger did not in fact derive from this a narrow interpretation of the unities of time and place, his insistence that theatrical events approximate actuality as closely as possible provided the theoretical foundation for this interpretation, justifying in some measure the French expression *unités scaligériennes*.[13]

Most radical in this regard was Lodovico Castelvetro, who claimed that the time of the performance should be the same as the time of the action, and that the scene should not vary but should be restricted to what could be seen by a single person. For instance, for Castelvetro, the twelve hours that were Aristotle's recommended outside limit for the time frame to be represented in a tragedy were to be taken literally—not, however, because Aristotle had said so, but rather because twelve hours was the longest amount of time an audience could reasonably be asked to remain in a theater without attending to "the necessities of the body, such as eating, drinking, excreting the superfluous burdens of the belly and bladder, sleeping and other necessities."[14]

This is not to say that such a strict correlation was always accepted; on the contrary, even during the classical period in which the unities enjoyed such preeminence, there were those who would criticize overly strict adherence to them. And at the time of Castelvetro, Alessandro Picolomini argued against his position, claiming that audiences know perfectly well that what they are seeing is not truth, that were it truth there would be no need for imitation and that exact temporal correspondence is therefore not necessary.[15] Such a view recognizes that the relation between the time and space of performance and that of the action is always mediated by a set of conventions, a position that Castelvetro's position failed to take into account. What is essential to notice, however, is that no matter what the position on the relation between these two times, the theorists involved recognized the existence of both. Whether they thought that difference had to be erased in the interests of perfect illusion, or whether they believed in the power of conventions to bridge that difference, there was a distinction. The other point they agreed upon was that—again, whether by means of convention or exact correspondence—the purpose of theater was to create that new reality and make it believable. Or, to build on Picolomini's distinction, if no one is really going to *believe* there is no difference between the reality in which one is observing a play and the reality being portrayed on the stage, then verisimilitude must serve another purpose: to make that reality *viable*.

The other great theoretical concept to emerge from the Italian Renaissance commentaries was decorum. This notion was introduced in 1550 in the commentary by Bartolomeo Lombardi and Vincenzo Maggi that followed Bernardo Segni's translation of the *Poetics* into the vernacular in 1549. In their *Aristotelis librum de poetica communes explanationes*, Lombardi and Maggi argued that verisimilitude also depended on the beliefs and expectations of the audience and that, hence, if the poet "introduces a king as saying or doing a given thing, what he says or does must belong to those things which are usually or necessarily attributed to kings."[16] The principle of decorum meant that dramatists, actors, and designers would not only have to do their best to ensure that their production imitated lived reality as closely as possible, they would also have to be aware not to deviate from the model of certain ideal, and hence morally charged, social types.[17] For the modern critic, then, the rule of decorum often seems to work in contradiction to the rule of verisimilitude, as the "insistence upon self-consistency in tragic and comic characters, which had the authority of both Horace and Aristotle, led to highly conventionalized characterizations in both tragedy and comedy and is one of the distinguishing features of most neo-classical drama."[18] While this may have been the case, it seems more important to remember that the theoretical justification for both rules was still a kind of realism, an attempt to bring to life or make viable a new theatrical space.

By the end of the sixteenth century in Italy, there was a wide variety of critical views being bandied about on the subject of theatrical mimesis, views that could be broadly categorized as falling into two camps: traditionalist and modernist. The traditionalist view saw Aristotle's *Poetics*, and its strictest interpreters, as prescriptive, as giving a recipe for how dramatic art ought to be. The modernists, exemplified by poets like Guarini, whose *tragicomedia, Il pastor fido*, sparked an enormous controversy on this topic, saw Aristotle's work as merely descriptive of theater in his own time and ripe for being superseded in the present. While the modernist position remained very much in vogue within Italy, it was the traditionalist position that tended to be exported, and that received its best welcome in France in the 1630s.[19]

THEORIES AND THEATERS IN PARIS

The traditional story told about the evolution of the theater in France was that the change from medieval to modern occurred in one sole coup, on 17 November 1548, when the Parliament of Paris issued a decree banning the performance of religious dramas. This opinion, canonized by Petit de Juvenille, was based on the assumption that at that time the sole type of theater that existed in Paris was precisely religious theater. This religious theater consisted mainly of the performance of *mystères* by a fraternity of bourgeois philanthropists called the *confrères de la Passion* who, that same year, had purchased some land that had belonged to the then defunct Dukes of Burgundy and built on it a theater, the theater that came to be known as the Hôtel de Bourgogne. According to this view, at around the same time a group of *literati* began to write comedies and tragedies in the classical style, borrowing ideas from Italy and performing the new plays in theaters designed according to Italian Renaissance models; and it was they who introduced the modern theater to France.

This theory was countered at the turn of the century by Eugène Rigal, who pointed out that, far from disappearing with the issuance of the ban on religious spectacle, the *confrères* continued to hold a virtual monopoly on public performances until the end of the century.[20] While the mainstay of the *confrères*' repertoire had fallen into disrepute, the medieval aesthetic remained in dominance at least insofar as the traditional, the non-erudite, and the bawdy continued to be the source of appeal for the masses at the Hôtel de Bourgogne. The new, for France, was represented by the court and the university, the tastes for antiquity imported, as usual, from Italy, but this style never spoke to the masses. "Il y avait donc lutte ouverte entre les deux systèmes; et, quoique le résultat n'en parût pas douteux, cette lutte pouvait se prolonger longtemps, retardant l'avènement définitif du nouvel état de choses"[21] [There was, then, an open war between the two systems; and although the result did not appear in doubt, the war was able to be prolonged for a long time, delaying the definitive arrival of the new order].

Indeed, the traditional narrative drew much of its power from the interpretation given by the immediate successors of the struggle for cultural dominance, the proponents of the classical style. Once again, the Abbé d'Aubignac:

> Au siècle de Ronsard, le théâtre commença à se remettre en sa première vigueur. Jodelle et Garnier, qui s'en rendirent les premiers restaurateurs, observèrent assez raisonnablement cette règle du temps ... Hardy fut celui qui fournit le plus abondamment à nos comédiens de quoi divertir le peuple; et ce fut lui sans doute qui tout d'un coup arrêta les progrès du théâtre, donnant le mauvais exemple des désordres que nous y avons vu régner en notre temps.[22]

> [In the century of Ronsard, the theater began to recapture its original vigor. Jodelle and Garnier, who became its first restorers, observed quite reasonably this rule of [the unity of] time ... Hardy was the one who furnished our comedians most prolifically with the wherewithal to amuse the people; and it was doubtless he who all at once stopped the progress of the theater, giving us the bad example of the disorders that we have seen reign in our time.]

For the Abbé, who saw the history of theater as unfolding naturally from the rediscovery of the greatness of classical antiquity in the Italian Renaissance and going on to achieve its apogee in the French classical style, it was not illogical to blame Hardy, whom he associated with the chaos of the *mystères* and *théâtre libre*, for the temporary setback that kept the classical style from achieving dominance until the 1630s. Representatives of the classical style often regarded Hardy as having polluted the French theater by conforming more to the liberties of the Spanish or English stage. But, as Rigal argues, Hardy's influences were more likely indigenous than Spanish or English; unlike the Spanish and English cases, for one thing, the theater of Hardy was staged using a simultaneous decor system, much like that of the medieval mysteries.[23]

It is clear that the Italian style made some inroads into French culture in the sixteenth century. Scaliger himself became a French citizen in 1528, and his major work was published in Lyon.[24] Authors such as Jean de la Taille, Robert Garnier, Jodelle, and Ronsard were clearly influenced by the Italians and defended the unities in their strictest form.[25] Du Bellay—poet, theorist, and spokesman of the *Pléiade*—would write in his *Défense et illustration de la langue française*, "Quant aux comédies at aux tragédies, si les rois et les républiques les voulaient restituer en leur ancienne dignité qu'ont usurpée les farces et les moralités, je serais bien d'opinion que tu t'y employasses"[26] [As far as the comedies and tragedies are concerned, if the kings and republics wished to restore them to their ancient dignity that the farces and moralities have usurped, I would be of the opinion that you should do it]. For the most part, though, actual performances in the new style were limited to private salons and the universities, and they were far from popular. Indeed, after 1567, the only reports we have of any such performances come from outside of Paris.[27] While there is disagreement over whether and to what extent the comedies and tragedies written in the classical style were even meant for performance (as opposed to being circulated in manuscript form to be read by friends and colleagues), Rigal insists that they were more than likely never performed in a popular setting, much less at the Hôtel de Bourgogne.[28] Rather, it was a fundamentally medieval brew of farces, moralities, histories and profane mysteries that continued to dominate the public stage in Paris until the very end of the century.[29] This situation was only brought to a close at the end of the century, when Alexandre Hardy combined many of the elements of classical tragedy with a more popular, medieval, "free" style, which then dominated the boards for thirty years.

Classical theory, set design, and most specifically the obsession with the unities did not really catch on, then, until the 1630s. In 1630, in fact, Chapelain published a letter in which he reestablished the theoretical importance of the notion of verisimilitude, using the term that would gain so much currency in the theory of the Classical Period, *vraisemblance*. According to Chapelain, the great discovery of the ancients was their "removing from the spectators any occasion to reflect on what they are seeing and to doubt its reality."[30] He also suggested, in the name of *vraisemblance*, that the scene never change place and that, like certain Spanish authors, the author should write in prose, in order better to imitate real language use.[31] Chapelain continued his crusade to reintroduce classical theory in 1635, referring in his *Discours de la poesie représentative* to the notion of *bienséance*. This was the term that had been used by authors such as Pelletier in 1555 and Vauquelin in 1605 to translate the Latin term decorum, but didn't reenter the critical vocabulary until Chapelain's use. In addition, Chapelain's use of *bienséance* revived the patently moralizing connotations of decorum, suggesting both suitability and moral decency.[32] *Vraisemblance, bienséance* and the unities, especially those of time and place, were to maintain a theoretical dominance in French theater, despite numerous debates and notable exceptions, for the rest of the century. But if the French obsession with the unities strikes us as idiosyncratic at best, it behooves us to keep in mind what Rigal recalled almost a century ago: French neo-classisicm emerged out of a period of conflict with another theatrical form; the obsession with the unities was a way of dealing with the particular context of the time, a context in which certain traditional staging practices, in many ways directly opposed to classical tenets, were still in use.

We will return to these practices below, but for now let us also recognize that the reemergence of classical theory did not necessarily constitute a complete realignment of the theater in its essential form. We know for certain that the decorators of the Hôtel de Bourgogne used a simultaneous decor at least some of the time up until the 1630s, meaning that different parts of the stage represented different places. Actors, as a result, were often obliged to speak their roles outside of the appropriate decor. However, whereas in the fifteenth century this was completely natural—presumably because, as d'Aubignac would have it, for them the actor and the decor were quite simply on the stage, not in some imaginary place requiring its own coherence—already in the seventeenth this practice fell into disrepute and the poets were expected to make arrangements that would prevent such discrepancies from occurring.[33] This suggests that while the theorists of verisimilitude had fallen silent, their theories persisted as a tacit imperative that actively partook the form of the theater.

So we can see that Italian theoretical innovation, while eventually of enormous influence in France, nevertheless met resistance along the way, a resistance that itself played a formative role in the form that the theater would finally take. Was this the same case with the technological innovations in scene design that the Italians had been developing throughout the sixteenth century? In fact, in neither France nor Spain was Italian technology immediately or broadly applied. The reason for this, most likely, was that these cultures had powerful traditions of spectacle that were themselves both entrenched, to a certain degree, and developing in their own right. These were open, popular theaters, with traditional expectations and conventions associated with them, such that the introduction of new technologies would also entail the alteration of tastes and habits, not to mention the introduction of costly new equipment. These innovations, therefore, remained for a long time the luxury of the courts and universities, and it was through the courts that these tastes eventually and gradually spread.[34]

The reigning tradition in France with which these innovations had to compete, as I have to some extent described in chapter 2, was that of the *mystère*, which was performed outside (although the *confrères* had been performing inside since the fifteenth century[35]), with massive sets and casts, and a design that included numerous fixed installations for the representation of different places, called mansions. This plurality of places on the set, or simultaneous decor, was a practice common throughout Europe during the Middle Ages.[36] When thinking of the spectators in such a form of performance, once must imagine people standing, walking about, entering and leaving the space of the performance—without ever experiencing a sharp border to distinguish it from the space of the spectators—participating as opposed to merely observing.[37] This system began to change in large part in France during the sixteenth century, when groups other than the *confrères de la Passion* also moved their performances inside[38]—and, as a result, had to deal with the added constraints of limited space and obstructed view. Specifically, in the case of the performances at the Hôtel de Bourgogne, the spatial requirements meant that fewer actors could be used, and that the actors who were on the stage had to leave the scene when their characters were not actually supposed to be there, in contrast to the traditional practice in which players would remain near their assigned mansion regardless of whether they were currently performing or not. In addition, rather than maintain the entire contingent of mansions—usually eleven or twelve—only the mansions needed for a given sequence were kept on the stage.[39] This was the situation at the beginning of the seventeenth century in the Hôtel de Bourgogne: a more or less empty central stage with five or six mansions surrounding it.

Nevertheless, while the decor might have been simplified, it remained fundamentally a simultaneous one. And when, in the late sixteenth century, tragicomedy and "irregular" tragedies—such as those in the style developed by Hardy—came into vogue, the presentation of places started to pose a problem common to many of the different theatrical forms of the time, including the Elizabethan drama and the Spanish *comedia*. Whereas these latter forms resolved the problem by means of a neutral stage in which location was indicated by dialogue, entrances and exits, or small, significant bits of scenery, the French fell back on their old standby, the simultaneous decor.[40]

However, the appearance of popularized comedy and tragedy was, I noted earlier, late in making its appearance in France, and the reason was the continued dominance of the *confrères de la Passion* in Paris. Although they had been officially prohibited from performing religious drama only shortly after building their new theater, the *confrères* did not at that point begin performing classical comedies and tragedies, but rather continued to present *mystères* under misleading titles.[41] In addition to illicit religious pieces, they entertained the people with traditional, bawdy, often satirical fare, as is alleged in this complaint from a disgruntled court officer of Henri III in 1588:

> Il y a un autre grand mal, qui se commet et tolère en votre bonne ville de Paris, aux jours de dimanches et de fêtes; ce sont les jeux et spectacles publics qui se font lesdits jours de fêtes et dimanches, tant par des étrangers Italiens que par des Français, et, par-dessus tous, ceux qui se font en une cloaque et maison de Satan, nommée L'Hôtel de Bourgogne, par ceux qui abusivement se disent les confrères de la Passion de J.-C. . . . Sur l'échafaud l'on y dresse des autels chargés de croix et ornements ecclésiastiques, l'on y représente des prêtres revêtus de surplis, même aux farces impudiques pour faire mariages de risées.

L'on y lit le texte de l'Évangile en chant ecclésiastique, pour (par occasion) y rencontrer un mot à plaisir qui sert au jeu. Et au surplus, il n'y a farce qui ne soit orde, sale et vilaine, au scandale de la jeunesse qui y assiste, laquelle avale à long trait ce venin et ce poison, qui se couve en sa poitrine, et en peu de temps opère les effets que chacun sait et voit trop fréquemment.[42]

[There is another great evil that is committed and tolerated in your good city of Paris on Sundays and festivals; these are the public plays and spectacles that are performed on these days, as much by Italian foreigners as by Frenchmen, and, above all are those which take place in a cesspool and house of Satan called the Hôtel de Bourgogne, by those who abusively call themselves the *confrères* of the Passion of Jesus Christ.... On the boards they erect altars covered with crosses and ecclesiastical ornaments, and they portray there priests dressed in surplice, even in lewd farces performing mock marriages. They read there the Evangelical text in ecclesiastical chants, in order to find therein (on occasion) a funny word with which to play. And what's more, there is not a farce they play that is not filthy, dirty and villainous, to a scandalous effect on the youth who frequent this place, who drink this venom and poison in long draughts, which then incubate in their breasts, and in just a little time work the effects that all know and see all too often.]

While the complaints of this one officer were probably not indicative of the general attitude toward the performances taking place at the Hôtel, his and perhaps those of others did have some effect, as shortly thereafter all performances there were prohibited for a period of about seven years. It is also interesting to note that one of the sources of his ire is the mockery made of the sacraments, particularly, in this case, the sacrament of marriage. Perhaps we can speculate that what is so infuriating to a pious man about the parody of the sacrament of marriage is that the enactment of the sacrament itself is already a performance; indeed, as I noted in the first chapter, it is one of the performances that has been most cited by philosophers discussing the illocutionary force of performative utterances. As one can imagine, placing a fake priest on stage and performing the sacrament according to practice, with the shared knowledge between the audience and the performers that the ceremony is a fake, would constitute an inherent mockery since it would demonstrate the potential non-performativity of a series of actions, gestures, and words that are supposed to be intrinsically performative. Compare this complaint, however, to the impromptu wedding performed in *Lo fingido verdadero*—which I discuss below in some detail—in which the manipulation of spatial frames allows Lope to portray a mock wedding (failed performative), which from a perspective once removed turns out to have been a real wedding (successful performative), which from yet another degree of removal turns out to be false (failed performative). One can only wonder how the disgruntled spectator would have reacted to that performance, only twenty years later.[43]

Perhaps one of the reasons that the spectacles preferred at the Hôtel de Bourgogne held on for so long was simply that the *confrères* were so politically astute when it came to guarding their privileges. When they were permitted to play, they often ensured that they would hold exclusive privileges, which they guarded jealously. Even when they failed to have other players banned, they often managed to skim a profit nonetheless. For example, when an itinerant troupe tried to set up a playhouse in the Foire de Saint Germain, the *confrères* tried to petition to have them closed. But when the public came to the aid of the troupe, and the municipal government gave them the right to play profane mysteries, the *confrères* still managed to ensure that they would have to pay a daily sum for each performance to the coffers of the *confrèrie*.[44]

It was not until the end of the century that the fraternity finally gave up its more or less complete monopoly on theatrical spectacle in Paris, and gave way to the repertoire of troupes playing a new sort of drama. However, this drama was not, as one might expect, of the neo-classical type favored by the academies and the court, although it incorporated elements of that theater. Rather, these innovators came from the countryside, itinerant troupes who had been perfecting a new style, a mixture of classical comedy and tragedy, farce and medieval staging techniques that would see its apogee in the *théâtre libre* of Hardy.[45]

According to Rigal, it was in the works of Hardy that the previously battling genres of the Renaissance tragedy and the medieval farces, *mystères*, and moralities were eventually synthesized,[46] and it is for this reason that, despite his detractors from the classical period on, Rigal held Hardy up to be the sole creator of the modern French theater.[47] Nevertheless, criticism in the twentieth century has shown that some of Rigal's claims concerning the dominance of Hardy on the Parisian scene during the first twenty years of the seventeenth century were probably exaggerated. For example, documents that have only surfaced since Rigal's time show conclusively that, before the time of Mahelot, whom I discuss below, Hardy was only in Paris from 1599 to 1600, and later from 1606 to 1612.[48] This is important for our purposes because Rigal had based his theories concerning the type of stage design that had been used during this time at the Hôtel on the assumption that (a) Hardy was in Paris for most of that time, (b) the Hôtel was the only functioning popular theater, and that therefore (c) whatever decor Hardy's plays required—needless to say a simultaneous decor—would have determined the decorative system used during that time.[49] He also surmised that Valleran, the director of the troupe that performed many of Hardy's pieces and that played almost exclusively at the Hôtel following the retreat of the *confrères*, would have rented already-existing scenery from the *confrères*, thus assuring the continuation of their decorative system. However, as Deierkauf-Holsboer points out, it is not likely that the *confrères* would ever have lent their decors to the actors renting the space free of charge, and no archival evidence exists to support the claim that they were rented.

Rather, it is more likely that Valleran had his own decor constructed, a decor that, based on what is known of the troupe's finances, would have to have been extremely simple.[50]

Thanks to the efforts of at least one and probably a few more stage designers at the Hôtel, we do have records of the decor used between 1622 and 1635, that is, more or less up to the beginning of the classical period. The records were begun by Mahelot, and they show that whereas even at that relatively late date a sort of simultaneous decor was still the rule, it was still not the only system, and that a synthesis of the medieval and Renaissance styles was developing.[51]

Whereas Mahelot's designs often allow for the simultaneous representation of several places, they are also clearly influenced by a knowledge of Vitruvius and, more specifically, of Serlio, whose three-scene paradigm can be found quite often in Mahelot's descriptions. As Deierkauf-Holsboer puts it, "[i]l est donc incontestable que la tradition médiévale s'est transformée sous l'influence de la Renaissance dans les décors de Mahelot"[52] [It is therefore incontestable that the medieval tradition was transformed by the influence of the Renaissance in Mahelot's decors]. The result is an essentially perspectival scene, with a central, empty playing space—which could represent whatever place was needed at a given moment, depending on who entered or what was said—surrounded by a series of compartments. Normally there were five of these, one large one in the back and two smaller ones on either side.[53] As Jacquot describes, these external scenic elements could be added or subtracted depending on the needs of a given piece. Mahelot only created new elements when the story demanded it; the fewer different places were required, the more his vision approximated an ideal that he would only realize when the piece entailed a simple unity: the symmetric perspective scene.[54] Needless to say, as the observance of the classical rules came back into vogue, the designs approached more and more this pure perspective scene and, simultaneously, the space of the stage became more and more abstract and mutable, changing only virtually and by means of the characters' indications, their dialogues, their costumes, their entrances and exits. By 1635, the last elements of the simultaneous decor had been phased out, and only the perspective scene was left.[55]

The Hôtel, then, as it appeared at the beginning of the classical period, was a rectangular building 32.5 meters long and 18.5 meters wide.[56] Its stage was 14 meters deep and as wide as the building, and was elevated 1.92 meters off the floor.[57] There was, in addition to the main stage, a smaller, upper stage which could be reached via stairs and which was supported by columns.[58] And finally the set had become exclusively a perspectival scene with an abstract background, a scene that could be changed at will into any place, any time. As Corneille writes in the preface to his *Clitandre*,

> Je laisse le lieu de ma scène au choix du lecteur, bien qu'il ne me coûtât qu'à nommer. Si mon sujet est véritable, j'ai raison de le taire; si c'est une fiction, quelle apparence, pour suivre je ne sais quelle chorographie, de donner un soufflet à l'histoire, d'attribuer à un pays des princes imaginaires, et d'en rapporter des aventures qui ne se lisent point dans les chroniques de leur royaume? Ma scène est donc en un château d'un roi, proche d'une forêt; je n'en détermine ni la province ni la royaume; où vous l'aurez une fois placée, elle s'y tiendra.[59]
>
> [I leave the place of my scene to the choice of the reader, although I would only need name it. If my subject is true, I have reason to keep it to myself; if it is fiction, then what appearance, following who knows what choreography, to give offense to history, to attribute to a country imaginary princes, and to tell of them adventures that can't be read in the chronicles of their kingdom? My scene, then, is a king's castle, near a forest; I determine neither the province nor the kingdom; once you have placed it somewhere, there may it remain.]

By the 1630s, in short, at an admittedly later date than in its neighboring cultures, French theater became theatrical. The experience of space it demanded and produced was no longer the full, participatory space of the medieval mysteries, farces, and moralities; it was now an empty, abstract space; a space that did not participate in reality, but rather reflected or imitated reality in a different dimension; a space, thus, in which all places could be theaters, and all characters could be actors.

THEORIES AND THEATERS IN MADRID

The differences between the French and Spanish theaters of the sixteenth and seventeenth centuries are well known. Whereas the popular theater in France was largely medieval in style right up to the end of the sixteenth century, Spain traces the origins of its modern theater to authors from the beginning and middle of the same century; whereas as France's experiment with the *théâtre libre* of Hardy was short lived and of relatively limited success, the Spanish *comedia*, which represented similar aesthetic impulses, was enormously popular and would go on to dominate cultural production in Spain throughout the seventeenth century; whereas the form of theater that would eventually become the norm in France was written and performed in full awareness and acceptance of a series of tight theoretical constraints controlling the versification as well as the content of the pieces, the Spanish poets were openly dismissive of theory, continuing to write in a comparatively free style—a mishmash of different rhyming and rhythmic schemes and prose, paying little or no attention to unities of time, space, or action—for the rest of the century.[60] Nevertheless, despite these obvious differences, the experience of spatiality in the theater of the seventeenth century in Spain was fundamentally similar to that which I have described as having emerged on the French stage. Granted, for reasons particular to its own cultural history, this form emerged sooner in Spain, and with a great deal less theoretical elaboration; but the space of the stage by the end of the sixteenth century was, just as in France by the 1630s, a fully theatrical one.

In both France and in Spain, the theatrical stage of the modern age can be understood as a synthesis of medieval and popular practices indigenous to their local cultures with new ideas coming from Italy. The principal reason for why Spain was faster in developing this synthesis most likely has to do with the fact that, as far as we know, it had nothing to compare with the enormously popular, highly entrenched form of medieval spectacle that dominated the stages of Paris in the sixteenth century. Spain's predominant forms of spectacle were much more dispersed, consisting of religious or political processions of the kind described in chapter 2, wandering troupes of country players, and courtly performances. When, starting at the end of the fifteenth and into the middle of the sixteenth centuries, the influence of Italian theorists as well as popular performers became increasingly important, transmitted via the courts of nobles and kings, the universities, and the travels of popular performers both Spanish and Italian, there were few structural, architectural or theoretical barriers in place to prevent their incorporation into existing practices.

In the realm of theatrical theory, Spain is perhaps best known for Lope de Vega's stinging, tongue-in-cheek rejection of classical rules in particular, and of the overtheorization of the dramatist's art in general, in his *Arte nuevo de hacer comedias en este tiempo*.[61] But Spain had its Renaissance theorists and commentators as well, and, perhaps not surprisingly, their central concern was, as with the French and Italian theorists, for the verisimilitude of the theatrical performance. While there was at no point a radical change in the thinking about theater in Spain, it gained a new dimension with the gradual incorporation of Aristotle's *Poetics*, which were known through the translation of Valla.[62] In addition, the playwrights of the early sixteenth century often show a knowledge of classical theory apart from Aristotle, such as Torres Naharro who, in his *Propalladia*, gives an account of the dramatic theory of Horace.[63] The styles and theories of the Latin comedies had already been available to university students for some time, as they had been traditionally used as tools in the instruction of Latin and rhetoric. These comedies were also thought to embody the Horatian ideal of instructing while delighting, by presenting characters who were representatives of certain vices and virtues, who played out their fortunes and misfortunes in a way quite similar to that of a morality play.[64]

Probably the best known poetical treatise in Renaissance Spain is Lopez Pinciano's *Philosophia Antigua Poetica*, the thirteenth book of which deals specifically with the theater. The form of the treatise is a series of letters Pinciano writes to a friend, recounting his conversations with two friends, Fadrique and Ugo. Fadrique is clearly the intellectual star of the trio, the eager, if somewhat less gifted, Ugo and Pinciano normally bowing to his greater taste and judgment. The letter in question deals with a trip the three friends take to the theater, where, being made to wait an inordinate length of time for the show to begin, they engage in a discussion of the merits of theater, its theory, and its performance. Perhaps the first thing of importance to note is the distinction they agree to between stories that are *told* in various ways, such as in epics, and those that are enacted before one's eyes. Inanimate or allegorical figures, which had provided the backbone of much spectacle leading up to the fifteenth century, are only appropriate for the former: "... en las acciones comunes épicas que no tiene[n] tanta necessidad de la verisimilitud se puede permitir, y au[n] son buenas tales personas fingidas; mas, en las actiuas adonde la cosa parece delante de los ojos, no es permitido"[65] [... in common, epic plots, which do not have as much need for verisimilitude, one may permit, and even consider good, such fake characters; but in active presentations wherein the thing appears before one's eyes, it is not permitted]. As is clearly stated, the active ingredient in this distinction is verisimilitude; in stories that are not acted out by bodies, the principle of verisimilitude does not have the same importance. The reason for this is that Pinciano is concerned, as were the French and Italian theorists, with the believability or viability of the action. He justifies this importance placed on believability by the argument that the purpose of theater is to move the audience, and if it is to do that it must first convince. The poet's words present reality (*la cosa*) via the mediation of his concepts; the actor needs yet another level of mediation, that of his bodily movements. As Ugo explains:

> Y éste baste por exemplo general de lo mucho que importa que el actor haga su officio con mucho primor y muy de veras; que, pues nos lleuan nuestros dineros de veras y nos hazen esperar aquí dos horas, razón es que hagan sus acciones con muchas veras; los quales solían hazer de tal manera los actores griegos y latinos, que los oradores antiguos aprendían de ellos, para, en el tiempo de sus oraciones públicas, mouer los affectos y ademanes con el mouimiento del cuerpo, piernas, braços, ojos, boca y cabeça, porque, según el affecto que se pretende, es diferente el mouimiento que enseña la misma naturaleza y costumbre; y, en suma, assí como el poeta con su concepto declara la cosa, y con la palabra, el concepto, el actor, con el mouimiento de su persona, deue declarar y manifestar y dar fuerça a la palabra del poeta.[66]

> [And let this suffice as a general example of how important it is that the actor perform his office with much skill and much truth; since they take our money in truth and make us wait here two hours, it is right that they should perform their roles with much truth; which is what the Greek and Latin actors used to do, such that the public orators learned from them in order to, at the time of their public speeches, move affects and attitudes with the movements of their bodies, legs, arms, eyes, mouths and heads, because, depending on the affect

one wishes to assume, nature and custom teach different movements; and in sum, just as the poet with his concept declares the thing, and with his word the concept, so the actor, with the movement of his person, must declare and manifest and give force to the words of the poet.]

In order to assure that this bodily mediation remains transparent, actors must become students of human nature, learning to imitate with precision the way other human bodies communicate their affects and emotions. In short, they must learn to do what all art forms do in their own way—imitate nature:

> ... el actor esté desuelado en mirar los mouimientos que con las partes del cuerpo hazen los hombres en sus conuersaciones, dares y tomares y passiones del alma; assí seguirá a la naturaleza, a la qual sigue toda arte, y ésta, más que ningina, digo la poética, de la cual los actores son los executores.[67]

> [... let the actor be vigilant in watching the movements that men make with their various bodily parts in their conversations, givings and takings and passions of the soul; in this way he will follow nature, which all art follows, and this more than any other, I say poetry, of which actors are the executors.]

Actors are the executors of an art that itself follows nature, that speaks, in some fundamental sense, the truth. But in order to communicate this truth in their special way, actors are charged with another, special kind of verisimilitude, a truth in action, a responsibility to imitate with the very movement of their bodies the truth of human action, emotion and sensation. These actors, in other words, are engaged in the production of this other space, the space I have called alternate but viable, in which spectators can see their own "conversations, givings and takings and passions of the soul" played out for them in ways that are recognizable because they imitate their own.

As in France, the theoretical development of this notion of mimetic space parallels the material or architectural development of a stage suited to contain it. Lope de Vega gives the following description of the Italian scenographer Cosmo Lotti's set design for his (Lope's) palace production of *La selva de amor*:

> La primera vista del teatro ... fue un mar en perspectiva, que descubría a los ojos (tanto puede el arte) muchas leguas de agua hasta la ribera opuesta, en cuyo puerto se vian la ciudad y el faro con algunas naves, que haciendo salva disparaban, a quien también los del castillo respondían. Víanse asismismo algunos peces que fluctuaban según el movimiento de las ondas, que con la misma inconstancia que si fueran verdades, se inquietaban, todo con luz artificial, sin que se viese ninguna, y siendo las que formaban aquel fingido día más de trescientas....[68]

[The first view of the theater was of a sea in perspective, that discovered for the eyes (of so much is art capable) many leagues of water to the other shore, in whose port could be seen the city and lighthouse with some ships, which shot off salvos, to which those of the castle responded. There could be seen as well some fish that floated along with the movement with which the waves, with the same inconsistency as if they were real, were agitated, all with artificial lights, none of which could be seen, although there were more than 300 used to create that simulated day....]

Now, the scene that Lope describes was not the typical stage decor of either the sixteenth or the seventeenth century. It was, however, typical of palace or courtly productions of both centuries, a form of spectacle with parallels in both England (where the masques of Jonson and Jones were also heavily influenced by Italian scene design) and the *ballet de cour* of the French absolutist monarchy.[69] In Spain these courtly productions constituted one of the three separate types of theater that abounded in the seventeenth century, the other two being the religious theater, or *auto sacramental*, and the *comedia nueva*.[70] And while the *comedia*, the popular theater that I am claiming represents the most innovative and modern of the three branches, was for the most part performed without the benefit of opulent or realistic scenery,[71] it nevertheless responded to the same implicit imperative contained in the Italian perspectival stage design: to reproduce the world as it is.[72] However, if the courtly stage was designed to imitate a given scene with exactitude, the *comedia* was experienced as imitating life via the speech and action of its characters. The sparsity of the set gave it a suppleness that court dramas lacked, as well as allowing it the economic flexibility to reach literally every level of society.

The *comedia nueva* has both roots that are autochthonous, in the courtly eclogues of Juan del Encina and the rustic farces of Lope de Rueda, and influences imported from Italy. Both Juan del Encina and Torres Naharro were in Italy at different points in their careers and were vehicles in the transmission of Italian culture back to Spain; moreover, Spain's military and political presence in Italy was such that one sixth of the Roman population in the early sixteenth century was Spanish.[73] Furthermore, Italian players came to entertain the Spanish court as early as 1548,[74] and were instrumental in setting up the first public theaters in Madrid in the 1570s.[75] And while it is probably fair to say that much of the realism of the speech and behavior of the characters of the *comedia* is attributable to the indigenous theaters of Juan del Encina and Lope de Rueda[76] (and, though probably never performed, that of *La Celestina*), much of the architectural shape of the *comedia*'s space is due to the Italians and to their tradition of perspective scenery.

The basic shape of the *corral*, the Spanish version of a theater, was already taking shape prior to 1565, at the same time popular performances also began to be structured with acts and prologues[77]—another obvious element of Italian influence. This shape could be seen in the performances of wandering troupes such as that of Lope de Rueda, who would erect a temporary construction of boards and curtains to create a stage with a *vestuario* (an all purpose backstage and dressing area or green room). But it was in 1565 that the history of the permanent, public theaters in Madrid actually began, with the formation of the *Cofradía de la Sagrada Pasión*,[78] which, like the *confrèrie* of the same name in Paris, was to earn money for its charitable works via the theater. Two years later, another *cofradía*, the *Cofradía de Nuestra Señora de la Soledad*, was formed, which shortly thereafter created a hospital for the care of the poor. Unlike the *confrèrie*, however, the brothers of these *cofradías* had no pretension of being actors and saw their role in the enterprise as a purely financial one. With the proviso that the funds were going to finance the hospital and their other charitable projects, the brothers were granted the right to build locales for the representation of all *comedias* in the city, for the use of which they could charge a rental fee.[79] Three locales, or *corrales*, were erected, one on the Calle del Sol and two more on the Calle del Príncipe.

Until a few years later, when actual buildings were constructed for the purpose of showing plays, these *corrales* depended upon an appropriation of public as well as private space. The first *corrales* were simply the open courtyards between houses, and at least some of the *aposentos*, or box-seats, were in fact the windows of those houses. In fascinating contrast to what would be considered "normal" property rights today, if an apartment owner wished to open his or her own window to watch the show, he or she would have to pay a fee to the *cofradía* in charge of the *corral*.[80] In other words, with the first *corrales*, the ephemeral space of medieval theater and the vagabond stage of Lope de Rueda were replaced by a legalistic and stable entity. While retaining details from its earlier form, the seemingly haphazard erection of boards to form a stage, the *corral* became institutionalized when the borders that defined it as the outside of other spaces became equally the markers of a legally-sanctioned inside.

In 1574 a theater was built in the Corral de la Pacheca (one of the two on the Calle del Príncipe). Alberto Nazero de Ganassa, the head of a troupe of Italian players who was in Madrid at that time, was said to have been involved in getting it built.[81] But it was not until 1579 that the *cofradías* erected their own theater, the Corral de la Cruz, followed three years later by the Corral del Príncipe. After 1584 these became the only two permanent theaters in Madrid.

Casiano Pellicer, in his *Tratado histórico sobre el origen y progreso de la comedia y del histrionismo en españa*,[82] gives this description of the Corral del Príncipe:

> A platform or stage was built, a green room [*vestuario*], raised seats (gradas) for the men, portable benches to the number of ninety-five, a gallery for the women, stalls and windows with iron gratings, passageways, and a roof to cover the gradas. Finally the patio was paved and an awning was stretched over it which protected against the sun, but not against the rain.

A curtain was stretched across the back of the stage that could be drawn to reveal other rooms, but in general the stage was plain and could represent many places without requiring a change in scenery.[83] The stage was 14 feet deep and 28 feet wide, with *tabladillos colaterales* [side stages] extending from the main stage on either side for ten feet. These side stages could be used for stage scenery when needed, or for seating extra spectators.[84] The main stage of the Corral de la Cruz was 16 feet deep by 27 feet wide, with 13 additional feet behind the main stage for the vestuario. It had 7.5 feet of lateral stage on either side. Two levels of balconies—most likely continuations of the levels where the aposentos were on the sides and the back of the hall—were to be found directly over the line dividing the *vestuario* from the main stage in both theaters.[85] Players could appear at "windows" on either of these balconies, or be seen there as if coming from a distance, or descending from "on high" (*en lo alto*).[86]

I have gone into some detail in the description of these two theaters in order to derive a more abstract, geometrical model of the experience of space that the theaters enabled. The diagram on the following page is a schematic map of what I call the four spaces of theatricality. S0 is the space of the audience. It is delimited by the line separating the stage from the various seating areas. S1 is the space of the stage; it is the space wherein the primary story of a play is carried out; and in a play within a play, it is the space in which the characters who play the inner audience exist. S2, the space of the play within the play, may be opened anywhere within S1. One could imagine, for example, the lateral stages becoming the place of the audience (S1) and the main stage becoming S2. Or the curtains at the back of the stage could open and S2 could appear therein. Finally, a fourth space, S3, is defined as that space within which no new spaces may be opened. In other words, the mise en abîme of nesting spaces that characterizes theatrical spatiality is potentially, but only potentially, infinite. In practice, there is always some ultimate interior space that cannot be opened further. This space, which, for reasons I explain below, I call the crypt, may also take the place of S2; there is, in other words, no requirement that it appear only within an explicitly metatheatrical setting; the only thing that is constant about the nature of this space is that it, alone among properly theatrical spaces, is solid, full, impenetrable. In the next section, I will explore in greater detail this space of the crypt, before moving on to a more complete exposition of all the levels of spatiality as they appear and interact in a specific example of modern theatrical production.

TALES FROM THE CRYPT

I have called the space of the medieval drama, and in fact the space of medieval perception, a full space, thickly laden with figures and impressed with meaning, capable of transmitting influences between bodies and distinctly unfit for housing sharp distinctions between the real and the imaginary. I would like, then, to

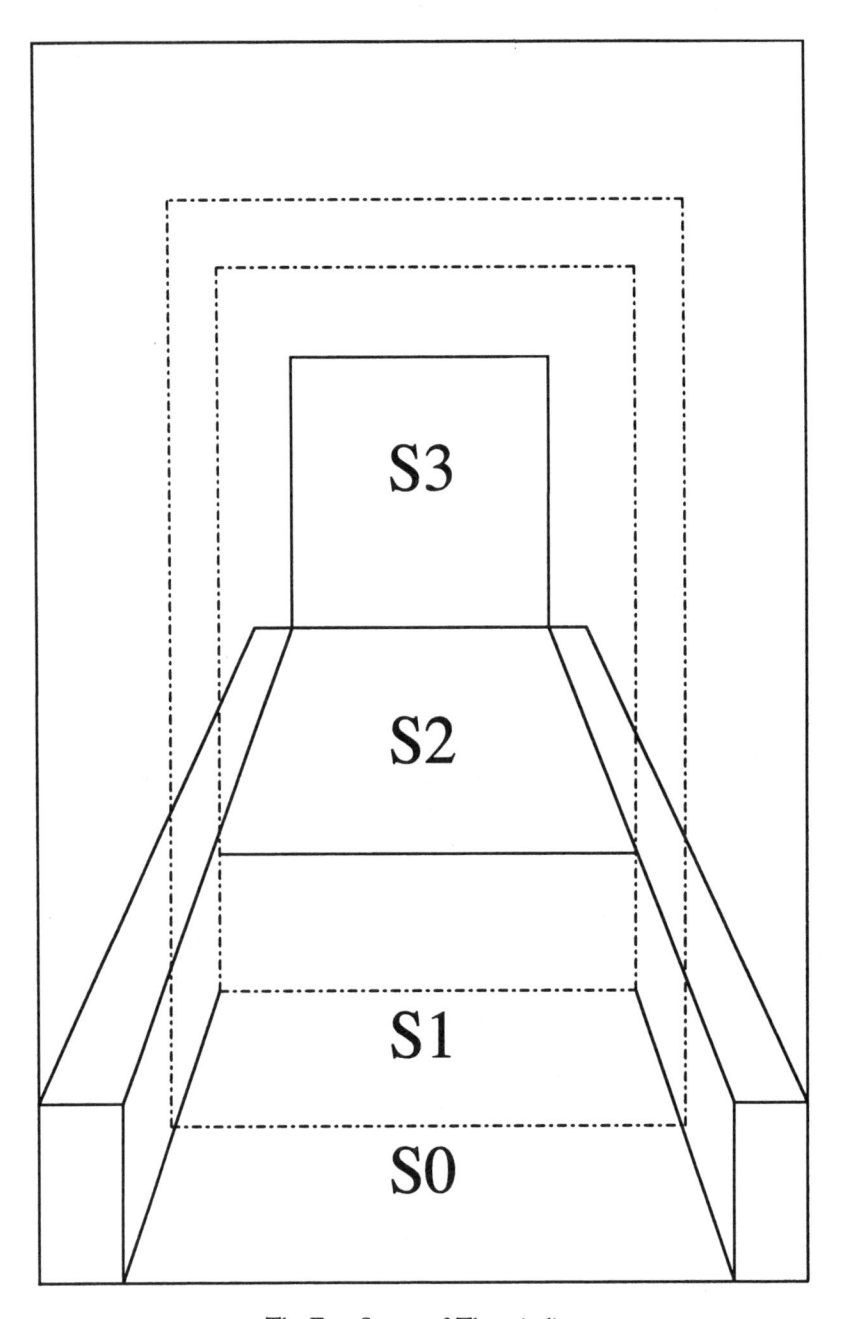

The Four Spaces of Theatricality

add to the exposition in this chapter another description of the way in which this experience of space began to change, for which I turn to George Kernodle's thesis concerning the emergence of Renaissance theatrical architecture from certain medieval forms of visual art. Let us refer to this thesis, or more precisely my adaptation of it, as *the flattening out of full space*.

To begin with, recall that one of the first medieval locales for the presentation of a dramatic sequence was the altar, which was or was closely associated with the crypt of a holy man and, ultimately, with the tomb of Christ. A crypt is a prototypically full form; to the extent that a performance appropriates it, the dramatic space is adapted to the exigencies of its symbolic architecture—the space is imbued, as it were, with the presence of the dead and their promise to the living. Because of its dual purpose of housing the dead and organizing the space of worship, the crypt became also a showpiece of sorts, at first completely three-dimensional but later succumbing to the same flattening tendency as did all showpieces.[87] In so doing its architecture became an integral component of the Renaissance facade and, eventually, of the modern stage.

Along with sepulchral architecture, another principal contributor to the Renaissance facade was a form of medieval street art called the *tableau vivant*. As we have seen in the context of the *Corpus Christi* processions, street theater in the Middle Ages was characterized by the creation of human still lifes, often devoted to episodes from the Bible. As they began to be filled with people rather than statues, these *tableaux* developed what we might call certain "dramatic conventions." These conventions, however, were never thought of as dramatic in the sense that we conceive of the word; rather, they were determined by their purpose as street decoration.[88] One of the conventions developed by the *tableaux*, perhaps adopted from elements of the liturgy, was the practice of "discovering" or revealing objects that had been concealed to that point. In addition to objects of importance for the scene, often—because the scenes did not generally include speech—what would be revealed was a banderole with dialogue written on it. For example, a scene in Ghent in 1458 depicted Peter walking over the water toward Christ. When he faltered and began to sink, the performer held out a piece of paper that read "Lord, save me!"[89]

Since *tableaux* would be staged in front of prominent pieces of urban architecture, the meaning of that architecture would become an integral part of the scene itself, whether a church wall from which angels might descend, or the city gate, from which, Kernodle claims, "was derived the shape of the triumphal arches of western Europe and of a number of *tableau* structures—part castle, part gate, part triumphal arch—which, in turn, were patterns for the regular theatres of the sixteenth century."[90] In a given scene, the significance of the gate would remain, while at the same time it would serve to frame the scene and set it apart from the surrounding space.

In other words, a *tableau* was a full space, only serving as a frame to the extent that the framing architecture retained its own meaning. There was, for the street theater, "no idea of a stage on which one built scenery—no conception of a background locating the action of a play."[91] Rather, it would always be organized around an emblematic scenic device, such as a garden, rocks, mountains, castle walls, etc. Like in the staging of the semi-liturgical dramas, these scenic elements were the central focus of the drama, from which the characters would emerge to make their gestures or speak their lines.

In order for this initial frame-like function to be become the equivalent of what Hardison referred to as the "protean Elizabethan stage," it must empty itself of this plenitude, of its meaningful attachment to places and emblems. This eventually occurs through a formal process of flattening out, a process that passes through several phases, including one that Kernodle identifies as that of the "arcade screen," which could "give splendour and stateliness to a scene, but it could not indicate a definite locale."[92] In the later Renaissance, this arcade became either more "realistic," by taking the shape of a non-specific building facade, or completely formal, becoming the proscenium stage. Against this background could be positioned arches, purely formal media inside of which the full space of a *tableau* could be unveiled,[93] provoking the sudden condensation of abstract into concrete, meaningful space.

From this genealogy emerges the facade, capable of absorbing the framing and signifying functions of previous forms:

> The remarkable fact about the facade is that it could take on the symbolic meaning of any of the older structures and that increasingly they were assimilated to its forms: they were made flatter and given framing columns and a canopy. The facade is the transitional form between the stylized realism of the medieval devices and the purely architectural symbolism of the Flemish and Elizabethan stages.[94]

What is important about this story of architectural change is that the full space of the medieval scene, while not replaced, is circumscribed and localized in a flattened, abstracted space, one that begins to serve the purpose of an empty space of universal representation. This flattened space now begins to designate the border between the real and the imaginary, it becomes a *screen*, delineating the limits of the stage whereon dramas are acted out for audiences whose attention rather than participation is demanded. The impact of the medieval device still exists, but now in the form of localized pockets of presence rather than as all-pervading full space. These pockets of presence became the "real" anchors of the protean stage; they are the place of hard materiality, the breakdown of interpretation, the locale of magic and of miracles and, for this reason may aptly retain the name of their origin, the crypt.

The power of the crypt, however, will only function in relation to the new spatial configuration. With this change, the medieval sense of space has been effectively turned inside-out; the new spatiality—an abstract, empty framework capable of objectively relating fragmented morsels of reality—will set the stage for the dominance of the new mode of being, and for the specific forms of spectacle that it enables.

In the *corrales* of the late 1500s, the stage became a permanent fixture that allowed for the emergence of this epistemological formation that I am calling a screen. By this I do not wish to imply that the *comedia* had ambitions toward what we would call a "realistic" reproduction of everyday life. For one thing, despite the prevalence of techniques of perspective in the visual arts of the time, there was no expectation that the simple paintings adorning the backdrops to performances in the *corrales* would be perspectively correct.[95] In fact, it is uniformly accepted that the much-touted special staging effects of the time were far more important for *autos* and court productions, where the traditional values of pageantry and spectacle reigned supreme;[96] the *comedia* was, for the most part, staged without the benefit of special effects.[97] The idea of screen, therefore, has nothing to do with the degree of mimesis involved in representation, but rather with the extent to which an audience was capable of *projecting* an alternate but viable reality onto that border and hence into the abstract space of the stage, and of *recognizing* in it models or representatives of its own values and modes of behavior.

Díez Borque remarks that what is perhaps most notable about the relationship between spectators and the stage at the time of the *comedia* is that the same spectator who went to the theater to be astonished [*embobado*] by the stage machinations (a similar desire led to the popularity of the *pièces à machine* in Paris) assumed, in fact, an enormously active role in constructing the imaginary space of the play, which he or she did by *reading* a whole array of verbal and scenic signs.[98] Spectators were expected to be able to imagine scene changes based on a verbal cue and an actor's exiting the stage and then entering through another doorway.[99] There are also countless examples in the texts of Golden Age plays of characters giving a play-by-play account of actions occurring just offstage; of changing, with a word, the typical second story window *en lo alto* into a distant mountain, a balcony, a rampart, or whatever might be needed for the scene; and of indicating a character's social standing through the register of speech adopted.[100] In addition to verbal cues, costumes were of particular importance in the creation of the play's imaginary space. Often a costume change was the only indication the audience would have that the actions of the play had changed locations.[101] Costumes also had a vital function in classifying a character within a given social category. The Spanish public at the time was extremely sensitive to such signifiers of class and could not, for example, tolerate or comprehend a scene in which the signs of social status presented by costume and speech would conflict; therefore, even when the plot called for a noblewoman to disguise herself as a servant, her speech would have to adopt the lower register for the time in which her character assumed that persona.[102] The rigidity of these codes provides powerful evidence that, while the public could understand that the fantasy space it projected upon the screen of the stage was fictional, that is, not itself reality, the representation was still held to certain standards that determined its *viability* as an alternate reality.[103] Such standards exist within the horizons of possible thought, such that, while the limitations of acceptability of the Spanish seventeenth century public might strike a late twentieth-century viewing public as quaint or provincial, we have our own horizons of limitations that demand that, even in a genre that is meant to explore the realm of the hypothetical such as science fiction, humanoid characters conform to a highly restrictive code of behavior, and will lose credibility if they exceed the limits of those codes. These standards only disappear when the performance ceases to be representational and becomes, rather like modern dance or certain kinds of avant-garde theater, pure performance.

According to Joan Copjec, film theory since Althusser has been content to conceptualize the screen as a mirror, as that space where a subject's reality is projected in a more or less distorted form, and in which space the subject recognizes him or her self.[104] But in order for this recognition to take place, the spectator has to identify with a perspective, a point of view from which the image makes sense; this point is termed the gaze.[105] The coordinates that define this point also define the horizon of possible thought described above, in that it is only when one is squarely situated within this horizon that the images constituting the screen one watches converge into a coherent whole that "makes sense." In the same way, the gaze that permits the viability of the imaginary space of the *comedia* and the spectator's recognition of this space as his or her own is one in which an individual is defined by certain fixed patterns of speech and clothing. Thus, one could conclude, the subject of representation—or of control, as Anthony Cascardi would put it[106]—is produced by the apparatus of the stage at that moment when he or she begins to recognize his or her self in an imaginary space, from a perspective defined by certain socially determined coordinates.[107]

As it happens, this is precisely where psychoanalysis parts company with extremely deterministic models of subject formation, and where Copjec intervenes in the exposition of the gaze in film theory. For Lacan, the distinction of the gaze is that it is more than merely a position to be assumed; it is, rather, an object to be desired.[108] That is to say, once a given reality is arranged for a spectator in the form of a screen, the spectator can never completely occupy that position from which everything, including his or her position, within the reality of the screen "makes sense." Whereas before the advent of the screen, a spectator would encounter a performance as a sight to behold and to enjoy in its presence, within the mode of being of theatricality the spectator becomes convinced that what he or she sees, that is, the characters he or she encounters, are, like his or her own "characters," merely appearances, and that there exists beyond the screen of appearances an essence that is somehow more real, but that is currently concealed or absent. Spectatorial subjects, therefore, are not transfixed by what they see on the stage, but rather by what they fail to see but desire to see anyway;[109] in other words, they are transfixed by what is concealed. The function of S3, the crypt, within the economy of theatricality, is to respond to this desire for substance, for presence, for the real. Like other stages of the time and since then—and like all media that today partake of the structure of the screen and that are, hence, fundamentally theatrical—the *comedia* tried to oblige precisely that desire by making the screen multi-leveled, and opening the rear curtain or trap door in order to effect "discoveries" that, more often than not, represented the fullest, most substantial possible entities: cadavers or mutilated bodies.[110]

The impulse to oblige this desire for the real is also behind the phenomenon of pornography, for what is most pornography but an attempt to make of woman (or, in general, the sexual other) a real *thing* instead of what she, like any and all living subjects, really is: a theatrical apparition, a screen for the projection of fantasies? In the typical porn film, for example, what is precisely *not* in question is the desire of the other—her desire is blatant, in your face, entirely unproblematic. Is it any surprise then that the extreme form of pornography, a form that persists in creating an enormous underground market despite all attempts to abolish it, is the snuff film? It is the snuff film that poses to theatricality its ultimate question, that brings it face to face with the paradox of its unfolding: death is the final escape from theatricality's eternal play of appearances (hence the death drive is the most fundamental level of drive), but on the screen, even death can be faked. The snuff film depends on a supplemental knowledge, a knowledge transmitted by the rumor of voices from outside the law, that the death on the screen was not faked, that one is in the presence, at last, of the real thing.

The stage of the *comedia*, then, was an abstract space delimited by the screen. This abstract space was consummately mutable, capable of portraying different places and times with lightening speed.[111] Next to the stage's essential vagueness, *apariencias*, *descubrimientos*, and bits of portable scenery could be used to indicate place synecdochically, anchoring in their hard specificity for a moment the amorphous space of the stage.[112] But this quotidian, anchoring function of *apariencias* (a function that still partakes, albeit in a less spectacular way, of the power of the crypt) was only part of the story. Of the five functions Allen lists for *apariencias*, the first on the list is "demonstrate results of violence."[113] And this was not only a tendency of the Spanish stage. Mahelot's stage design normally consisted of five reduced *mansions* or compartments surrounding the proscenium, which itself acted, as we have seen, much like the abstract stage of the English or Spanish stages.[114] These compartments, as in the case of the Spanish *apariencias*, could be opened to reveal scenic elements, and often players could enter and perform inside them. In Mahelot's descriptions, however, what predominate are sacred or sepulchral places: one "tourne autour du tombeau," or "autour de l'autel"[115] [moves around the crypt, or around the altar]. In his notice for *Arétaphile*, he writes: "il faut au milieu du theastre un palais caché où il y ait un tombeau et des armes"[116] [one needs in the middle of the theater a hidden palace where there is a crypt and some weapons]; or in the notice for Mairet's *Silvanie*, a "toille de pastoralle" [pastoral backdrop] hides yet again her tomb.

Other forms of spectacle tried to cultivate the power of the crypt as well, and in doing so were perhaps more in keeping with their medieval ancestry. Hagiographic drama would use the crypt to fuse the death and beatification of its subjects; *autos sacramentales* would use it to recreate the presencing effect of religious ceremony; and courtly masques and ballets would use it to add to the power and mystique of the sovereign. The *ballet de cour*, as Jacquot explains, depends on the interaction between the space of the stage, ruled by illusion and the manipulation of perspective, and the space of the audience, "[m]ais certaines zones conservent leur mystère, et les personnages qui en proviennent, ou qui s'y meuvent, paraissent d'une essence différente, ont l'air s'appartenir à un autre monde"[117] [but certain zones retain their mystery, and the characters who emerge from them, or who move about in them, seem to be of a different essence, they give the impression of belonging to a different world]. Such was the case of the space above the stage, which was not visible to the audience but from which characters would descend—characters who could, for the audience, only be of divine origin. The depths of the stage are "discovered" only little by little, revealing surprises housed within surprises, the effect being complete when characters emerge from the deepest place and into the space of the audience.

Finally, the effects of the crypt could be accentuated by the use of music. While it is next to impossible for us to speculate as to the exact nature of all the music played during or between performances, we know that music abounded; and indeed, it is often referred to directly in stage directions. Pinciano specifies music as an essential aspect of decor; as Fadrique puts it, "[e]s ta[m]bién la música parte del ornato, en la qual se deue considerar que, especialmente en las tragedias, nunca se aparte de ella misma, sino que vaya cantando cosas al mismo propósito, para que la acción vaya más substanciada"[118] [music is also part of the decor, which, especially in tragedies, should never be lacking it, but rather should always be accompanied by singing suitable songs, in order that the action be more substantiated]. As I show in the case of *Lo fingido verdadero*, this substantiating effect of music was important enough for Lope to mention it virtually every time he opened the crypt.

TRUE PRETENSE: LOPE'S *LO FINGIDO VERDADERO* AND THE STRUCTURE OF THEATRICAL SPACE

At first glance, Lope's *Lo fingido verdadero*, or *True Pretense*, is a hagiographic drama, a tragicomedy based on the legendary events of the life of Saint Genesius, reason enough for a reading stressing its theological aspects.[119] The fact that Lope actively engages the *teatrum mundi* metaphor in the first act would only confirm the accuracy of such an emphasis. From this perspective, *Lo fingido verdadero* would appear to be an extended dramatization of the metaphor made most famous by Calderon's *El gran teatro del mundo*, in which human existence is compared to a dramatic production written and directed by the almighty *autor de comedias*, God. One's only obligation in this drama is to play the role assigned to the best of one's ability—that is, the poor man should be the best possible poor man, the king the best possible king, etc.—in the knowledge that at the end of the drama one will be judged by God according to the way one played one's role.

Carino, one of a string of ill-fated Roman emperors who populate the chaotic first act of Lope's play, challenges this vision of the universe while at the same time challenging God, placing himself above the human comedy and claiming for his role as emperor a perpetuity rivaling that of the heavens. His servant offends him by reminding him that while his performance may last longer than that of the actors on a stage, it is a performance nonetheless, and will come to an end:

> ¿Luego tú piensas que reinas
> con mayor estimación?
> La diferencia sabida,
> es que les dura hora y media
> su comedia, y tu comedia
> te dura toda la vida.
> Tú representas también,
> mas estás de rey vestido
> hasta la muerte, que ha sido
> sombra del fin.[120]

> [So you think you reign
> with greater esteem?
> The difference, of course,
> is that their comedy last
> an hour and a half,
> and your comedy lasts you
> your entire life.
> You also are playing a role,
> but you will be dressed as king

until death, which has been
a shadow of the end.]

Carino becomes fully conscious of the ephemeral nature of his role only at the moment of his death, from which perspective the difference between his time on earth and an actor's on the stage seems moot:

> Representé mi figura:
> césar fuí, Roma, rey era;
> acabóse la tragedia,
> la muerte me desnudó:
> sospecho que no duró
> toda mi vida hora y media.[121]
>
> [I played my part:
> Caesar, I was Rome, I was king;
> the tragedy ended,
> death denuded me:
> I suspect that my whole life
> did not last an hour and a half.]

The saint and martyr, Ginés, provides the counterpoint to Carino's belated lament by demonstrating an awareness of life's brevity and falsity, and of the fictive, ephemeral nature of one's role in that life. However, in this respect, Lope departs somewhat from the Calderonian model, as the final moral of the play is not merely that the quality of Ginés' performance of his role saves him, but also the fact that he attains, via his performance, a consciousness of the distinction between earthly roles and heavenly roles:

> Pueblo romano, escuchadme:
> yo representé en el mundo
> sus fábulas miserables,
> todo el tiempo de mi vida,
> sus vicios y sus maldades;
> yo fuí figura gentil
> adorando dioses tales;
> recibióme Dios; ya soy
> cristiano representante;
> cesó la humana comedia,
> que era toda disparates;
> hice la que veis, divina;
> voy al cielo a que me paguen,
> que de mi fe y esperanza
> y mi caridad notable,
> debo al cielo, y él me debe
> estos tres particulares.

Mañana temprano espero
para la segunda parte.[122]

[Roman people, listen to me:
I represented in the world
its miserable tales,
all the time of my life,
its vices and evils;
I was a heathen figure
adoring such gods;
God received me; now I am
a Christian player;
the human comedy is over,
which was all nonsense;
I made the one you see, divine;
I am going to heaven that they may pay me,
what of my faith, hope,
and notable charity
I owe to heaven,
and it owes me
these three particulars.
Early tomorrow I await
the second half.]

Life, cosmic or heavenly life included, is still theater; the distinction is that earthly life is theatrical life that is unaware of its theatricality. If this were a simple morality play, the lesson would be that, like Ginés, we should learn to disregard the attachments of our earthly roles and strain to play only the eternal role, the role ordained by God. Lope's play, however, is not a morality play, and at every turn it resists and subverts such a theologically allegorical reading.

For one thing, Ginés is something special: a martyr and a saint. And to become like him would require a special effort: it would require one to rend the very fabric of representational space; not merely to transcend worldly matters enough to recognize their ephemerality, but rather, and more fundamentally, to shatter the rigid theatrical frameworks in which we perform our lives, tell our stories, and receive the very moral message Lope is sending us. In other words, by understanding his message, by grasping and identifying with his characters, we are already revealing ourselves as condemned to our earthly theatrical states, for Ginés attained sanctity by failing to make the very frame distinctions that make him comprehensible to us as a character: by experiencing as real what were meant to be mere representations; by feeling the successful, illocutionary force of what were meant to be failed or suspended performatives.

My reading of Lope's play, then, is as a demonstration, a performance, of the spatial structure of theatricality, and an argument for why, in the theatrical mode of being, truth may only be attained by way of pretense. Act 1, the act that establishes the *teatrum mundi* metaphor, is an exposition of S1, a space distinguished from the audience's space by a screen—a space characterized by its own place, Mesopotamia, and its own time, that of the Roman Empire. It is an unproblematic space, an unsurprising space, a space of fiction, romance, and perhaps of moral lessons as well. In this space we witness the meteoric and in some ways ludicrous rise to power of the Emperor Diocleciano, his love for the bread seller Camila, and his loyalty to his friend and fellow soldier Maximiano.

Act 2 then, logically, becomes an exposition of the first interior effect of the theatrical distinction I have called the screen. We know we are in theatrical space because Ginès, actor of great renown, is called to perform before Diocleciano; the space of the stage becomes the place of another stage, and some of our characters become actors while others become spectators. Lope, however, is not merely concerned to demonstrate the metatheatrical flexibility of theatrical space; his emphasis is rather on the complexity of negotiating between the various framed levels and on the effects that this complex negotiation has on the identity of character. Almost immediately after it has been formed, then, S2 shows signs of disintegrating, collapsing back into S1. For his first play, Ginés decides to perform a love story, but casts as the lover (Fabia) of his Rufino his leading lady Marcela, with whom he is in love "in real life." To further complicate matters, he casts the man she loves in real life, Octavio, as Octavio, the man Fabia loves; and he casts Marcela's real father, Fabricio, as Fabia's father, Fabricio. The only signs he leaves us to indicate the difference between reality (for S1) and playacting (for S1) are his and his love interest's stage names. So our first indication that the newly constructed S2, the space of the love story being performed before the emperor, is breaking down comes when Ginés, playing Rufino to Marcela's Fabia, errs in his role by calling her Marcela:

> Bien sé, Marcela, que nace
> el hacerme aqueste agravio
> de que quieres bien a Octavio;
> Octavio te satisface,
> Octavio te agrada, ingrata;
> por él me dejas a mí.
>
> *Marcela:*
> Ginés, ¿representas?
>
> *Ginés:*
> Sí.
> Mi pena a quien mal me trata.[123]
>
> [Well I know, Marcela, that
> your injuring me in this way

is born of your love for Octavio;
Octavio satisfies you,
Octavio pleases you, ingrate;
for him you leave me.

Marcela:
Ginés, are you acting?

Ginés:
Yes.
My grief to her who treats me so badly.]

Ginés's response is really quite astute. He is acting or, more accurately, acting out his grief to the one who is its cause. He is, in other words, communicating, conveying a truth by means of a pretense. But the truth is not the naive truth of the pain of unrequited love; it is the truth that the "acting" of "Ginés, are you acting?" is not an absolute term. Whether Ginés is acting or not depends on the space he occupies relative to another observer: for S0 he is acting, for S1 he is not.

Diocleciano and his entourage are no less confused. They too begin to argue (in S1) as to whether or not Ginés is acting, Diocleciano himself eventually concluding in the affirmative:

Mas pienso que es artificio
deste gran representante,
porque turbarse un amante
fue siempre el mayor indicio.[124]

[But I think it is artifice
of the great actor,
because that a lover should become confused
was always the best index of his love.]

A spectacular argument, because it could equally prove that Ginés was acting when in fact he was not (since his confusing his lines is adduced as proof of his technical excellence, the extremes of verisimilitude), and that he was not acting when in fact he was (since his confusing his lines is also the ultimate proof of his actual love). This paradox, however, is inherent in the nature of acting in theatricality and to verisimilitude as its index of excellence: for to achieve perfection in one's art is to erase any trace of art, and hence of one's perfection.

Lope's play, however, goes beyond demonstrating this paradox in theater in order to reveal it as an inherent aspect of life as theatrically experienced. Once verisimilitude has been accepted as the standard of artistry in the theatrical space, the paradox that plagues it plagues any and all interaction, by undermining the lines between the real and its simulation. Such is the problem with performatives. A performative should perform something; it should, in other words, provoke a socially tangible change. But how do we know when and how to distinguish "real" performatives from ones that are merely performed, that is, acted out? Marcela, still playing Fabia in S2 for the gazes S1, performs with her lover Octavio a series of promises that in Spanish society of the time would have had the power of creating the legal bond of marriage.

> *Marcela:*
> ¿Prométesme ser mi esposo?
>
> *Octavio:*
> Mano y palabra te doy.
>
> *Marcela:*
> ¡Ay cielo, si verdad fuera
> la comedia![125]
>
> [*Marcela:*
> Do you promise to be my husband?
>
> *Octavio:*
> My hand and word I give you.
>
> *Marcela:*
> Heavens, if only this comedy were real!]

Again the promise takes place in S2, and is witnessed by the audience in S1 as a fictional performance. As such it would be what we could call a failed performative, in the sense that Austin specified was peculiar to an actor on a stage. However, Marcela's comment reveals a real desire, real for S1, and prefigures the realization of that desire and that performance in that space (S1) when they actually do run off together, hence consummating their marriage. The failed performative in S2 is thus revealed to have been a success in S1. However, in order for this revelation itself to have been a success, the vacillation between the two levels must have been experienced by us, the audience S0, as a fiction of the stage, as in some sense fundamentally distinct from our own reality (if not, how could it have been both a failure and a success?). And if it is indeed, as it must be, experienced as a fiction, as a pretense, then the successful performative of S1 is revealed yet again to have been a failure.

The stakes for the Ginés of S1 multiply exponentially when the performatives being uttered change from the topic of love to the topic of eternal salvation. In act 3, Ginés begins to rehearse for his role as a Christian martyr, and while doing so utters a performative in S2 that again threatens to be successful in S1:

¡Cristo mío, pues sois Dios,
Vos me llevaréis a Vos,
que yo desde ahora os sigo![126]

[O my Christ, since you are God,
You will take me unto yourself,
as I from now on follow you.]

The performative power of this utterance, however, is only revealed via the aperture of yet another space, S3, the crypt. This occurs shortly after Ginés undertakes his role in front of the emperor's entourage, when the voice of an angel calls out:

Dios oyó tu pensamiento,
que Dios su lenguaje entiende,
Ginés, y lo que pretende
tu alma, le da contento.
Sube, sube, llega a verme;
que te quiero bautizar.[127]

[God heard your thought,
as God understands its language,
Ginés, and what your soul desires,
He gives happily.
Come up, come up, come to see me;
as I want to baptize you.]

Now, the audience in S1, of course, thinks the angel is an actor, as do we, the audience in space S0. But while we are correct in our assumption, they are not; because in the reality of S1 it really is an angel. This *real* angel (again, real for S1 only insofar as S1 exists for S0) calls Ginés into S3, where he is baptized, transforming via this performative his character in S1 (a pagan actor) to its character in S2 (a Christian martyr).

As should be expected at this point, when S3 opens, we are faced with an entirely different sort of space from those that came before it. The crypt, the place of the angel's magical apparition and Ginés's transformation, the space of this mediation between the previous framed realities, is not an empty, abstract, mutable space like the space of the stage, but is, rather, the concrete, particular, full, and richly stationary space of medieval *tableaux vivants* and of mystères such as that of the *Glorieux corps*. The stage directions for the first revelation S3 read

Con música se abren en alto unas puertas en que se ven pintados una imagen de Nuestra Señora y un Cristo en brazos del Padre, y por las gradas de este trono algunos mártires.[128]

[With music some doors open up high on which can be seen painted an image of Our Lady and a Christ in the arms of the Father, and along the stairs leading to this throne several martyrs.]

As I mentioned before, while we cannot know what actual music was played, it is significant that in each of the scenes centered on this *apariencia* (which was certainly "discovered" behind doors on the balcony above the *vestuario*) Lope calls for music, which, as Pinciano pointed out, substantiates the scene much in the way that the *tableau* scenery itself creates the effect of substance. These same doors open a few minutes later to reveal the scene of Ginés's baptism:

Descúbrese con música, hincando de rodillas, un ángel; sostiene una fuente, otro un aguamanil levantando, como que ya echó el agua; otro una vela blanca encendida; y otro un capillo.[129]

[Accompanied by music, an angel is revealed, on his knees; he is holding a fountain, and another is holding a pitcher although he has just poured the water; another is holding a white, lit candle; and another a hood.]

It is this historically-past referent, a medieval *tableau vivant*, which marks the stopgap in a potentially infinite telescoping of interior spaces and which, perhaps, retains some of the power it once had: a power to evoke the miraculous, to make present the objects of faith. This space, the space of the crypt, remains locked behind the trap doors and rear curtains of the new stage designs, opening occasionally and in climactic moments to bring movement and uncertainty to a screeching halt, to reveal the answers to a plot's concealed secrets, and to sate an audience's desire for the real with its powerful iconography. Thus it is with the final, shocking, and yet expected "discovery" of the play, in which Ginés is revealed, impaled, and gives his last speech.

The moment of Ginés's conversion in this S3 is witnessed by the audience of actors in S1 as a realistic performance in S2. The comment of one of these spectators, "No hay diferencia desto al verdadero caso"[130] [There's no difference between this and the real thing], becomes a description of enormous complexity when one realizes that in order for it to be true, or to make any sense at all, it must also be false—that is, the audience in space S0 *must* be able to tell the difference between the performance in S2 and that in S1 (the "real thing"), in order for a character in S1 to claim that a performance in S2 is indistinguishable from his or her own reality (if not, we would not know what he or she was referring to). The audience who comprehends this must be able to unpack the liar's paradox[131] it contains, and must be able to identify simultaneously with its own gaze and with that gaze that animates and justifies the action of S2, the gaze of a staged version of itself, a virtual audience. It is the ability to negotiate this distance that opens the permanent possibility that we ourselves are animated and made real by precisely such a disembodied gaze, a gaze on which our very reality rests, but one whose existence we can never know for certain.

This chapter has been concerned with tracing the development of the theatrical experience of space out of the experience of presence characteristic of medieval spectacle. As such, it has concentrated on how the conventions of spectacle changed during the sixteenth century to produce a theater based on metatheatrical staging practices, practices that assume and help construct viewers capable of navigating an often bewildering edifice of imaginary spaces that open onto further interior spaces in what I have called a permanently potential mise en abîme. This telescoping of separable spaces requires audiences to negotiate different levels of reality, which they do by means of characters or avatars, virtual selves that become conditioned to this new, fundamentally scopic organization of space, in which they watch and are watched watching; they become bodies saturated by the gaze. Furthermore, these avatars acquire symbolic representativity in the political sense, a representativity that manifests itself in different forms of political "subjectivity"—symbolic forms—because these avatars exist on the same plane as symbols, maps, or political demarcations of territory. The connection between theatricality and the various political, philosophical, and aesthetic notions of subjectivity is the theme of the next chapter.

CHAPTER 5

Theatricality versus Subjectivity

What is modern about modernity? Is there a quality, an essence of life, or an organizing principle to western culture after the sixteenth century that distinguishes it as a whole from the cultures of prior centuries? The grounding assumption of history since the seventeenth century, when European thinkers began to think of history as distinguishing the present from the past, has been an affirmative answer to this question. As Lee Patterson argues,[1] the form of this affirmation has more often than not been to claim for the modern age—to which the "we" in question always belongs—a quality, essence, or principle that is *lacking* in the pre-modern age. The Middle Ages become the negation against which modernity is positively defined. And as Patterson also argues, the most popular contemporary name for that quality, essence, or principle is *subjectivity*.

But what exactly is this subjectivity? Is it grammatical? Do modern people refer to themselves with personal subject pronouns while medieval people had the primitive tendency to talk about themselves in the third person, or to use the personal pronoun in writing exclusively as an abstract universal, displaying no subjective insight or emotion? Or perhaps the term refers to a properly philosophical distinction: modern individuals experience themselves as autonomous agents acting upon a material world, much like a grammatical subject acts upon a grammatical object; whereas the medievals found themselves awash in an undifferentiated unity with the world. Or, if this seems far-fetched, could it be that subjectivity is a term from political theory, referring either to the subject of a state or, in a more critical-theoretical vein, to an individual whose self-consciousness is formed or produced through a sociocultural process of subjection to an anonymous power structure seeking only to reproduce itself?

This chapter argues that the vocabulary of subjectivity is inappropriate for theorizing the distinction between the pre-modern and the modern—not, as with Patterson, because other ages can be shown to have it as well, but rather because "it" as a concept has neither historical specificity nor theoretical coherence. Subjectivity, as it tends to be used in contemporary cultural studies, history, discourse analysis, and even philosophy, has become an empty reference point, a catchall explanation and (just as often, today) condemnation of the contemporary, rendered useless by its overdetermined vacuity. To say that modernity is characterized by subjectivity is to say nothing at all.

The purpose of this chapter, and indeed of this book, is to propose an alternate way of understanding the—very real, I believe—differences between the western world before and since the sixteenth century. Instead of conceptualizing a quality, essence, or principle that we have and they did not, I suggest that what occurred was a shift in dominance between two modes of experiencing space, that is, between two modes of spatiality: presence and theatricality. The theory of theatricality as a mode of spatiality has several advantages over theories of subjectivity. First, it is highly specific. Rather than claiming applicability as a term of philosophical, aesthetic, and political analysis, theatricality applies to one domain: the way individuals experience the spaces they inhabit. At the same time, when this extremely specific mode of spatiality has been mapped, it will become clear that many of the modern phenomena described by philosophy, political theory, and aesthetic criticism as functions of subjectivity are in fact dependent on precisely the mode of spatiality described by theatricality. Theatricality, in other words, does much of the work that subjectivity purports to do without suffering from its theoretical incoherence or lack of specificity. In the following pages, I discuss in detail the three principal manifestations of the subjectivity complex—the philosophical, the political, and the literary/aesthetic—in order to argue in each case for the conceptual superiority of theatricality. In the first section I argue that the philosophical critique of subjectivity, derived principally from Heidegger, fails to distinguish adequately between experience and the conceptualization of experience, and as a result foments a constant confusion between the history of thought and the history of being. From Heidegger, however, I also borrow the notion of phenomenology that best describes the methodology of this project: an ontology based not on *a priori* concepts but on the description of the everyday practices that frame and structure—reveal, in his terminology—our historical existence; in the present case, these would be the practices and conventions of theatrical spectacle. In the next section I make a claim for the centrality of theatricality to the political organization of modern states, and show how the theory of subjectification, in both its psychoanalytic and historicist forms, presupposes a theatrical experience of space. Finally, in the third section, I suggest that in the arts, and specifically in literature, theatricality describes precisely that experience of space implied in the ironic frame-distinctions constitutive of fiction, perhaps the paradigmatic form of modern literature. From these three moments I conclude by deriving a notion of theatricality as a term of media analysis, and suggest that the mode of being subtended by theatricality is still dominant in contemporary western culture and still structures the most fundamental interactions between ourselves, other people, and our world.

PHILOSOPHICAL SUBJECTIVITY

The critique of subjectivity, one of the great tendencies of philosophical thought in the twentieth century, can more or less be divided thematically into three groups: *deconstruction and pragmatism*, which despite their differences are unified by a desire to do away with the notion of an autonomous self-consciousness serving as a foundation for all knowledge; *historicism*, which, building on the traditions of both Hegel and Nietzsche, seeks to undermine the confident universality of subject-centered thought by pointing to its dependence on historically specific practices and assumptions; and *psychoanalysis*, which describes a human agency whose most basic motive force, its will or desire, is in eternal and hopeless conflict with itself.[2] Whereas the first two categories involve attempts to reveal the philosophical inconsistency of subjectivity as a description of how human beings interact with the world, the latter, especially in the work of Jacques Lacan and his followers, has instead involved a redefinition of the term toward an ostensibly more accurate description of this relation. Lacanians, then, do not reject subjectivity; they merely defend a different—and perhaps more nuanced, although still universalistic—notion of what the human subject is and how it works. Because the psychoanalytic definition of subjectivity has become so idiosyncratic, I will not deal with it in this section, but will concentrate instead on the first two categories. I will discuss the psychoanalytic model below in conjunction with theories of subjectification.

When proponents of deconstruction, pragmatism, or historicism attack subjectivity, they are not, as I am, claiming that the word has no coherent point of reference. The philosophical tradition is in fact quite unified about what subjectivity is. What they are claiming is that what the term refers to—a set of ideas about how the human individual relates to the world and, more specifically, has knowledge about the world—is a fundamentally misconceived set of ideas about the human individual and its relation to the world.[3] The most forceful originator of this claim (in both its anti-metaphysical and historicist forms) is Martin Heidegger. Heidegger's basic argument is that, essentially beginning with René Descartes, the modern philosophical tradition has described the grammatical, first-person subject as the foundation of all possible knowledge, thereby making the world in which the subject and all other thinking and perceiving beings dwell a secondary object, a "standing reserve" of resources in which the subject moves about, picking and choosing at will and constructing his or her own surroundings, and a "world picture" (*Weltbild*): a screen of representations constituted and compared by the subject for their relative accuracy in depicting the real:

> What it is to be is for the first time defined as the objectness of representing, and truth is first defined as the certainty of representing, in the metaphysics of

Descartes.... The whole of modern metaphysics taken together, Nietzsche included, maintains itself within the interpretation of what it is to be and of truth that was prepared by Descartes.[4]

This way of understanding the world has, moreover, traditionally been understood as liberating: "The essence of the modern age can be seen in the fact that man frees himself from the bonds of the Middle Ages in freeing himself to himself."[5] Still,

> [w]hat is decisive is not that man frees himself to himself from previous obligations, but that the very essence of man itself changes, in that man becomes subject. We must understand this word *subiectum*, however, as the translation of the Greek *hypokeímenon*. The word names that-which-lies-before, which, as ground, gathers everything onto itself. This metaphysical meaning of the concept of subject has first of all no special relationship to man and none at all to the I.[6]

Heidegger's first problem with the subjective model is that it is philosophically inconsistent. By becoming self-naming, self-supporting, the subject attains a nominal freedom from the bonds of the world, tradition, culture, etc. But the modern philosophical tradition, the tradition that achieves its apex with Kant, also figures this liberated self as the *meta-physis*, the foundation of the (human) being's every engagement with the world. According to Heidegger, there is no basis for this claim: subject as *hypokeímenon*, as ground, as that which comes before and hence as foundation, has no necessary relation to the subject as self, and the Greeks knew this, even if we have forgotten it.

The Cartesian description of the human's relation to the world is, then, philosophically wrong, because it is based on a false etymological connection between the grammatical subject and subject as metaphysical ground. It is also, however, phenomenologically wrong, that is, an inaccurate description of Being. The modern subject is a masterful subject, a subject that controls its environment, that determines its involvement with the world. But for Heidegger, human existence (*Dasein*) finds itself always already thrown (*geworfen*) into a world that preexists and exceeds it in every way. Dasein's being is not to be understood over and against the world, a world existing as an object for its use, but rather as a part of the general "worldliness" of the world. In this sense, then, modern philosophy has distanced itself from a truth that was better understood by the ancients:

> To be beheld by what is, to be included and maintained within its openness and in that way to be borne along by it, to be driven about by its oppositions and marked by its discord—that is the essence of man in the great age of the Greeks. Therefore, in order to fulfill his essence, Greek man must gather (*leg-*

ein) and save (*sozein*), catch up and preserve, what opens itself in its openness, and he must remain exposed (*aletheuein*) to all its sundering confusions. Greek man *is* the one who apprehends [*der Vernehmer*] that which is, and this is why in the age of the Greeks the world cannot become picture.[7]

With such a statement, Heidegger would appear to establish an absolute rift between himself and other, say radically historicist, critiques of subjectivity. For if the historicist attitude is to claim, like Rorty, that such and such a formulation was adequate for its time but is simply no longer proper, or, like Foucault, that any given set of truths is dependent on a particular historical regime of power, then it is certainly inconsistent to posit one historical period as being privileged over another in its ability to grasp the Truth. But what Heidegger does share with all those engaged in the critique of subjectivity is an antipathy toward Modernity and its trappings, in particular toward its ordering of the categories of knowledge. In the work of both Foucault and Heidegger, this antipathy is expressed by way of often nostalgic descriptions of past epistemes as well as utopian pronouncements of coming ones. It is interesting, for instance, to note the astonishingly similar tone between Foucault's famously lyrical invocation of the end of Man on the last page of *Les mots et les choses* (in which Man is imagined as a face drawn in the sand by the side of the sea, soon to be swept away by the tide), and this passage from note 9 to Heidegger's "The Age of the World Picture":

> Man cannot, of himself, abandon this destining of his modern essence or abolish it by fiat. But man can, as he thinks ahead, ponder this: Being subject as humanity has not always been the sole possibility belonging to the essence of historical man, which is always beginning in a primal way, nor will it always be. A fleeting cloud shadow over a concealed land, such is the darkening which that truth as the certainty of subjectivity—once prepared by Christendom's certainty of salvation—lays over a disclosing event [*Ereignis*] that it remains denied to subjectivity itself to experience.[8]

For Heidegger as for Foucault, the subject, or Man as its fundamentally self-reflexive framework for all knowing (for instance, the "sciences of Man"), are ephemeral notions, far from the foundations of thought and experience they present themselves as. Similarly, the critique of subjectivity as a philosophical movement also seems to be driven by a utopian impulse, a conviction that beyond the philosophically mistaken or politically anathematic imposition of the subjective model on human Being, another kind of freedom looms large. I do not share this optimism. Nor, on the other hand, do I share the conviction that the philosophy of subjectivity conditions a kind of experience that is in some way more limiting, more restrictive, than other possible philosophical formulations. The reason for this is, quite simply, that being subject in its philosophical sense is not a mode of experience, it is a mode of *talking about* experience.[9] Whereas the kind of work that Foucault undertakes in *Surveiller et punir* and *L'histoire de la sexualité* is very much about how humans experience limitations on their freedom, this is an entirely different discourse from that of the critique of subjectivity; it is a discourse that, when it uses the term subject, uses it in a different way. The philosophical discourse of subjectivity does not deal with practices, real experiences, or "techniques of power"; it deals with other philosophers.[10] And by far the philosopher of preference, when one wants to go about critiquing subjectivity, is Descartes.

Intellectualism versus Experience

Descartes, however, is considered the founder of the discourse of modernity by more than merely those who wish to use him as a straw man for their philosophically-subversive projects. Descartes' formulation of *cogito ergo sum* as the foundation for all knowledge is acknowledged by many thinkers as the initiation of modern thought, be they critics, staunch defenders, or ostensibly neutral observers of modernity.[11] One thinker who would appear to belong to the latter camp is Charles Taylor, who advocates what he calls a "cultural" approach to the problem of modernity.[12] A cultural approach, clearly modeled on the methodology of cultural anthropology, sees the advent of modernity not as a moment in a necessary historical progression (a progression of which "we" moderns are the most recent product), but as a culturally specific and historically contingent constellation of intellectual, social, and economic factors. From this perspective, it makes little sense to be for or against modernity—and, in fact, those who have taken explicitly critical or affirming positions vis à vis modernity can be shown to have fixated on one or another aspect of this constellation. In Taylor's reading, modernity's leitmotif of inwardness and detachment from the self allows for the emergence of both the themes of self-control and self-exploration, themes which he sees as grounding the opposing attitudes toward modernity: namely, those of the critics construing modern identity as fundamentally characterized by self-control; and those of the defenders construing it as characterized by self-exploration.[13]

Taylor's point is that, regardless of which side one chooses to be on, there are commonalities to the description of the self favored by modernity. This self is pictured as a separate, autonomous sphere of inwardness,[14] capable of being separated from itself—as agent and object—and acting upon, manipulating, or exploring itself in a state of disengagement:

> What one finds running through all the aspects of this constellation—the new philosophy, the methods of administration and military organization, the new spirit of government, and methods of discipline—is a growing ideal of a

human agent who is able to remake himself by methodological and disciplined action. What this calls for is the ability to take an instrumental stance to one's given properties, desires, inclinations, tendencies, habits of thought, and feelings so that they can be worked on, doing away with some and strengthening others, until one meets the desired specifications. My suggestion is that Descartes's picture of the disengaged subject articulates the understanding of agency that is most congenial to this whole movement and is part of the grounds for its great impact in his century and beyond.[15]

I accept completely Taylor's suggestion that our approach to the problem of modernity be a cultural, and thus nonevaluative, one—hence my criticism of the utopian drive in both Heidegger and Foucault. Where I differ from Taylor (and from most discussants of modernity) is in his tendency to intellectualize, to conflate how people might actually have conceived of themselves—that is, as interior beings, as disengaged agents—with how the philosophical tradition talks about how people conceive of themselves.[16] There are several responses to this objection: that Descartes and other thinkers are reflecting the general thought of their time; that they have a "finger on the pulse" of their era and are a conduit for the mentality of their time; or that there is a separation between practices and behaviors on the one hand and theories of those behaviors on the other, but that the relationship between these theories and practices is "dialectical," in that the theory both reflects and alters the practice by, for example, shaping government or other "public" forms of interaction; or, finally, that philosophy is not about what "the people" actually experience or think, but about what philosophers think—that it is, in other words, a self-contained tradition, and that any influences it might receive from sources exterior to that traditional are largely irrelevant.

To the extent that the last of these objections is true, the thought it describes becomes trivial and ultimately irrelevant to my discussion. Most thinkers, however, implicitly endorse one of the first two positions, that philosophy either "reflects" the tenor of its time or exists in a dialectical relationship with it. I can accept both as being likely descriptions, though I emphasize the latter because it is more inclusive, allowing for interaction and mutual influences between thought about life and everything else occurring in life. Nevertheless, accepting that there is a dialectical relation between thought and lived experience does not sanction a conflation between the two poles. When Taylor claims of Descartes' disengaged subject that it was not unique to him, that "for all the challenges and disagreements to his dualism in modern thought, with the central idea of disengagement he was articulating one of the most important elements of the modern era,"[17] he does not specify the nature of this element: was it an element of experience or of the discourse about experience (or, for that matter, of the isolated tradition of philosophical inquiry)?

This indeterminacy in the concept of subject is precisely what leads thinkers to more "interdisciplinary" approaches, approaches that seek to describe the nature of subjectivity by tracing it not just in its philosophical but also in its historical, literary, and political manifestations. Anthony Cascardi's *The Subject of Modernity* is an ambitious attempt of this sort.[18] In his introduction, Cascardi argues that the paradigm of modernity is more than historical and more than philosophical, because "the phenomenon that grounds modernity (the subject) is itself more than any of these things."[19] Nevertheless, what in my view stymies his project from the outset lies at the heart of this very claim, namely, that the subject is somehow a *phenomenon*. In what sense can the subject be considered a phenomenon, something that presents itself to the senses? Or, if the word phenomenon is to be taken as Heidegger redefined it in *Sein und Zeit*, as "that which already shows itself in the appearance as prior to the 'phenomenon' as ordinarily understood and as accompanying it in every case" and "can, even though it thus shows itself unthematically, be brought thematically to show itself,"[20] does this not require that it be approached not via an intellectual history of the kind Cascardi proposes, but rather by a history of the practices and behaviors that constitute what Heidegger calls our preontological understanding of Being?[21]

If Cascardi grounds his discussion of modernity in the philosophy of subjectivity,[22] he is acutely aware of the difficulties surrounding the nature of the claims made on behalf of subjectivity. Because, as he grants, "[t]he disadvantage of understanding modernity strictly in terms of the 'philosophical discourse' (Habermas)[23] is that the invention of subjectivity is something that only transformations in the structure and organization of social values could have produced," the description of modernity must rely not on the "veracity of an abstract order of concepts," nor on the "validity of a series of autonomous historical 'facts' but [rather on the ability] to comprehend the way in which the subject is positioned between these two orders."[24] But, if the subject is *something*, and Cascardi clearly believes it is, what exactly is it?

Cascardi's answer to this question is emblematic of the difficulties encountered by just about anyone who tries to define subjectivity, given that he seems to be arguing for the existence of a series of "real" and ultimately contingent historical events as creating the "conditions of possibility"[25] for a discursive formation called the modern subject, a discursive formation that in turn imposes its own form dialectically on the events and history in question, in effect creating itself as a phenomenon by naming itself.[26] In the first instance, then, he makes a claim about Descartes' "invention" of subjectivity that falls into our first category of objections listed above, that category in which subjectivity is the philosophical "pulse-taking" of a more widely held worldview:

> Rather, the case to be made about Descartes as the inventor of subjectivity is closer to the one that Alasdair MacIntyre has made for Luther, viz., that he is able to grasp the moral experience of his public and in so doing leads to the acceptance of a discourse in which their experience may be comprehended in stock 'Lutheran' ways.[27]

Such a reading implies that the experience of self common to Descartes' public is adequately grasped by his notion of subjectivity (a notion which, as we will see below, Balibar claims cannot really be attributed to him in the first place). But what is this experience? Is Descartes' public in fact beset by worries concerning the ultimate grounds of knowledge, or finding itself justified in its beliefs only on the assurance of an autonomous, thinking substance inhabiting its extended body? Or are these models intellectual manifestations of other, more inchoate experiences?

Cascardi's argument would seem to follow the latter tack when he "probes behind" Heidegger's interpretation of subjectivity to "see that it is the disorienting experience provoked by the loss of belief in the existence of natural forms that in turn precipitates the search for a 'transcendental' position from which to evaluate competing points of view."[28] But again this formulation forces us to ask: who lost belief, who sought this transcendental position? The answer Cascardi must eventually give us is that the intellectual tradition's concept of subjectivity is at once false and true: false in that it is an abstraction with little to do with the social practices, cultural changes, and individual beliefs that brought it about; true in that it became the vocabulary through which social change was codified and political organization legitimized:

> In retrospect, we can see that insofar as the invention of subjectivity marks the beginning of the modern age by laying claim to an absolute break within time, it is aligned to a concept of modernity that is equally abstract and false; for, strictly speaking, there is neither a temporal nor an absolute break, only what amounts to the consciousness of such a break, combined in the case of Descartes with the attempt to subordinate it to 'rational' ends; yet it is this very attempt that points up the gap between history and subjectivity and that subsequently allows us to grasp the abstraction's 'truth.'

By trying to comprehend itself as an abstraction, in other words, the subject becomes one:

> it becomes possible to see that the invention of subjectivity based on the concept and practice of representation provided a way in which a series of social and historical conditions could conveniently be framed.... Phrased in other terms, it could be said that the metaphysical position of the subject was itself

invented in order to grasp the process through which its own historical origination took place.[29]

Now, this formulation is temptingly paradoxical and, in fact, resonates in many ways with the psychoanalytic concept of subjectivity that I discuss in more detail below. Nevertheless, to claim for subjectivity the status of an abstraction that engenders its own existence is to disavow it as a *phenomenon*, precisely that status Cascardi wished to attain for it at the outset of his book. Subjectivity is not a phenomenon, because it neither presents itself to us as an appearance nor underlies or structures our experience in our everyday lives. Even if it can be claimed, as I think it can, that something very like the philosophical notion of subjectivity evolved in the modern period and intervened retroactively to shape human interaction in the political realm, this claim must be distinguished from the more straightforward description of selfhood that the philosophical discourse and all those who borrow from it are claiming for themselves.

Phenomenology and Subjectivity

If subjectivity is not the phenomenon that distinguishes modernity from its predecessors—if it is not, in fact, a phenomenon at all—can it even be claimed that there exists a phenomenological distinction between these historical modes of being? What would be the nature of the phenomenology capable of producing such a distinction? In the form propounded by Edmund Husserl and his followers, phenomenology fit unproblematically within the tradition of the philosophy of subjectivity as established by Kant and, before him, Descartes.[30] Phenomenology was to be considered a science, the most fundamental science, in fact, in that the knowledge that human subjects could accrue about the world was seen as being dependent upon a more primordial description of how the human subject experienced the phenomena of the world. This subject responsible for all experiencing and for the organization of these experiences was in many ways a direct descendent of Kant's transcendental subject of apperception, itself grounded by Kant on Descartes' foundation of knowledge on self-certainty.

The problems with returning to this notion of phenomenology in order to confront the problem of modernity should be obvious: first, it is a methodology that assumes as given (in fact, universalizes) a concept of subjectivity that might itself be at the heart of the historical debate concerning modernity; second, the purpose of the Husserlian science of phenomenology is to determine the ultimate and determinate contours of experience, all experience. Such a project aims to find the commonalities that transcend historical difference, not to explain that historical difference. Phenomenology in its traditional sense, then, cannot be helpful in defining the difference between historical periods.

Nevertheless, there is a sense in which phenomenology is appropriate to the project at hand, and this is the sense proposed by Heidegger as a reaction to the teachings of Husserl. For Heidegger, the basic assumptions of Husserl's phenomenology were flawed because they inherited precisely that Cartesian worldview of the "world as picture" that had condemned modern philosophy to such a fundamentally skewed understanding of Being. As he states in *Basic Problems of Phenomenology*, "[s]elf and world belong together in the single entity, Dasein. Self and world are not two entities, like subject and object . . . but self and world are the basic determination of Dasein itself in the unity of the structure of being-in-the-world."[31] If Dasein cannot extract itself from the world, there can be no "objective" point from which to study the world and, more specifically, Dasein's modes of interaction with it. Phenomenology, then, cannot be the most fundamental of sciences; it must, rather, constitute an entirely different way of knowing than the objectivity claimed for themselves by the sciences. Rather than objective study, Dasein's knowledge about its world, and hence about *the* world, must be grounded in "interpretation."[32] This interpretation did not involve primarily a study of Dasein's "subjectivity," that is, what Husserl would have referred to as its intentional sphere, the realm of beliefs, desires, and intentions constituting its interiority. Rather, phenomenological interpretation is about Dasein's coming to understand itself in terms of the skills and practices that make up its everyday existence.[33]

If, for Husserl, phenomenology was about articulating in an exact way the structure of subjectivity such as to ground more perfectly the objective foundations of knowledge, "[i]n Heidegger's hands, phenomenology becomes a way of letting something shared—that can never be totally articulated and for which there can be no indubitable evidence—show itself."[34] It is in this sense that we must take Heidegger's famous dictum from *Being and Time* that "*[o]nly as phenomenology, is ontology possible.*"[35] For in this statement, not only is the traditional understanding of phenomenology reworked, the generic meaning of ontology is also, and more profoundly, subverted. In light of Heidegger's understanding of Dasein's Being as always being-in-the-world, a world thick with the cultural and historical specificities of Dasein's own self-understanding, ontology cannot be understood as the objectively "true" description of all that is, but rather as the revelation to Dasein of the grounds of its own being-in-the-world. This revelation occurs through the interpretation known as phenomenology. In this methodology,

> that which already shows itself in the appearance as prior to the 'phenomenon' as ordinarily understood and as accompanying it in every case, can, even though it thus shows itself unthematically, be brought thematically to show itself; and what thus shows itself in itself (the 'forms of the intuition') will be the 'phenomena' of phenomenology. For manifestly space and time must be able

to show themselves in this way—they must be able to become phenomena—if Kant is claiming to make a transcendental assertion grounded in the facts when he says that space is the a priori 'inside-which' of an ordering.[36]

Heidegger's point is that phenomena can no longer be accepted as those appearances that unproblematically reveal themselves to a receptive subject, who then synthesizes them into what we could call "bites" of knowledge via the *a priori* "forms of the intuition" of space and time. Because Dasein, perceptions, and the modes of "presencing" of things are all part of the structure of "world," phenomenology cannot be a mere description of what is perceived but must instead go beyond this level to describe the modes of presencing themselves. What Kant thought of as the "a priori 'inside-which' of an ordering," such as the space in which something is perceived to take place, can no longer be granted the tranquility of aprioristic certainty; space itself must be understood as phenomenon in the new sense, as that which underlies or accompanies the appearance of things, itself subject to all the changes besetting Dasein's unsettled world.

The first ramification of such a radical reworking of the notion of phenomenon is that it undermines any concept of a stable, trans-historical basis to the human being's changing perceptions. This is why in his later writings Heidegger decided that the attempt to isolate the ultimate causes of being and intelligibility was futile, and turned instead from "transcendental hermeneutic phenomenology to thinking being historically."[37] But even in the late twenties, when Heidegger was writing *Being and Time*, traces of this radical historicism are evident in his work:

> In its factical being, any Dasein is as it already was, and it is 'what' it already was. It *is* its past, whether explicitly or not. And this is so not only in that its past is, as it were, pushing itself along 'behind' it, and that Dasein possesses what is past as a property which is still present-at-hand and which sometimes has after-effects upon it: Dasein 'is' its past in the way of *its* own Being, which, to put it roughly, 'historizes' out of its future on each occasion. Whatever the way of being it may have at the time, and thus with whatever understanding of Being it may possess, Dasein has grown up both into and in a traditional way of interpreting itself: in terms of this, it understands itself proximally and, within a certain range, constantly.[38]

To philosophize about Being, then, requires a phenomenology that reveals the nature of those phenomena that accompany the revelation of a world, fundamental phenomena such as space and time; this phenomenology must, at the same time, be a historically conscious one—one, in other words, that approaches Being as a historically variable set of circumstances. Furthermore, this description of Being cannot be philosophy as it has been traditionally done—either the analysis of current phenomena or language in search of universally valid truths, or the history of an intellectual tradition—rather it must turn to the skills and practices that comprise the preontological understanding of Being in which the world is revealed to us.

The work this book tries to do should be understood as a phenomenology in precisely this sense: the phenomenon it tries to reveal is the spatiality of the modern age; the skills and practices it explores are those of theatrical convention. But in light of this explanation, it is worthwhile clarifying the status of theatricality's counter-concept. Presence cannot refer to some "'mimetic' union with the natural world,"[39] a level of interaction with the world more intimately immediate than that of more recent times. Rather, what I have called presence and the form of mimesis proper to it are aspects of another way of being-in-the-world, one whose basic experience of space is as full and impressionable rather than as empty and infinitely divisible. Such a use of the term is also consistent with Heidegger's thought. Presence as the pure apperception of matter depends precisely on the "epistemological assumptions" that Heidegger's work seeks to shed. "For Heidegger, unlike Descartes, Husserl, and Sartre, the object of mere staring, instead of being that which really is, is an impoverished residue of the equipment we directly manipulate."[40] The reason for this is that, unlike these thinkers, and in direct contradiction to most intuitive approaches to experience, it is not the experience of space that is prior to all other experience; rather it is spatiality that grounds and precedes the experience of space.

Spatiality and Theatricality

To broach the concept of spatiality in Heidegger's thought, it is useful to sum up briefly two of his basic concepts: that which is present-at-hand (*vorhanden*) and that which is ready-to-hand (*zuhanden*). The present-at-hand refers to those objects that lie about us in our everyday environment unencumbered by a specific use or purpose. The ready-to-hand names those objects in our environment whose existence for us is determined by a particular use or purpose. Perhaps the most radical aspect of Heidegger's thought in Division I of *Being and Time* is the claim that the ready-to-hand has ontological priority over the present-at-hand. In other words, Dasein's "factical" existence, its existence as a being-in-the-world, is first and foremost an interpreted being, a being in a world of things that mean, not a bestowing of meaning on previously uninterpreted objects. Space is the name for that "in-which" that orders our apperception of things that are present-at-hand, the undetermined ground of scientific knowing or the *a priori* form of the intuitions; spatiality, on the other hand, is an aspect of worldliness, of the culturally and historically variable complex that makes up Dasein's being-in-the-world.[41] Heidegger's revolution is to argue that space is an impoverished and derivative manifestation of a broader and more fundamental spatiality.[42]

However, while spatiality is an aspect of a worldliness that is, as I argued above, culturally and historically contingent, Heidegger nevertheless describes certain aspects of spatiality as common to all of Dasein's experience. While this is not *a priori* problematic,[43] it is worthwhile to note precisely what those aspects are that Heidegger finds indispensable to spatiality. The first aspect of Dasein's spatiality he identifies is the "concernfulness or familiarity" with which Dasein encounters things in its world:

> Dasein is essentially not a Being-present-at-hand; and its 'spatiality' cannot signify anything like occurrence at a position in 'world-space', nor can it signify Being-ready-to-hand at some place. Both of these are kinds of Being which belong to entities encountered within-the-world. Dasein, however, is 'in' the world in the sense that it deals with entities encountered within-the-world, and does so concernfully and with familiarity.[44]

The entities Dasein encounters in the spatiality of its world are not first and foremost neutral, objective things. Rather, they are always encountered as laden with a certain prior value, meaning, or concern. Those things that Dasein encounters that are not meaningful to it in this way are specifically deprived of this familiarity, for it is that which is familiar that Dasein knows first. Familiarity, therefore, is an aspect of spatiality, an idea that is hard to criticize if one concedes Heidegger's initial distinction of spatiality from space on the basis of worldliness: if Dasein encounters the world primarily through those entities and objects that mean something to it, then it follows that this spatiality would be characterized by familiarity.

The second aspect is even more specific. This is what Heidegger calls de-severance (*Ent-fernung*):

> Proximally and for the most part, de-severing is a circumspective bringing-close—bringing something close by, in the sense of procuring it, putting it in readiness, having it to hand.... *In Dasein there lies an essential tendency towards closeness.* All the ways in which we speed things up, as we are more or less compelled to do today, push on towards the conquest of remoteness. With the 'radio,' for example, Dasein has so expanded its everyday environment that it has accomplished a de-severance of the 'world'—a de-severance which, in its meaning for Dasein, cannot yet be visualized.[45]

By specifying such a characteristic or tendency of Dasein, Heidegger is making a much more radical and decisive statement about spatiality, one that goes beyond a logical or "analytic" extension of the original definition. One way to understand this statement is to reword the original notion of Dasein's worldliness to emphasize the idea that Dasein does not encounter the world in an *immediate* way. This is another way of saying that Dasein's experience of the world is always *mediated*, that is, encountered through the intervention of some medium. As Heidegger makes clear with his example of the radio, this medium may take the form of what we specifically refer to as a medium in current language, that is, a technological intervention between our bodies and the world, what McLuhan called an "extension of man."[46]

If this is the case, however, then we must question Heidegger's claim that such media are essentially involved in de-severing, that is, bringing closer or bridging the distance between us and the world, for certainly we can imagine media whose purpose and effect is precisely the opposite: to distance the world in some way, to make it impinge less on our everyday lives (McLuhan cites sunglasses in a different context;[47] one could also mention earplugs). Nevertheless, it is certainly fair to accept as a caveat Heidegger's use of the word "tendency," that "*In Dasein there lies an essential tendency towards closeness*" and that this closeness is a function of Dasein's essentially *mediated* relation to the world.

Theatricality is the historically-specific description (i.e., mine) of the historically-specific form of mediation that structures the spatiality of Dasein's experience in the modern world. The practices and conventions associated with all visual culture—but most strikingly with spectacle—that I described in the last chapter as undergoing massive and systematic change in the period around the sixteenth century are the basic elements of the form of mediation I call theatricality. The theater was the paradigmatic medium of this change, a medium which, as I will discuss below in greater detail, has been retained in the present in the form of the screen. If we are to understand the relation of philosophy to the practices and conventions that structure our basic involvement with the world in either of the first two ways listed above (i.e., as in some way *relating* to them, either by influence or dialectically), then we can explain the "emergence of subjectivity" in its purely philosophical sense as a linguistic or conceptual manifestation of the new spatiality.[48]

Let us return to some of the ways contemporary philosophy, whether critical, apologetic, or neutral, has described the philosophy of subjectivity. One of the primary associations with subjectivity was the notion of disengagement. As Taylor puts it,

> Reason and human excellence requires a stance of disengagement. 'Disengagement' here is a term of art, meaning a stance toward something which might otherwise serve to define our identity or purposes, whereby we separate ourselves from it by defining it as at best of instrumental significance.[49]

But, as I argued in the previous chapter, the ability to separate oneself from a virtual copy of oneself is hardly a self-evident operation. Rather, its use in philosophy must be understood as a metaphoric adaptation of a skill that was developed by regular people themselves adapting to a new form of visual entertainment, a new medium. It is precisely the spatiality conditioned by the experience of the theater that allows for a philosophy predicated on the instrumental manipulation or exploration of the self by the self.

As Richard Rorty's purpose in recounting the narrative of the invention of subjectivity is to mount a polemic against epistemology, he stresses slightly different aspects of Cartesian subjectivity, principally the mind/body distinction and the concomitant notion of a disembodied mind that represents the world to itself, having certain knowledge only of how those representations appear or feel to itself. Prior to Descartes and Locke, he explains, there was no "conception of the human mind as an inner space in which both pains and clear and distinct ideas passed in review before a single Inner Eye."[50] Such a way of understanding the self was thus, for Rorty, an invention of the seventeenth century. And perhaps it was. But it should also be clear by now that it was an intellectual invention made possible only by a theatrical experience of spatiality, one in which viewers had learned to become disembodied spectators of an action that only involved them as characters, as virtual rather than actual participants. Rorty quotes Descartes' third *Meditation* in an effort to show where the notion of incorrigibility (of the total and exclusive pertinence of a belief, thought or feeling to its owner) comes from:

> Now as to what concerns ideas, if we consider them only in themselves and do not relate them to anything else beyond themselves, they cannot properly speaking be false; for whether I imagine a goat or a chimera, it is not the less true that I imagine the one rather than the other.[51]

However, the operation of separating a content from its presentation in order to relativize the former is an exact analogy to the framing operation of the theatrical screen, which allows for the suspended performativity of all that occurs within the frame without in anyway affecting the validity of the world outside the frame. The spectators, in other words, may feel free to doubt the validity of the actions they see represented on the stage, but can in no way doubt the existence of the stage itself, or the fact that they are present in the audience watching the performance.

Finally, in Heidegger's critique of subjectivity, one of the principal lines of argument is that the world is somehow always rearranged in the world-picture such that it, the world, is relegated to being a mere function of Man's self-representation: "The subiectum, the fundamental certainty, is the being-represented-together-with—made secure at any time—of representing man together with the entity represented, whether something human or non-human, that is, together with the objective."[52] The problem with subjectivity is not, then, that it makes a picture of the world, or at least not primarily. Its real problem is that in this picture the world is subordinated to man, an act of subordination that is repeated at the level of individual self-representations: "Here to represent [*vor-stellen*] means to bring what is present at hand [*das Vor-handene*] before oneself as something standing over against, to relate it to oneself, to the one representing it, and to force it back into this relationship to oneself as the normative realm."[53] But again, for this model of representation—in which the representer represents him or herself together with the object of representation—to have become the basic model of representation requires, according to Heidegger's own philosophy, a fundamental change in the spatiality of the world containing and conditioning those thinkers who verbalized this model. This change was the emergence of theatricality, that form of spatiality in which viewers constantly confront pictures containing copies of their selves, and in which they are free to manipulate that world at a distance or be manipulated by in it as characters.[54]

In his well-known essay, "Citizen/Subject," Étienne Balibar has taken Heidegger and the Heideggerian critique of subjectivity to task for what he calls a fundamental confusion concerning the status of the subject in Descartes. His basic claim is that the term subject (*sujet* in French, *subiectum* in Latin) appears nowhere in Descartes' *Meditations*. Nor, indeed, is the thesis of the ego as a subject to be found in his oeuvre.[55] The origin of Heidegger's mistake, according to Balibar, is his creative forgetting of one of the two possible meanings of the Anglo/French word subject/*sujet*, which has, in Latin and German (and, for that matter, in Spanish, as we will see below) two possible translations. The Latin and German pairings are *subiectum/subiectus* and *Subjekt/Untertan*, meaning, respectively, subject as one who orders (be it grammatically, philosophically, or politically) and subject as one who obeys. By associating the Cartesian *cogito* with the subject as *hypokeímenon*, or absolute ground of being, Heidegger has imported a false association (because, according to Balibar, the metaphysics of substance as a univocal term is foreign to Descartes, whose "subject" is rather an entity divided into poles of experiencing self as cause and effect[56]) while simultaneously negating an appropriate one (the *cogito* a being *subiectus* to a divine sovereignty[57]). Once he has established that the proper meaning of the Cartesian subject is not the philosophical *hypokeímenon*, but rather the individual subjected to a theological and political sovereignty, Balibar is free to pursue his main objective: to demonstrate the emergence of a properly political agency (an enlightened subjectivity), the citizen, out of the political servitude of the seventeenth-century subject.

The problem with this argument is that it is not Heidegger but Balibar who is confused. Balibar complains that Heidegger has imported an inappropriate meaning of the word "subject" into the Cartesian text, and that he, Balibar, is correcting that mistake by indicating the more appropriate meaning. However, it was Balibar himself who claimed that "subject" appears nowhere in the *Meditations*, regardless of the interpretation. But while Descartes may not use "subject" in the *Meditations*, he does use the word *foundation*,[58] making it clear that the *cogito* is for him precisely such a foundation of all possible knowing as that advanced by Heidegger's interpretation of the *hypokeímenon* as ground, or that which comes before.

Unfortunately, there does not seem to be any purpose for Balibar's "creative forgetting" of the differences between the political and philosophical uses of the subject. His argument concerning the transition from political subjection to citizenship in the political theory of the eighteenth century would be just as valid without masking it as a critique of Heidegger's critique of subjectivity. As it is, however, Balibar's argument is indicative of a general failure to distinguish what are in fact two completely different fields of inquiry. The subject of political theory is deeply implicated in the political and social organization of sixteenth and seventeenth century society; in the skills and practices of the marketplace and the "public sphere" of debate; and in the ongoing processes of state-formation. To try to associate this subject entirely with the philosophical discourse of subjectivity is to risk descending inextricably into a morass of semantic confusions. There is, however, a commonality to both theoretical projects: the type of individual who is the focus of both the philosophical and the political theorization of subjectivity is one who inhabits a theatrical world.

POLITICAL SUBJECTIVITY

Political theories of subjectivity are concerned with presenting models of how individuals, as well as their roles and duties, have been conceived in relation to the new formations of power specific to the modern world. As such, they are principally concerned with developing a model of agency and with asking the question of how much and what kind of agency is granted to whom in the context of a given political organization. As in the case of philosophical subjectivity, a distinction can be made among those who seek to describe this relationship: between thinkers who are neutral or apologetic toward modern forms of political agency and thinkers who are critical of them. Which of these stances one takes is largely a function of how one describes the political organization of modernity and its denizens (or vice versa). The prevailing tendency among those who are neutral or apologetic toward modern political subjectivity is to focus on the process of state-formation, the differences between modern and pre-modern forms of statehood, and the causes and effects of these new political organizations. Among the critics of political modernity, the tendency is to focus on the place of the individual within the social and political complex, demonstrating how the much-touted liberties of modern forms of political organization in fact conceal a more profound imposition of servitude. For these critics (belonging to a tradition spanning Marx to Foucault) one's political subjectivity (and hence agency) in modern society is attained only at the cost of a fundamental subjection (*assujetissement*) of the self to the interest of some power complex.

The aim of this section is to demonstrate that, whereas the subjects of the early modern state (whose political system was absolutist) and of subjection theory are precisely *not* examples of philosophical subjectivity, both state-formation and subjection theory assume an individual who is modern in that he or she is *theatrical*. The modern state as a massive, centralized administrative body requires a different kind of interpersonal bond than had existed in the localized, personal domains of feudal power. This interpersonal bond, which I will call *theatrical identification*, a form of social cohesion utterly dependent on the spatiality described above, is also the active ingredient of the modes of subjectification analyzed by critics from Althusser to Foucault to Butler. Finally, theatrical identification also corroborates the psychoanalytic theory of ideology, and provides the historical underpinnings for an understanding of how—as Maravall argues of the baroque culture—a cultural product such as the theater could function as a tool for ideological manipulation.

Theatricality and State-Formation

In *Power and Civility*, Norbert Elias eloquently expressed the indissoluble connection between modes of individual consciousness and the institutional processes of state-formation:

> The sociogenesis of absolutism indeed occupies a key position in the overall process of civilization. The civilizing of conduct and the corresponding transformation of human consciousness and libidinal makeup cannot be understood without tracing the process of state-formation, and within it the advancing centralization of society which first finds particularly visible expression in the absolutist form of rule.[59]

Certainly, as Elias says, the sociogenesis of a new form of political organization implies a corresponding change in the self-understanding of individuals caught up in that political organization. But is it not precipitous to claim—as I and many of the political theorists and historians whose arguments I rely on in this section are claiming—that this form of political organization, absolutism, and its corresponding model of individual existence, the subject (used here in its strictly political sense as subject to a sovereign), are modern—thus implying a direct relation between them and democratic forms of political organization and selfhood?[60] What could be more different, we might ask, from today's relatively egalitarian and freedom-oriented political systems than the strict hierarchies and totalitarian power structures of seventeenth-century absolutism? Nevertheless, despite the obvious differences in the exercise of power between the seventeenth century and the late twentieth century, the absolutist state was modern in that it was a *state*. It was during the sixteenth and especially seventeenth centuries that the fundamental modern form of political organization, the nation-state that still dominates world politics in an uncontested manner today, came into existence.

Whereas the political culture of Europe prior to the sixteenth century was largely uniform, due to an interlocking web of ruling families and extensive contacts via trade,[61] it was nevertheless almost entirely decentralized.[62] Indeed, western Europe during the Middle Ages comprised at times more than 500 independent political units. By the turn of the twentieth century, that number was closer to twenty.[63] The process of state-formation in Europe, then, was primarily one of centralization and consolidation of often preexisting polities. This process, while decidedly gradual and confronted with near constant resistance on the part of entrenched interests,[64] nevertheless represented a change of almost unprecedented magnitude in most every aspect of social and political life.

The word we are using to name this new formation—state in English, *estado*, *état*, *stato*, and *Staat* in Spanish, French, Italian and German, respectively—began to be used with increased frequency throughout Europe in the sixteenth century in response to the growing awareness of the existence of a new form of political organization.[65] In 1595, Pierre Charron defined *l'état* as "a domination, an ordering involving command and obedience, and . . . the foundation, the internal link, and the guiding spirit of human affairs; it is the bond within society which cannot exist without it, the vital essence which brings life to human and natural associations."[66] For the legists of the seventeenth century, the notion of the state connoted large territorial unity under the dominion of a single sovereign; the separation and continuity of the office of royalty apart from the king's mortal person; and a people living under the sovereign enjoying a sense of community.[67] Many of these connotations have been retained in the definitions of the modern state produced by contemporary sociologists, perhaps the most influential being that of Charles Tilly. According to his definition, the state is distinct from previous forms of domination in that it: "1) controlled a well-defined, continuous territory; 2) it was relatively centralized; 3) it was differentiated from other organizations; [and] 4) it reinforced its claims through a tendency to acquire a monopoly over the concentrated means of physical coercion within its territory."[68] However, sociologists such as Tilly are normally not concerned with discussing the issues of "consciousness" or "libidinal" constitution that may result from or enable macro-social changes in political organization. So in order to attempt to categorize the nature of the social bonds providing cohesion for the new formation, we need to extrapolate somewhat, both from the language of today's theorists and from that of the theorists of the time.

When discussing the change from feudal to absolutist rule, theorists almost universally refer to some variant of the personal/procedural dichotomy. Take, for example, the description of Dyson:

> Western Europe had, nevertheless, witnessed a shift from personal forms of domination (which found their expression in medieval, patrimonial and clientelist polities) to organizational forms of domination—from personal ties to formal procedures of rule; from a politics that centred on the personal relations of notables and estates to one that was based on bargaining between mass parties and organized groups and reflected a consciousness of class; from ascription to achievement in assessment of status; and from deferential to utilitarian attitudes.[69]

This change from personal to procedural (or objective, administrative, organizational, etc.) forms of domination also implied, in Maravall's words, the notion of a "transpersonal and objective collectivity, which, as such, possesses its own conditions of existence, disengagement and conservation."[70]

The change from personal to procedural forms of domination also involved a shift in the nature of the roles played by individuals within the system. The principal linguistic marker of this shift at the time was a change from the denomination *vassal* to that of *subject*, corresponding to a shift from *lord* to *sovereign*. Whereas the relationship between a lord and his vassal had involved what we might call an "imaginary" bond, in that the lord's personal *image* was always present to the vassal and the vassal knew his lord by sight and sound, the relationship between a sovereign and his subject was a more symbolic one, that is, one requiring the mediation of a highly organized set of representative symbols.[71] Whereas the feudal organization was based on a system of special privileges afforded to people on the basis of their particular status within a locality, the absolutist theory of sovereignty assumed a general equality of subjects alike in their subordination to one ruler.[72] This is not to say that under the new system people all of a sudden became subjects and hence equal in the eyes of the king. As I mentioned above, there is no reason to believe that any change of this magnitude ever occurred rapidly or, for that matter, completely. Rather, as the general shape of political power shifted gradually over the years, new ideals of political relationships developed within the discourse of political theory to reflect the highly complex changing realities. The discourse of sovereignty and subject presented one of these ideals. The fact that this ideal was (and is today) almost always belied by the interference of particular interests and the actual retention of traditional power structures does not lessen the impact of the fact that the traditional elite were resorting to new, modern methods for the maintenance of their privileges.[73]

Finally, the transpersonal "libidinal economy" of the new state generated what can be called, with the benefit of hindsight, protonationalistic communities.

Maravall refers to this sentiment, corresponding to the new concept of sovereignty, as a feeling of belonging, along with other "members" of one's state, to the same "body."[74] The word that began to appear at the time to refer to this corporeal entity and that resonated with the libidinal charge such an entity conjures was *patria, patrie* in French, or, roughly, fatherland.[75] Francisco Baudouin and Juan de Mariana both wrote of the importance of expressing one's solidarity with one's land by knowing its history,[76] a notion that would not have made sense in the particularity of the feudal relationship, in which one inhabited the history of one's land. And Alonso Villegas, in his *Comedia selvagia*, writes, "no solo para nosotros nacíamos, sino para la patria y amigos" [not only for ourselves were we born but for our fatherland and friends]. But these "friends," Maravall adds,

> que acabamos de encontrarnos mencionados, no son los amigos personales, unidos en un lazo de trato directo. Son, muy diferentemente, millones de compatriotas, desconocidos personalmente, lejanos, de cuya existencia individual no se tiene testimonio directo, y, sin embargo, con los cuales, la evolución política del vínculo protonacional lleva a reconocer un nexo de amistad.[77]
>
> [whom we have just mentioned, are not the personal friends with whom we are united by a direct bond. They are, quite differently, millions of countrymen, unknown to us personally, distant, of whose existence we have no direct testimony, and with whom, nevertheless, the political evolution of a protonational vinculum leads us to recognize a nexus of friendship.]

This transpersonal collectivity has another sociological correlate, which it is worth discussing briefly at this time: Jürgen Habermas's theory of the public sphere.

If, as Maravall argues of the urban society of the seventeenth century, the "mass" nature of society led to a pervasive anonymity, in which "bonds of neighborhood, friendship and kinship" are seriously diminished,[78] these bonds are gradually superseded by an arena in which the "transpersonal collectivity" discussed above is played out in practical, everyday ways. This arena has been called by Habermas the public sphere.[79] What Habermas calls the structural transformation of the public sphere takes place in three moments. To begin with, he argues that the distinction between public and private in the sociological sense, that is, in the sense of dealing with the nature and history of institutions, did not exist in the European Middle Ages.[80] The classical (later adopted to modern) distinction of types of authority into *dominium* (authority of a man in his home) and *imperium* (authority of a ruler over his people, the model for the theory of sovereignty) cannot be applied to manorial authority. In the medieval system, "[t]here were lower and higher 'sovereignties,' eminent and less eminent prerogatives; but there was no status that in terms of private law defined in some fashion the capacity in which private people could step forward into a public sphere."⁸¹ The clear distinction between the public and private exercise of power only regained its usefulness with the rise of the modern state and the emergence along with it of a civil society.⁸²

It was at this time, then—during the sixteenth century when the institutions of the modern state were developing throughout Europe—that the renewed distinction between a public and a private sphere became common. However, this distinction still had entirely to do with the exercise of political power: "'Private' designated the exclusion from the sphere of the state apparatus; for 'public' referred to the state that in the meantime had developed, under absolutism, into an entity having an objective existence over and against the person of the ruler."⁸³ Public, in this narrower sense, refers to what Habermas calls the sphere of public authority, which he distinguishes from the "authentic" public sphere, a sphere composed of private citizens who came together as a self-conscious *publicum* in order to "compel public authority to legitimate itself before public opinion. The *publicum* developed into the public, the *subjectum* into the [reasoning] subject, the receiver of regulations from above into the ruling authorities' adversary."⁸⁴

It is worth noting that this third moment, in which the authentic public sphere emerges as an arena for the contestation of authority and for the demand for legitimation, parallels what Balibar called the transformation of the subject into the citizen, a process that he claims requires precisely the distinction between public and private spheres.⁸⁵ And, just as with Habermas, the conversion of subject to citizen demands that the *subiectus* of "public" authority become a private *subiectum* in the public sphere.⁸⁶ But whereas Balibar (properly, I believe) points to the derivative nature of the subject's philosophical connotations, calling Kant's *Subjekt* a "reinscription of the citizen in a philosophical and, beyond that, anthropological space, which evokes the defunct subject of the prince even while displacing it,"⁸⁷ Habermas's invocation of subjectivity seems to be of the opposite order, a reification to which he grants a sort of causal agency.

> For the experience about which a public passionately concerned with itself sought agreement and enlightenment through the rational-critical public debate of private persons with one another flowed from the wellspring of a specific subjectivity. The latter had its home, literally, in the sphere of the patriarchal conjugal family.⁸⁸

This subjectivity—which, "as the innermost core of the private, was always already oriented to an audience"⁸⁹—would seem to serve Habermas as the explanation for how private individuals, within the context of an emergent public sphere of civil society, would be empowered to represent their private, economic interests in a sphere that had previously only existed for the public, that is, universal, representation of sovereign power. The problem is, of course, that subjectivity, as a derivative reification, has no explanatory power here; at best it is a name that can be given to the effect of this insertion of private interests into a public sphere of representations.

The question, therefore, remains: on the basis of what impetus, on what model of interaction, was a "public" composed of "private" interests empowered to eventually impose its will on what had heretofore been exclusively a sphere for the public representation of sovereign power? The answer would seem not to lie (tautologically) in the ascription to the private citizen of a core subjectivity, but rather in the adjective Habermas uses to describe that subjectivity: audience-oriented (*publikumsbezogen*).[90] "Private" interests may be represented "publicly" because the very division that engenders the public and the private spheres is at its core a theatrical division. Indeed, the sphere of public authority that precedes the emergence of the "authentic" public sphere is already a theatrical entity in that the modern state, as a protonationalistic, transpersonal collectivity, only exists in a "world" whose spatiality is theatrical. In such a world, individuals are capable of believing in emotional bonds with people they have never met, in honoring a prince whose presence they have never felt, and participating in a public debate about a society that concerns their private interests precisely because these other people, this prince, and this public debate occupy an imaginary (i.e., not real) but viable space in which they too can interact via the intervention of their avatars or characters. They can, in other words, *identify theatrically* with rulers, laws, unknown friends, ideas, their nation, without ever once encountering these entities face to face. And these individuals have learned to do this, or better, *have become the individuals who are defined as such by doing this*, through the accumulative imposition on social life of the new fundamental medium—the theater.

In order to give an example of the extent to which this theatrical consciousness was formative of political theory at the time, let us turn to Hobbes' famous treatise concerning political representation in the *Leviathan*.[91] Hobbes begins his treatment of this topic by defining a person, from the Greek *persona*, meaning "disguise or outward appearance," as he "*whose words or actions are considered either as his own or as representing the words or actions of another man or of any other thing to whom they are attributed, whether truly or by fiction.*"[92] Of these possibilities, the former are called natural persons (whose words or actions are their own) and the latter are called artificial persons (who are representing the words or actions of another). He also states explicitly that the model for this definition of personhood is the stage, and that "to *personate* is to *act* or *represent* himself or another; and he that acts another is said to bear his person or act in his name."[93]

Hobbes' purpose with this model of personhood is, of course, to explain how one person in society can be granted the power to represent another person's interests. He accomplishes this through a further analysis of artificial persons, some of whom, those he calls actors, have their words or actions owned by other persons, whom he calls authors.[94] Political representation occurs when actors act for their authors. This model of representation is also what allows Hobbes to theorize the unity in multiplicity that is the state.

> A multitude of men are made one person when they are by one man or one person represented, so that it be done with the consent of every one of that multitude in particular. For it is the unity of the representer, not the unity of the represented, that makes the person one. And it is the representer that bears the person, and but one person; and unity cannot otherwise be understood in multitude.[95]

This, of course, becomes the fundamental basis for the Leviathan, the sovereign who represents the interests of all, with absolute authority:

> And in him consists the essence of the commonwealth, which, to define it, is *one person, of whose acts a great multitude, by mutual covenants one with another, have made themselves every one the author, to the end he may use the strength and means of them all as he shall think expedient for their peace and common defense.* And he that carries this person is called SOVEREIGN and is said to have *sovereign power*; and everyone besides, his SUBJECT.[96]

The point to recognize here is not merely that Hobbes has adopted the language of the theater to make an argument concerning political organization. Rather, it is that the Hobbesian model of political organization, so fundamental to modern, western, democratic ideas of statehood and citizenship, is predicated on the actor/character distinction of the new spatiality.[97] It is only as characters that the collective wills of the citizenry can be represented in the abstract body of the state; it is only as characters that we can identify ourselves with that abstract body at all.[98] The modern state, in its most influential theorization in the work of Hobbes, is inconceivable outside of the framework established by theatricality.

Theatrical identification, then, is the mode by which theatricality subtends the actual formation of the superindividual entity known as the state. As such, theatrical identification played an enormous role in the development of social cohesion necessary for the maintenance and reproduction of the forms of power of the state, as well as of the traditional privileges of elites who had managed to adapt to the new forms of political organization. On the other hand, theatrical identification allowed for the organization of private interest into groups or classes united by a sense of community, group purpose, or solidarity, who thereby offered the new power formation its first and lasting form of contestation, hence the properly "dialectical" nature of theatricality and its ability to explain both the "positive" and "negative" elements of both philosophical and political subjectivity. It remains for us, however, to look at the other aspect of the political theory of subjectivity: subjectification theory, to see if the processes it seeks to describe are also historically dependent on theatricality.

Theatricality and Subjectification Theory

Perhaps the most powerful and persistent voice in the late twentieth-century critique of subjectivity has been that of Michel Foucault, whose work was, from its inception (despite attempts to categorize it into "archaeological" and "genealogical" periods) concerned with the way institutions and discourses shape the individuals whose lives they encompass. However, it was not until the last decade of his life that he explicitly identified the aim of his work as an exploration of the ways in which power produces "subjects."[99] What is fascinating about his use of the "subject" is that it clearly borrows (and in this it has become a model for much contemporary work in cultural studies) from both the philosophical and the political uses of the term. However, being an unbridled critic of modernity, as we discussed in the first section of this chapter, Foucault refers exclusively to the negative or, more accurately, restrictive connotations of the word: "There are two meanings of the word 'subject': subject to someone else by control and dependence; and tied to his own identity by a conscience or self-knowledge. Both meanings suggest a form of power which subjugates and makes subject to."[100] It should be clear by now that his first definition comes from the seventeenth-century theory of sovereignty we discussed above, while the second definition derives from the philosophy of subjectivity, which had located individual freedom in self-consciousness. Nevertheless, Foucault's presentation of this model of subjectivity implies, by means of his phrase "tied to his own identity," that the freedom of self-knowledge is not a freedom at all, but rather another form of bondage (an example of the Foucauldian trope par excellence). The quintessentially modern paradigm of the interests of the individual suspended in opposition to the interests of the state is, for Foucault, itself a total power-structure working entirely in the service of the state: "But I'd like to underline the fact that the state's power (and that's one of the reasons for its strength) is both an individualizing and a totalizing form of power."[101] In light of this implication of the state's agency in both aspects of the social whole (i.e., on the side of both the one and the many), for Foucault the

> political, ethical, social, [and] philosophical problem of our day is not to try to liberate the individual from the state and from the state's institutions but to liberate it both from the state and from the type of individualization which is linked to the state. We have to promote new forms of subjectivity through the refusal of this kind of individuality which has been imposed on us for several centuries.[102]

This analysis of the problem and its subsequent "manifesto" has become the core discourse, along with that of Althusserian Marxism, of subjectification theory, the theory of how individual subjects are not merely oppressed by power, but rather produced by it.

The first obvious question such a project raises is this: if one's agency is already in the service of the power structure one seeks to subvert, what is the source of the desire that induces one to subvert the power structure in the first place? This apparent paradox returns in almost any formulation of subjectification theory, as in, for example, Judith Butler's rendition of it in *The Psychic Life of Power*.[103] "Subjection consists precisely in this fundamental dependency on a discourse we never choose but that, paradoxically, initiates and sustains our agency."[104] Butler recognizes that if we truly accept the initial premise of subjectification theory—that our agency is formed by the discourses of power—then we cannot, as Foucault advanced above, merely pursue different forms of subjectivity, but rather must confront the apparent paradox that our agency has its origins *in this very pursuit*. According to Butler, then, regardless of the specific form that a given process of subjectification takes, the fact of this recurrent paradox suggests that there is a consistent aspect to that process, an aspect she calls the figure of a "turning," or more precisely a "turning back upon oneself."[105] While the subject is always constructed by this turning, the paradox lies in that there is no subject who makes the turn; the subject is, then, always retroactively produced by its turning back on itself.

With this formulation, Butler has turned implicitly (and will turn explicitly) to a different model of subjectivity from those we have been discussing until now, namely, a psychoanalytic model. The "psychoanalytic valence" her Foucauldian model assumes is provoked by the realization that the turning back on oneself, the making of oneself an object, requires what she calls a "passionate attachment" to the source of one's subjection.[106] One must, in other words, desire to enslave oneself. A model of subjectification characterized by a turning back on oneself, a making object of oneself, and a passionate attachment to the source of subjectification is in many ways indistinguishable from the model of subjectivity that psychoanalysis, principally in its Lacanian form, has been advancing for years.

The term "subject" for the principal object of psychoanalytic study and practice was introduced by Lacan in the early years of his teaching as a response and an alternative to what he saw as the specifically American bastardization of Freud's thought: ego psychology.[107] The subject had the advantage of not pertaining to any one single aspect of the Freudian psyche (i.e., to the id, the ego, or the superego), but instead referred to the grammatical shifter "I"; the subject, in other words, is a being whose existence is referred to by the symbolic order of language. This being, in addition, insofar as it speaks and can speak about itself, is divided by language into the subject referred to in its utterances (the *sujet d'énoncé*) and the subject assumed to be making those utterances (the *sujet d'énonciation*).[108] Because of this existential condition, the being is condemned to a life of endlessly seeking self-identity but never finding it. In all levels of its existence, the being described by psychoanalysis is characterized by a fundamental misrecognition of who it is. Its essence, however, is precisely this instability, its lack of essence, its lack of ultimate ground or identity.

This subject, then, is, like Butler's, characterized by a "turning back on itself" that is at one and the same time formative of the self it turns back to find.[109] It is also, therefore, a subject that makes of itself an object to be both explored and manipulated. Finally, as it must seek outside of itself models on which to found its own identity, it invests these models with its desire, and in turn desires to become what it perceives these models as desiring;[110] in short, it develops a "passionate attachment" to the very figures who are also present to ensure its ultimate conformity to a set of social norms—to those, in other words, to whom it is subjected.

The point of my argument is not to criticize Butler's appropriation of psychoanalytic theory; as it is, she goes on to draw interesting and highly relevant parallels between this model and several other philosophical models, principally Nietzsche's and Hegel's. Rather, I am concerned to show that even a model of *subjectification* based explicitly on Foucault's work (Foucault being a notorious critic of psychoanalysis's methods and assumptions) appears to lead inevitably to a basically psychoanalytic model of subjectivity. And this model, at least at the fundamental level of subject formation we are dealing with here, is not a historical one.[111]

A human being, any human being, is, for Lacan, a being who, in its being, has been split by the signifier. The aspects of "turning back," taking oneself as an object, and forming passionate attachments with those who subject one, are fundamental and universal aspects of the sociogenesis of beings who inhabit a linguistic universe of any kind. If this is what it means to be a subject, then it makes no sense to speak of a particular age as being the age of subjectivity, or of the subject as being the defining aspect of a historical period. And, in fact, neither Foucault nor Butler make this mistake. Foucault is content to speak of "new forms of subjectivity" (implying that subjectivity is constant and only its forms are variable), and Butler has always been committed to a model of agency born of a fundamental subjection of one kind or another.[112] But, if we remain committed to the idea that (the universal, psychoanalytic notion of) subjectivity is at least characterized by the basic aspects discussed above, then we can agree with Butler that "[n]o individual becomes subject without first becoming subjected or undergoing 'subjectivation' (a translation of the French *assujetissement*),"[113] a statement that would seem to doom Foucault's desire for other subjectivities, subjectivities without subjection, to futility. The problem, again, lies in the confusion between two uses of the word subjectivity, a confusion exacerbated by Foucault's conflation of philosophical and political subjectivity into subjectification theory.

My inclination is to leave the notion of subjectivity entirely to psychoanalysis, where it retains a stable, relatively unambiguous meaning (one perfectly compatible with certain forms of agency), and to show that the "becoming subject" of subjectification theory depends on a particular historical form that "subjectivity" can assume, a form in which the identification so central to the psychoanalytic theory of subjective constitution takes on specifically theatrical contours. Now, theatrical identification is not "better" or "worse" than any other form of identification. It is just the form to which our specific historical spatiality has conditioned us. And, as such, it is useful to determine its functioning. In fact, because "ideology" is, as I will argue in more detail below, a manifestation of theatrical identification, any kind of critical-theoretical approach to culture needs to begin with an understanding of theatricality.

Theatrical Identification

Recall that one of Heidegger's principal criticisms of the subjectivity bias of modern philosophy was that in its representational worldview, the world was never allowed to impose itself on the viewer, but instead the viewer constructed a picture of the world, a picture that was always organized around the presence of the viewer within its frame. This notion, as I mentioned in passing above, is an exact correlate of Slavoj Žižek theory of the "fantasy screen." In this theory, the human subject interacts with the world and with other humans in the world via the mediation of a fantasy screen, a screen that orders and interprets everything for the subject in accordance with a particular idea the subject has of itself.[114] The purpose of this screen is to render compatible the subject's two ontologically-incompatible points of identification: the symbolic and the imaginary (correlates of the ego-ideal and the ideal ego; the dimension of meaning and that of the body; the role one plays and the actor one thinks one is, etc.). The screen works to cover over the fundamental gap between these two points of identification, convincing the subject that it is, in fact, whole, complete, self-identical. In this sense, the fantasy screen is also the active ingredient of any ideological edifice that may be manipulating the subject, as the subject can be made to desire any thing, person, or idea that plays the role of the stopgap and thereby helps to create the illusion of self-identity and completion.

Such a model of how a subject situates itself visually in relation to the world and other people is, I am claiming, utterly theatrical. And the mode of identification that emerges as a result of the screen is, therefore, also theatrical. Theatrical identification (while it can still be considered as a sub-type of the identification described by Lacan as fundamental to all linguistic beings) is distinct in that it occurs within the confines of a spatiality that allows for the production of characters; it depends upon, in other words, the screen as a division between the space of the audience's and actors' bodies (wherein sits the theatrical version of the subject of the enunciation) and the space of the stage (whereon the subject is represented by the theatrical version of its subject of the utterance: a character). The characters on stage (or on a movie screen, in the theater of world affairs, or sometimes right in our living rooms) become the site of our imaginary performance of ourselves for the approving (or disapproving, depending on the fantasy) gaze of the audience, an audience playing, in our personal fantasy, the role of our ego-ideals, that place from which we are desired.

But as much as we might desire it, and as much as the "producers" of our theatrical experience might wish to comply, the illusion is never entirely convincing. We are besieged by uncertainties about ourselves, about the extent to which we fulfill our roles or are desired and appreciated by our audience. We are constantly and inadvertently "separated" from a full identification with our characters, and it is this separation that provides the "breathing space" of our individual agency.[115] In other words, it is precisely the endemic failure of our fantasy screens to adequately account for all of lived experience that provides for our freedom, a freedom we sorely wish to avoid, to be sure. The role of ideology is to cover these inconsistencies and failures at all costs, and it does so via the interplay of concealment and revelation that has its material, conventional counterpart in the space I have called *the crypt*.[116]

This notion of the crypt, which I have expounded in detail in the previous chapter, provides an answer to questions such as that posed by Oscar Pereira in his dissertation on the idea of the actor in the Spanish Golden Age. How, he asks, does a medium so apparently contrary to essentialist notions of the person as the modern theater become coopted as an instrument of reification of an essentialist social order?[117] The theater is contrary to essentialist notions of personhood insofar as the spatiality conditioned by the stage undermines the certainty of social roles by demonstrating those roles to be a function of relatively positioned frames. The theater can be made to function as an instrument of reification precisely by convincing the spectator that behind its play of appearance there is a certain and stable reality, a reality that conforms to the desire of ultimate self-identity. However, no representation can perfectly accomplish that. The closest a representational apparatus can come is to represent the breakdown of its own representationality. This is where the crypt comes in. As the space that stands in for the breakdown of theatricality, it can emerge to fulfill, in an instantaneous and ephemeral way, the desire for a bedrock of stability in a world of relative frameworks. This is why, as I argued in the previous chapter, the ultimate form of pornography, whose injunctive is to "show it all," is the snuff film, whose desperate ploy is to shut down the shifting frameworks of representation, to claim "this is it, this is the real thing." For, in the final analysis, this is the foundational role of the crypt in theatricality: to stand in for the real, the unrepresentable, and hence the foundation of all representations.

Through the functioning of theatrical identification, then, theatricality is the very condition of possibility of ideological manipulation, which puts an interesting—if not tautological—twist on claims, such as that of Maravall, that the theater was used precisely as a tool for the manipulation and "guidance" of the masses during the absolutist monarchies of the baroque period. That is to say, the very notion of this sort of mass-cultural manipulation is itself an option only within the spatiality of theatricality. However, not only does theatricality condition the instrumentalization of culture for the purpose of guiding behavior, it also makes possible the relativization of frames of reference constitutive of both modern drama and fiction. It is because of this common factor that these two effects have been identified as aspects of an emergent "subjectivity" that now conflates not only philosophical and political concepts, but literary and aesthetic ones as well.

AESTHETIC SUBJECTIVITY

Convinced that philosophers and political theorists are speaking of one and the same thing when, in their respective fields, they outline the contours of a modern subjectivity, literary and cultural theorists have been quick to follow, assuming that if a new creature of spirit took shape in the early modern period, it would certainly have left its traces in the cultural production of its time. In general, we can identify two dimensions of the cultural-critical interest in subjectivity: the first, a correlate of subjectification theory, seeking to show how culture was involved in the production of subjects; the second, a correlate of philosophical subjectivity, seeking to identify elements of the new sense of interiority and autonomous selfhood in modern writing and art. These dimensions, of course, seldom appear in a pure form; more often than not a given critic will be making a claim that borrows in some degree from both sets of assumptions.

For the purposes of this project, the most appropriate example of the former tendency in cultural criticism is the argument that European culture of the seventeenth century was by and large involved in the manipulation or guidance of large populations in ways conducive to the propagation and reproduction of a power structure specific to the absolutist state. Perhaps the most influential proponent of this idea—although one who does not engage specifically in the rhetoric of subjectivity—is the Spanish historian, José-Antonio Maravall.

Cultural Subjectification

Maravall's project should be approached with some knowledge of its position within the field of Spanish cultural history. Throughout the middle of the twentieth century, this field was dominated by the thesis of Americo Castro that Spain's history had to be understood in its particularity, as a unique product of the 700 odd years of the "convivencia" between Christians, Moors, and Jews known as the "reconquista."[118] For Castro, Maravall's desire to analyze Spanish history as an aspect of broader, pan-European processes of change was doomed to failure from the outset, because these different cultures "lack a common denominator endowed with a dimension capable of being written into history."[119] In contrast, Maravall gives primacy to the idea of historical periods encompassing all of Europe, despite the individual characters of particular cultures.[120] And the historical period he lays out with the greatest detail is the period he calls the baroque, removing from the term its common connotation of artistic style or genre: "My examination presents the baroque as a delimited epoch in the history of certain European countries whose historical situation maintained, at a specific moment, a close relation, whatever the differences between them."[121] It should be clear that I have no quarrel whatever with this grounding assumption, which does not mean that I have arbitrarily chosen a side in some great debate about the nature and purpose of historiography. Rather, it is my position that there is in fact nothing incompatible between Maravall's and Castro's visions of history; it is just a matter of what perspective one chooses. There are aspects of Spain's history that are unique and there are aspects that are not; the history I am telling is concerned with those aspects that are not. The only time these stories actually contradict one another is when they make mutually exclusive claims about the efficient causality of certain events or tendencies, claims which, as I explained in the previous chapter, are not particularly relevant to my project.[122]

In Maravall's telling, then, the baroque, a period stretching from the end of the sixteenth to the end of the seventeenth centuries, was a cultural complex or structure spanning all of western Europe and having repercussions in eastern Europe and the occupied lands of the American continent.[123] As a cultural complex, it was instigated and maintained by active groups in a society that was undergoing massive social and economic upheaval as a coordinated response to the possibilities of social unrest these upheavals represented.[124] The active groups in question were the traditional elites who, in the face of growing mobility, both horizontal (or geographical) as well as vertical, turned to the nascent political form of the absolutist monarchy as a tool to ensure the ultimate maintenance of their privileges:

> This interpretation serves to explain the mobilization of an extensive social operation whose aim was to contain those forces of dispersion that threatened to disrupt the traditional order. To such an end, the absolute monarchy was latched onto as an efficient instrument; first mobilized to discipline the course of development taking place in the Renaissance, it was applied in the new circumstances of crisis toward subduing the different elements that could be

raised up against the prevailing order. Thus the absolute monarchy was converted into the foundation, or, rather, into the keystone of the social system: in the absolutist regime of the baroque, the monarchy capped off a complex of restored seigniorial interests, supporting itself on the predominance of land ownership that became the base of the system.[125]

Therefore, while elements of the traditional nobility would always be in conflict over the relative augmentation or diminution of their privileges, the monarchy was in essence a force for the conservation of a traditional order—which is not to say that the methods were traditional. The methods of the new alliance were, in fact, akin in many ways to the kind of psychological manipulation[126] we encounter today in everything from advertising to nationalist propaganda, in that their purpose was to have their target audience form a "passionate attachment" to a particular version of the world.

Of this cultural complex dedicated to manipulating the passions of the people, perhaps the most powerful example was the theater:

> The stage productions of these plays were meant to give a new, undiscriminating public—el vulgo—what it supposedly wanted: lots of action, a variety of verses and other forms, and, above all, the dramatic structuring of concepts with which most spectators learned to identify.[127]

It was via this dramatic structuring of concepts that the baroque theater was supposed to instruct its public in the values it was meant to hold, the roles it was meant to aspire to, and the political structure it was meant to invest with its protonationalist sentiments.

But what exactly was the mechanism, the *"resorte,"* that Maravall constantly refers to as enabling this manipulation? In the quote above we are told that spectators learned to identify with a certain dramatic structuring of concepts. Was this identification different from that of previous forms of spectacle? Or was the content of the spectacle what was different? Mitchell Greenberg, whose work on French theater—as well as his later work on Spanish and English theater—supports Maravall's conclusions as to the guiding tendency of the theater of that period, also points to identification as the active ingredient of this manipulative process:

> In that pleasure [of the spectacle] great amounts of libidinal energy are released by the spectators' identification with characters, plots and peripeteia; but also, due to the formal constraints of the Classical theater, this energy is reharnessed just as quickly as it is released.[128]

As he expounds on this process, his version of identification begins to take on specifically Lacanian hues:

> The theater functions, we have said, like a mirror. It holds up to view both the individual desires of the spectators and the societal Law that informs these desires and prohibits their fulfillment. The spectators in front of this spectacle—a spectacle that is, in its symbolic dimension, a representation of the Prince, of the law—are rather like Lacan's famous infant in front of the 'mirror' that presents him with an image of himself as 'total,' One, unified, in which he jubilates.'[129]

This use of the Lacanian mirror stage in conjunction with an Althusserian notion of being "hailed"[130] by one's image or one's name, is, as I discussed in chapter 1, central to feminist film theory's idea of the screen's power in constructing subjectivities. The problem here is that Greenberg wants to account for the ideological power of the theater by reference to the Lacanian model of subjectivity, but at the very same time he wants to explain the modernity of that theater with reference, again, to subjectivity: "all these particulars worked together to produce a different nexus of social dynamics out of which a new subject emanates, a subject characterized most forcefully as a psychological configuration of human potential."[131] As I argue above, the subject of the Lacanian subjectivity Greenberg describes cannot account for the novelty he also wishes to attribute to it. However, what *is* new is the kind of identification the Lacanian subject engages in during the baroque, that is, modern, period, a kind of identification conditioned by the conventions of the theater itself. The theater, then, does not merely reflect or depend on the existence of some new model of subjectivity for the manipulation of the passions. Rather, it is part of the cultural "world" whose specific spatiality allows for the theatrical identification central to this particular form of manipulation.

Another form the guidance thesis can take is advanced by Pereira, who argues that the theater, and baroque culture in general, presented the mass audiences of the time with models of a subjectivity that, like the philosophical model developed by Descartes, described the self as essentially instrumentalizable. According to Pereira, with the dissolution of the personal forms of domination that characterized the feudal period, the conditions were ripe for the emergence of what he calls "an instrumental model of subjectivity,"[132] a model characterized by the distancing of the self from the body and the subordination of the latter to the requirements of the former.[133] This instrumental model was specifically the fruit of a realization among ordinary people of a scission between interior and exterior, that is, of the consciousness of a real distinction between a public space imposing certain constraints on one's conduct and a private space not necessarily requiring the same self-control.[134] During this period—the Renaissance—literature and theater begin to mediate between the newly distinguished private sphere and sphere of public authority, simultaneously promoting precise models of subjectivity and "constituting individuals and imaginary communities."[135] But whereas in the Renaissance the model of the self as an adaptable, instrumentalizable entity had been disseminated in the spirit of a new autonomy and "self-fashioning,"[136] in the baroque, the model was coopted by a cultural elite bent on assuming the role of "author" to the public's "actor."[137]

In the regime that will eventually emerge to take control of this model of subjectivity, the baroque monarchy, the mechanisms of literature and the theater "serán los encargados de promover la visión imaginaria de una república de súbditos dependientes de la potestad absoluta del rey; la imagen central será: el mundo es un teatro ... en ambos casos el objetivo es una formación de la conducta mediante la manipulación de las pasiones y el control de la exterioridad"[138] [will be responsible for promoting an imaginary vision of a republic of subjects dependent on the absolute power of the king; the central image will be: the world is a stage ... in both cases the objective is a molding of behavior by means of the manipulation of the passions and the control of exteriority]. Literature and the stage, then, serve the interests of the new power structure by disseminating models of subjectivity, models that happen to be the same as those developed by the theorists of the passions in the sixteenth century and Descartes in the seventeenth century, and in which subjects see themselves as existing in a relation of absolute dependence.

There are several major problems with this argument, the first two having to do with the role and purpose of the concept of subjectivity, the third having to do with the mechanism of manipulation Pereira is trying to describe. To begin with, if one is going to argue that subjectivity emerges from the dissolution of personal relations of domination and from a consciousness on the part of the people that there is a difference between the public and the private spheres, this still leaves open the question of what brought about both the change in relations and the distinction between public and private spheres (especially as an idealistic response would be precisely that the emergence of subjectivity brought these conditions about...). Secondly, if one argues that the existence of private and public spheres led people to a consciousness of interiority and exteriority, because they were forced to become aware of a distinction between how one behaves and controls one's behaviors in public and how one behaves and controls one's behaviors in private, one will have to defend the notion that medieval people always behaved exactly the same regardless of whether they were in their own homes or in the public square, and were therefore unaware of any distinction between interiority and exteriority.

Finally, to say that literature and theater disseminate versions of this subjectivity that benefit the interests of the elite tells us little, because it leaves unanswered the question of how these versions of subjectivity are effective at changing behavior at all. It assumes that an audience will, first, recognize itself in the propagated model and, second, alter its behavior to fit the new model. As it is, Pereira defends his association between the theater and the philosophy of subjectivity on the strength of an analogy between the I/body model and the author/actor model. This model is expressed on the baroque stage as a relation of domination that the writer tries to impose on the public "by means of the manipulation of the bodies of the actors who are on the stage."[139] But how does the portrayal of this manipulation translate into actual manipulation? Does the analogy between a certain model of subjectivity and the theater mean that the theater was capable of propagating this model?

The difficulty here lies again in the confusion between a philosophical model of subjectivity (one in which the subject is conceived of as an interiority, an instrumentalization of self, etc.), its "reflection" in a cultural genre, and the appropriation of that genre toward the *subjection* of individuals.[140] In terms of determining what's modern about modernity, Pereira's thesis provokes the same question as Greenberg's: if subjectivity is the name we give to what is new, what is it about it that allows for the manipulation of subjects through culture? Is it the mere fact that the new models of subjectivity also take on aesthetic forms and appear reflected in popular culture? The portion of both Pereira's and Greenberg's (as well as Maravall's) theses that argues for a notion of the theater and of literature in general as manipulating the masses has little to do with subjectivity, and can be better explained, as I have argued, by the theory of theatrical identification. The portion of their theses that identifies, in literature, signs of an emergent subjectivity, while it has little to do with the "subjectification" of individuals to a power-structure, can, nevertheless, also be explained with reference to theatricality.

Theatricality and Frame Distinctions

In the two centuries since Romanticism began to make its mark on the arts in the West, the aesthetic realm has become the dimension of self-expression par excellence. Perhaps this is why it is also in the aesthetic realm that the notion of subjectivity seems to carry the greatest explanatory power. Luiz Costa Lima's book, *Control of the Imaginary*, argues that western literary culture since the Renaissance has been predicated on a fundamental prohibition of the fictive in mimetic work, a prohibition that we now take for granted but that was never intrinsic to mimesis prior to this age. To explain this change, he also turns, at least in part, to the theory of subjectivity.[141]

Costa Lima's thesis is that the reigning aesthetic values of the Renaissance, classicism and formalism, were in danger of coming into conflict with another tendency—aesthetic as well as political and epistemological—of the time: the emergence of subjectivity. The doctrine of verisimilitude, and its corresponding prohibition of the fictional, became a tool for reconciling the expression of individuality with classicism and formalism:

Moreover, that reconciliation was successful only if imitatio permitted the control of the individual subjectivity and if one of its possible discourses, the fictional, were controlled aprioristically as well, through its subjugation to legitimate models. Only thus could classicism and formalism be rendered compatible with expression of individuality.[142]

What is new in the equation, then, is what Costa Lima calls the "experiencing of subjectivity,"[143] a development traced by some critics to the twelfth century. The core of the subjective experience is a conferral of agency and responsibility onto the individual, most fundamentally in cosmological and theological matters:

> To the extent that the notion that truth had been inscribed by the Divinity in the things of this world and therefore revealed itself in unequivocal signs was being abandoned, phenomena were increasingly allowed multiple meanings; and it was the subject who was made responsible for apprehending the correct one.[144]

Whereas the phenomena of the world had been previously ordered according to an immanent logic whose matrix was God, from the late Middle Ages the burden of "discovering a guiding logic" is increasingly bequeathed to the individual (a thesis that, albeit with different chronology and terminology, echoes that of Foucault in *Les mots et les choses*).

This thesis is supported by evidence from twelfth-century legal discourse, according to the work of Howard Bloch;[145] from medieval poetry—as manifested in the growing identification between the "I" of the poem and the individual person of the poet—according to the work of Paul Zumthor; and from the many personal self-references of Juan Manuel, according to Menéndez Pidal.[146] This individual, increasingly liberated from strict adherence to social hierarchy, is, according to this thesis, also increasingly liberated to engage in the production of a discourse entirely of his or her own choosing, a discourse that would be, properly speaking, fictional. It is precisely in order to protect social order against the potentially anarchic forces of fictional freedom that the Renaissance theorists issue their prohibition—which is not to say that a prohibition against fictionality equates to a negation of subjectivity. On the contrary, "*the pure expression of subjectivity can itself act as a veto of fictionality.*"[147] And this, in the end, is the work that Costa Lima believes the Renaissance prohibition was engaged in: the adaptation of subjectivity, of individual agency, to the strictures of social control, an adaptation that required its purification via the erasure of all potentially chaotic elements. Fictionality was one such element.

But what exactly is fiction, and what distinguishes it from other forms of mimesis? For Costa Lima, the meaning of fiction can be explained through Goffman's theory of frames. Frames, for Costa Lima, as for Goffman before him, are the essence of representation, in that representations are themselves the numerous frames we move into and out of on a daily basis, that organize and condition our perceptions and interpretations.[148] The ability to comprehend fiction as fiction thus depends on a process called "keying." Paraphrasing Goffman, Costa Lima defines keying in a particularly concise way as "a device by means of which an agent carries out a series of actions that, from the standpoint of the primary frame, would convey a specific meaning that in fact does not apply."[149] The metaphor of framing should be taken quite literally here. If we are watching a play, we can experience an action, say (taking our example from the previous chapter) the performance of a wedding ceremony, as if it were "really" happening, without ever in fact believing that the man and woman involved are "really" married. Rather, we understand that in the "aesthetic sphere" of the drama their characters are now husband and wife, but that this has no standing in our reality, in which the two may in fact detest each other (although this is equally a possibility of their marital life in the aesthetic sphere). This apparently simple act of comprehension, however, requires what from some perspectives could be an extremely complex process; this process is keying.

As I discussed above, the example of a wedding taking place on a stage is not innocent, because both wedding ceremonies and stages are elements in John Austin's formulation of his theory of performative language.[150] The phrase "I declare you man and wife," while not performing an action via a threat or a direct order, in fact causes something to occur in the moment of its enunciation, something that all those around—witnesses—experience as meaningful. This occurs because the statement has what Austin calls illocutionary force. The keying of frames involved in the comprehension of fiction, much like the "etiolations"[151] of language uttered upon a stage, suspends the performativity of utterances and actions. In other words, we understand them *as if* we inhabited their space, but at the same time we recognize that we do not inhabit that space and are not affected by them in the same way we would be if we did.[152]

As Costa Lima puts it, "[t]his opening out to otherness through the feigned 'I' of a character, and/or through the transformation of language, requires on the part of the recipient a keying of frames he is familiar with. (Fiction is not realized if the recipient is ignorant of this flexibility)."[153] In fact, at least for the modern age, such an inability to distinguish, say, "between fantasy and reality" has been taken as one of the primary indicators of madness. Charles Palliser's charmingly naive homicidal maniac in *Betrayals*, for instance, is utterly incapable of recognizing the framing function of his television screen. He is convinced that the family whose lives he peeks in on every week for his favorite show is in fact a real Scottish family; when actors from the show appear on other shows he has to come up with explanations that account for, "in real life," such a remarkable coincidence; and when a fictional character is mentioned in the context of a fictional show, he can make allowance neither for the fictionality of the character nor for that of the show. He records in his journal the following event from an episode of *Biggert*—his favorite detective show—in which the protagonist Biggert has just discovered an actual murder committed on stage by an actor playing the character Sherlock Holmes:

> At that moment Biggert came jumping up out of the audience and arrested Sherlock Holmes for the murder of Maturin. Sherlock Holmes of all people! I couldn't believe it! I thought he must of been framed, but apparently not, because he broke down and admitted it, standing on the stage in front of hundreds of people. We saw Dr. Watson looking at him in horror. How the man must have felt betrayed![154]

In this scene there are a number of frames that normally would be active, suspending performativity, but which are all, in his case, inoperative: the frame separating the space of the program from that of the man's living room; the frame separating the space of the play from that of the audience; and the frame separating the fictional reality of Sherlock Holmes from that of the play, from that of the program, and from that of the living room. The result for a modern reader is amusing; but is it too much to suggest that medieval reception (aside from the obvious fact that it would not be acquainted with TV) would be incapable of interpreting the keying necessary to comprehend this scene?

The point is not that a medieval viewer of a modern play would succumb to the "psychotic" reaction of Palliser's character, but rather that Palliser's parody of this failure of framing, that is, his framing of it, would not make sense to a viewer from a cultural "world" devoid of such frames. A medieval viewer of a spectacle portraying the martyrdom of Saint Genesius, for example, would not "mistake" the performance for the real thing, and somehow "believe" that Saint Genesius was in fact being tortured on stage. Rather, the relationship between the performance and the "real thing" would never be a question for him or her. Both would have an equal and noncontradictory claim on his or her experience of reality. A representation of the failure of this framing function would therefore be meaningless.

The notion of the framing function also provides another way of thinking about Vico's distinction between the "primitive" and the modern psychology in terms of the ability to think ironically:

> Irony certainly could not have begun until the period of reflection, because it is fashioned of falsehood by dint of a reflection which wears the mask of truth. Here emerges a great principle of human institutions, confirming the origin of poetry disclosed in this work: that since the first men of the gentile world had the simplicity of children, who are truthful by nature, the first fables could not feign anything false; they must therefore have been, as they have been defined above, true narrations.[155]

As a culture becomes more advanced, from Vico's perspective, it grows distant from its primordial simplicity by way of its increased tendency toward *reflection*. Whereas a culture's first narrations are true in that they partake unproblematically of the world, as a culture becomes more reflective—as individuals begin to reflect upon themselves, begin to incorporate themselves as characters into their narrations—the distinction between a true and a false narration begins to take shape. Irony is a result of the further realization that a falsehood can come in the guise of a truth, and that truth can come to us by way of a pretense, or a lie.

This close relation between truth and fiction is also at the center of Lacan's understanding of truth, an understanding that, like Richard Rorty's pragmatism, refuses to evaluate truth on the basis of a correspondence to the real, but rather places it in relation to the field of intersubjectivity.[156] In the well-known joke Lacan uses to illustrate the truth-potentiality of a falsehood, one man says to another, "Why are you telling me that you are going to Krakow so that I'll think you're going to Lemberg, when in fact you're really going to Krakow?"[157] In the intersubjective situation, like in the inter*active* one, truth has the structure of a fiction because the interacting agents are skilled in keying the various frames they are acting in, treating certain utterances as fictional by deactivating their performative potential, and treating others as true by activating that potential. In this sense the fictive utterance par excellence is the exclamation of one of the audience members in Lope's *Fingido verdadero*, "There's no difference between this and the real thing," an utterance whose intrinsic paradox can only be unraveled by an auditor conscious of his or her own duality as actor and character, an auditor who can say, "This statement is true for the character I am who identifies with the action in space 1, only insofar as it is false for the character I am who is sitting here in space 0." But this maneuver is also the maneuver par excellence of theatricality. Fictionality, therefore, as I am defining it in agreement with Costa Lima—as depending on the keying of frames—is a mode of expression characteristic of theatricality.[158]

To say this is certainly to risk provoking paroxysms among scholars specializing in earlier historical periods, who are likely to react with horror at the thought that I might be denying the existence of fiction prior to the early modern period. But this will only be the case if one ignores the specificity of this claim on the part of fiction. If one defines fiction as, say, Wolfgang Iser does, as "an act of boundary crossing which, nonetheless, keeps in view what has been overstepped," then one will have no problem choosing, as he does, the fifteen-hundred-year history of pastoral as a prime example of the fictional discourse.[159] The advantage of a definition that centers on the notion of the keying of frames, on the other hand, is that it identifies a phenomenon that is more specific than that implied by the imaginative crossing of boundaries, or the use of the material of reality in a way that contradicts reality. For the trope of the fictional is to say to the participant not only that "what is contained within this frame looks like reality but really is not," but rather and more radically that "the distinction between reality and its imitation is inherent in what is contained within this frame, and in order to understand it, you must activate the same distinction within you, and approach me, fiction, simultaneously from both sides."

It is in this sense that *Don Quixote*, often referred to as the first novel, is also one of the first works of narrative fiction: it is fictional in that it puts into written form the spatiality characteristic of the theater. Cervantes' reader has constantly to ask him or herself throughout the course of the narrative in which frames the novel's utterances are to be placed. Are the laudatory poems at the beginning just bad poetry or are they parodies of the very notion of laudatory poetry? Once it is accepted that they were, in fact, written by Cervantes and not by the various personages they are attributed to, one has to decide to what extent, if any, the voice of the poems wants to be taken seriously. When the knight is made to appear ridiculous, who among the various levels of narration is responsible for this portrayal; and when he appears noble, who has come to his rescue? More explicitly, Cervantes seems to be putting into play precisely the distinction—between a reader who can key frames and one who cannot—that I am claiming distinguishes fiction from prior forms of literary imagination. For it is precisely the constant negotiation between literary frames that is required of the reader of *Don Quixote*, the book that also constitutes the Achilles' heel of Don Quixote the character: the specific nature of the knight's insanity is his inability to distinguish fiction from reality.

But if what I am arguing is true, not only was this failure to distinguish not a form of insanity for the Middle Ages, the distinction itself was not yet a possibility. This is precisely the perspective of Foucault, who diagnoses Don Quixote's madness as being the result of his existing in the wrong historical episteme. As a character from an age in which language and the world were perceived to partake of the same substance, Don Quixote draws no frame distinction between the world he travels and the words he reads,[160] and for that reason becomes the next age's paradigm of a madman:

> *Don Quixote* is the first modern work of literature, because in it we see the cruel reason of identities and differences make endless sport of signs and similitudes; because in it language breaks off its old kinship with things and enters into that lonely sovereignty from which it will reappear, in its separate state, only as literature; because it marks the point where resemblance enters an age which is, from the point of resemblance, one of madness and imagination.[161]

Foucault's idiom is different, but the notions translate: if in the new age (the Classical Period for Foucault, which he distinguishes from the modern as well) identities and differences can play with signs and similitudes, it is precisely because the relation of the former to things is bracketed and separated via a framing function. To maintain language's kinship with things in the way that Don Quixote does makes of one a madman, a "man of primitive resemblances" in the eyes of the new order; but the new order also has its madness, the realm of "madness and imagination"—opened up by language's detachment from things, and by the emergence of theatrical frames—that from the perspective of resemblance's solid certainties must look threatening indeed.

The "aesthetic sphere," a term Costa Lima takes from Rousseau, is, of course, the space opened up by the screen of theatricality. To the extent that modern culture is predicated, as Costa Lima would have it, on a prohibition of fiction, it is a prohibition of an experience inherent to the modern experience of spatiality. For fiction, conceived of as a relativization of frames of experience, is an aspect of theatricality, not an indicator of subjectivity.[162] Its prohibition is precisely an expression of the unsettling force of theatricality's mediation of the world, and it shares, in that sense, the same motive force that compels our relations to the crypt. Literature—and aesthetic expression in general—develops new vocabularies for the description of new experiences. If this is true, then what has been identified in literary and aesthetic theory as the effects of a newly formed subjectivity can be more adequately described as the presence in language of a new experience of spatiality, the experience I have called theatricality.

THEATRICALITY AND MEDIA THEORY

If, as I argued at the beginning of this chapter, Dasein has not a tendency to *closeness*, as Heidegger claimed, but a tendency to mediation with the world, then theatricality is the name for Dasein's fundamental mediation with the world (or better, the mediation with the world that is Dasein) in the modern age. In *Understanding Media*, McLuhan writes:

> Today, when we want to get our bearings in our own culture, and have need to stand aside from the bias and pressure exerted by any technical form of human expression, we have only to visit a society where that particular form has not been felt, or a historical period in which it was unknown.[163]

This is what, with my description of presence in the Middle Ages, I have tried to do: approach the modern experience of spatiality via a detour through another time, and show by means of the estrangement that other time provides, some of the peculiarities of our own world.

If the theater has become, in the form of theatricality, our fundamental "bodily extension" in the modern age, are there further ways to describe it in its function as a medium? For instance, McLuhan himself divides all media into the categories of "hot" and "cold," hot signifying those media that overwhelm and shut down the senses, cold signifying those that open and invite further exploration, drawing the individual into a deeper and deeper participation.[164] In the context of such a classificatory schema, television is shown to be a cold medium and film a hot medium, on the basis of the difference in their respective levels of screen resolution. Taking a step back, however, I would argue that both film and television (as well as computer technology) are essentially cold media insofar as they partake of the phenomenological entity I have called the screen.

In a more recent intervention into media theory, Bolter and Grusin have argued that the present situation is characterized by a "double logic of remediation," the tendency in our culture to a simultaneous hypermediation and erasure of mediation.[165] Although their study focuses on the plethora of media in which we now find ourselves immersed, they are quick to point out that the phenomenon of remediation cannot be limited to contemporary culture, and that, in fact, its roots must go back as far as the origins of modernity: "Remediation did not begin with the introduction of digital media. We can identify the same process throughout the past several hundred years of Western visual representation.... All of them [various practitioners of representation] seek to put the viewer into the same space as the objects viewed."[166] Bolter and Grusin identify this trend as a crucial aspect of western representational practices since at least the Renaissance, and they cite examples as historically varied as Albrecht Dürer, Cartesian perspectivalism, Alberti's optics, and baroque trompe l'oeil.[167] But the question remains: if these practices share the desire of placing the viewer in the same *space* as the objects viewed, how are we to grasp the bizarre—for if not to us, we can certainly imagine an entity to which it might seem bizarre—notion that the solid materiality of a physical surface, for example, is subject to erasure and transformation into an imaginary, yet viable, alternate reality?[168]

In fact, it is precisely because the theatrical screen becomes the basic mediating force in early modernity that people can begin to express the world and their relation to others in it in terms that invite comparison with the participatory experience of cold media. McLuhan's example of the dark glasses, which "create the inscrutable and inaccessible image that invites a great deal of participation and completion,"[169] are an exact analogue of Lacan's invocation of the veil in the regime of the gaze—that when one wants to cause a man to desire something, one should show him a veil. Both of these are distillations of a general dialectic of concealment and revelation that became, as I mentioned above, one of the central leitmotifs of the baroque. As Maravall argues,

> [t]he receivers of the baroque work, being surprised at finding it incomplete or so irregularly constructed, remained a few instants in suspense; then, feeling compelled to thrust themselves forward and take part in it, they ended up

finding themselves more strongly affected by the work, held by it. In this way they experienced an incomparably more dynamic influence of the work being presented, with a much greater intensity than when other tacks were taken.[170]

This technique, he claims, was central to an overall strategy of bending the public "toward certain desired objectives."[171] But if, as I also argued above, this technique is indeed so central to modern ideology, and to the processes of identification so basic to people's experience of selfhood, then a knowledge of how visual culture works today is dependent on how it, the theater, functioned in the social context of its day. While many of the specific values or behaviors the stage may have been propagating were peculiar to its time, the structure and function was the same as they are today. Thus, if we, like the subjects of seventeenth-century Europe, are modern, it is primarily because we are still theatrical.

Epilogue:
A Future without Screens?

It should be clear by now that from the perspective offered by this book, a perspective in which the distinction of modernity is a phenomenological one—as opposed to a sociological, economic, philosophical, or poetic one—it does not make sense to speak of the present as "postmodern." Indeed, while this term may have currency in the context of a vocabulary that emphasizes "totalizing narratives" or the centrality of the categories of Man or Reason— although I would still question whether these organizing principles are as dead as their antagonists have claimed—in the context of the vocabulary of theatricality and presence, I see no indication that we have stepped out of a basically theatrical experience of the world.[1] The paradox of saying that we are living in a theatrical age, of course, is that in much of the modern world, *the theater* is essentially dead or dying, surviving only as an occasional pursuit of the cultural elite, or suffering intermittent resuscitations by political or cultural revolutionaries, convinced that they will strike a blow against oppression by at last leveling the carceral fourth wall. The vast majority of us, however, absorb our visual entertainment via television and the movies, with an ever-growing percentage also logging onto the Web for any variety of reasons, business or pleasure.

To say that we are still theatrical, then, is to make an observation utterly independent of whether or not we still go to the theater because the same viewer who learned to negotiate theatrical space in the seventeenth century would, after a few lessons in close-ups and montage, feel pretty much at home in a world of television and movie screens. And the point of contact is, I have suggested, the screen. The screen is more than just an element of technological innovation; it is a word we can use to identify a phenomenological entity, an essential ingredient of a particular organization of space. The screen has become so fundamental to modern ways of being that even situations of extreme interpersonal intimacy, from face-to-face conversation to sexual intercourse, can be seen as particular instantiations of the general rule, specific encounters in which part of the fiction is that there is no fiction, that there is, in effect, no screen there.[2] At the same time, we must recognize the persistence of presence in the form of what I have called the crypt, for certainly we achieve moments of ecstasy, of immediacy, moments when actions, gestures, and words have an impact that does not follow the route of theatrical identification. But these moments, sublime and ephemeral as they are, are couched in and revealed to us from within the confines of a theatrical organization of space. And insofar as our desire is also theatrical, it is a desire for the crypt, a desire that has been described by psychoanalysis as the epiphenomenon of a more fundamental drive toward death.

This, then, is the spatiality of modernity. But can we speculate as to what might follow? If our modern world is disclosed to us through screens, then what would a postmodern world resemble; what vocabulary might we use to describe it? The theatrical, literary-artistic, and philosophical avant-garde since the early twentieth century has tried to force the issue, has tried to create an art and a thought that pierces the theatrical divide, that reconnects directly and viscerally with human essence as opposed to its mere appearance, with the unconscious lurking beneath consciousness, with the political reality underlying ideology. And to a large extent art and philosophy were determined by this desire to get beyond representation for much of the rest of the century. But such a desire only attests to the persistence of theatricality. Neither Artaud nor Heidegger, Stelarc nor Deleuze, can successfully force the issue, make the sea rise and wash Foucault's face of man from the beach.[3] The sea will do what the sea will do, which is not a statement of political conservatism because real political battles are being fought as the sea is now and will continue to be fought. The interests of people in the here-and-now is the issue of politics, and no one's interests can predictably be served by entering a different mode of being, even if such a change could be forced. Knowing how our spatiality works, though, can facilitate the effort to work effectively within it, and, if so desired, to effectuate change. Understand theatricality, and theatrical identification! Learn how it functions on your desires! Appropriate it to your own purposes, and you may achieve a modicum of freedom! This, at least, might be one way of translating the imperative of *Ideologiekritik*, from the Frankfurt School to Žižek, into the vocabulary of theatricality.

The way out of theatricality, then, is not through the fourth wall, since presence has always tantalized us from that vantage. If I could imagine, just for a moment, what a world without screens would look like on the basis of the kinds of media that exist today, I would say that it would not involve a return to presence or to the immediate in any sense, but rather a fall into pure mediation, mediation without reference to the original body, the primary self. Such a reality would be a virtual reality without the oxymoronic connotation, a virtuality in which all aspects of being would exist free of any anchor in the physical, a virtuality in which ultimately life, consciousness, and human history would be sustainable. This is the dream of artificial intelligence and of the new age cyber-prophets who speak of the network girdling the globe as a nascent life form. Like Hegel's Absolute Spirit, object and subject would coincide: in place of consciousness would be transparency, and perhaps, in the distant future, something like Asimov's giant computer would encompass the edges of the universe, answer all possible questions, and in a last gasp say, "Let there be light." On the other hand, it is only because we are theatrical that such fictions even begin to make sense.

NOTES

INTRODUCTION

1. The result of such a procedure is, of course, to effectively remove the distinction between an inside and an outside of perception, which is precisely what Heidegger intended.

CHAPTER 1

1. See my critique of that tendency in "Psychoanalysis and the *Comedia*: Skepticism and the Paternal Function in *La vida es sueño*," *Bulletin of the Comediantes*, 52.1 (2000): 97–122.

2. Quoted from, "The Universal Avatars Specification," Working Draft #2, Revision 1-1-97, by Moses Ma, Velocity, Inc.—moses@i-game.com; Dan Greening, Chaco Communications, Inc.—greening@chaco.com; Abbott Brush, IBM, Inc.—brush@vnet.ibm.com; Maclen Marvit, Worlds, Inc.—maclen@worlds.net. White paper at http://www.chaco.com/community/avatar.html. "Second selves" is the term used by Sherry Turkle in her *Second Self: Computers and the Human Spirit* (New York: Simon and Schuster, 1984). More recently this technology has been developed into such popular "games" as *The Sims*.

3. Slavoj Žižek, *The Indivisible Remainder. An Essay on Schelling and Related Matters* (London: Verso, 1996) 194.

4. This said, it should be noted that neither I nor Žižek is saying that the body and a virtual self are the same: "The second trap, the opposite of the first, lies in too hastily proclaiming every reality a virtual fiction: one should always bear in mind that the proper body remains the unsurpassable anchor limiting the freedom of virtualization" (197).

5. Judith Butler, *Gender Troubles: Feminism and the Subversion of Identity* (New York/London: Routledge, 1990) 25.

6. Butler 136.

7. Judith Butler, *Bodies that Matter: On the Discursive Limits of "Sex"* (New York/London: Routledge, 1993) ix.

8. *Bodies* 1.

9. *Bodies* 2.

10. *Gender Trouble* 237.

11. *Gender Trouble* 137.

12. *Bodies* 13.

13. *Gender Trouble* 140.

14. *Gender Trouble* 124.

15. See my discussion of Butler and Foucault in chapter 4, in which I argue that Butler's more recent work has become more Lacanian in this regard.

16. John Austin, *How to Do Things with Words*, 2nd ed. (Cambridge, Mass.: Harvard University Press 1975, 1977 printing) 22.

17. Jacques Derrida, *Margins of Philosophy*, trans. Alan Bass (Chicago: University of Chicago Press, 1982) 326.

18. Andrew Parker and Eve Kosofsky Sedgwick, "Introduction: Performativity and Performance," *Performativity and Performance* (New York/London: Routledge, 1995) 7.

19. Parker and Sedgwick go on to differentiate their interrogation of the relation between doers and watchers in a performative situation from what they call "a more familiar, psychoanalytically founded interrogation of the gaze," since it "involves more contradictions and discontinuities than any available account of interpellation can so far do justice to" (7). I hope to show that the notion I am invoking of the gaze is itself substantially different from this "more familiar notion" associated with Althusser's theory of interpellation and its appropriation by feminist film criticism. For a summary of these ideas, see Sandy Flitterman-Lewis, "Psychoanalysis in Film and Television," *Channels of Discourse: Television and Contemporary Criticism*, ed. Robert C. Allen (Chapel Hill: University of North Carolina Press, 1987) 170–210. For a critique of this appropriation and a perspective closer to mine, see Joan Copjec, *Read My Desire: Lacan Against the Historicists* (Cambridge, Mass.: MIT Press, 1994) ch. 2.

20. See my discussion of this metaphor in ch. 3.

21. Erving Goffman, *The Presentation of Self in Everyday Life* (Edinburgh: University of Edinburgh Social Sciences Research Centre, 1956) 6.

22. Goffman 10.

23. Goffman 155.

24. Goffman 161.

25. Goffman 6.

26. Goffman "Preface."

27. Jean-Paul Sartre, *Being and Nothingness*, trans. Hazel E. Barnes (New York: Washington Square Press, 1956) 369.

28. Sartre 320.

29. As Sartre says at another point, "The unreflective consciousness does not apprehend the *person* directly or as its object; the person is presented to consciousness *in so far as the person is an object for the Other*. . . . I am for myself only as I am a pure reference to the Other" (349).

30. Sartre 343.

31. Sartre 344.

32. Sartre 360.

33. As he puts it in "On Narcissism: an introduction" [*General Psychological Theory* (New York: Collier Books, 1963) 56–82]: "Thus we form a conception of an original libidinal cathexis of the ego, part of which cathexis is later yielded up to objects, but which fundamentally persists and is related to the object-cathexes much as the body of a protoplasmic animalcule is related to the pseudopodia which it puts out" (58).

34. "For that which prompted the person to form an ego-ideal, over which his conscience keeps guard, was the influence of parental criticism (conveyed to him by the medium of the voice), reinforced, as time went on, by those who trained and taught the

child and by all other persons of his environment—an indefinite host, too numerous to reckon (fellow men, public opinion)" (Freud 76).

35. "That which he projects ahead of him as his ideal is merely his substitute for the lost narcissism of his childhood—the time when he was his own ideal" (Freud 74).

36. According to Philippe Lacoue-Labarthe ["Theatrum Analyticum," *Glyph* 2 (1977): 122–143], "the great discovery of this critical movement was that Freud had remained a pure and simple prisoner of the Western system and of the mechanics of representation—of Greco-Italian scenography, of classical dramaturgy, etc.—and that he had even added to its coercive power by presenting it as a structural necessity of the human subject in general" (123).

37. Jacques Lacan, *The Four Fundamental Concepts of Psycho-Analysis*, trans. Alan Sheridan (New York & London: W. W. Norton, 1981) 144.

38. Jacques Lacan, *The Seminar of Jacques Lacan. Book I: Freud's Papers on Technique. 1953–1954*, trans. John Forrester (New York & London: W. W. Norton, 1991).

39. Lacan reads Descartes' *cogito ergo sum* as the description of a speaking thing chasing endlessly after its unconditioned being: "Il ne s'agit pas de savoir si je parle de moi de façon conforme a ce que je suis, mais si, quand j'en parle, je suis le même que celui dont je parle" [It's not a question of knowing whether I am speaking of myself in a way that conforms to what I am, but if, when I speak about myself, I am the same as he of whom I speak."] *Écrits* (Paris: Éditions du Seuil, 1966) 517.

40. It is important to realize that Lacan was not always consistent in his teaching concerning the transference (in fact, it is a term with a particularly unstable history no matter whose writings one consults). While in Seminar XI he stresses its ambiguous character as both a mode of staging the fantasy and that which prepares the way for the analyst's disruption of that staging and, hence, the emergence of the unconscious, in his earlier work the term seems to refer entirely to the breakdown of the staging and not to its actual enactment. What is clear from Seminar XI is that transference involves the analyst occupying the place of the Other in the analysand's mind, for "as soon as there is a subject supposed to know, there is transference" (230). Žižek has referred to it, suggestively, as a mode of "suspended performativity" of words, in which a contractual arrangement between analyst and analysand allows the latter to lay down his or her guard and speak as if his or her words would have no effect: "this is why I can say anything to my analyst, reveal all my obscene fantasies about him, knowing that he will not be offended, he will not 'take it personally'" (Žižek 197). One should note here that just because the subject has laid down her guard does not mean that what emerges is the more "true" for that reason. Rather, what emerges is more fantasy, this time even less concerned with the need to have a correlate in observable, lived "reality." And it is in this mode that the sudden awareness of the analyst, of the bodily presence of another being, is able to have its effect.

41. *Seminar I* 42.

42. See his article, "Du <<Trieb>> de Freud et du désir du psychanalyste," *Écrits* 851–854.

43. Kaja Silverman, *The Threshold of the Visible World* (New York & London: Routledge, 1996) 132.

44. *Silverman* 133.

45. *Seminar XI* 85.

46. *Seminar XI* 92.

CHAPTER 2

1. If one purpose of this chapter is to suggest that "theater" refers to an exclusively modern phenomenon, it is worthwhile to note that in the cultures under examination, this contention finds philological support as well. Theater—*théatre* in French, *teatro* in Spanish and Italian—derives originally from the Greek *thea*, the action of looking. In classical Latin, the Greek *theatron* became *theatrum* and referred to any space in which spectacles were played out before a public. In France it is not until the end of the fourteenth century that the word begins to be used, alongside the religious *mystères*, to refer to profane spectacles and to the places in which they took place as well. In Spanish and Italian, the word is first used somewhat earlier—1275 in Spain, and 1348–53 in Italy—although the usage reflects the same generality as in the classical context: "teatro do hazían juegos," or, in Boccaccio's words, "edificio, destinato alla rappresentazione di opere liriche o di prosa." In both France and Spain, the word only achieved wide usage in the sixteenth and seventeenth centuries, when it began to be applied metonymically to the burgeoning profession and the canon of works being presented on the stage. See the corresponding entries in J. Coromines and J. A. Pascual, *Diccionario crítico etimológico castellano hispánico* (Madrid: Gredos, 1983); Le Robert, *Dictionnaire Historique de la Langue Française* (Paris: Alain Rey, 1992); and Manlio Cortelazzo and Paolo Zolli, *Dizionario etimologico della lingua italiana*, (Bologna: Zanichelli, 1988).

2. This position may strike some scholars currently working in medieval studies as retrograde. Indeed, the recent trend has followed the more "continualist" position that I ascribe to Patterson, over and against a belief in medieval "alterity." See, for example, Jody Enders, *The Medieval Theater of Cruelty: Rhetoric, Memory, Violence* (Ithaca and London: Cornell University Press, 1999), and *Rhetoric and the Origins of Medieval Drama* (Ithaca and London: Cornell University Press, 1992); see also, Robert S. Sturges, *Medieval Interpretation: Models of Reading in Literary Narrative, 1100–1500* (Carbondale and Edwardsville: Southern Illinois University Press, 1991). A recent exception to this trend is Lawrence Clopper's study, *Drama, Play, and Game: English Festive Culture in the Medieval Period*: "My thesis is . . . that we have applied modern senses of theatrical terms to medieval texts and documents with the result that we have 'theatricalized'—made into theater—activities that do not properly belong in that category as we understand it" (4). One way or the other, the implicit "debate" between similarity and alterity is itself as old as the concept of the Middle Ages. See Hans Robert Jauss's contextualization of this debate in "The Alterity and Modernity of the Medieval Literature," *New Literary History* 10 (1979): 181–229, along with the other essays collected in that volume, dedicated to the issue of "Medieval Literature and Contemporary Theory," especially Rainer Warning's "On the Alterity of Medieval Religious Drama" 265–292. Other recent speculations on the possible affinities between the Middle Ages and contemporary critical concerns are the subject of the volume *The New Medievalism*, eds. Marina S. Brownlee, Kevin Brownlee, and Stephen G. Nichols (Baltimore and London: The Johns Hopkins University Press, 1991); see esp. Nichols' introduction, 1–26, and the final article by Gumbrecht, "Intertextuality and Autumn/Autumn and the Modern Reception of the Middle Ages" 301–330, which offers some epochal theses as to the nature of this apparent affinity. See also in this regard Michel Zink, *The Invention of Literary Subjectivity* (Baltimore and London: The Johns Hopkins University Press,

1999): "So one can imagine a special accord, an encounter between the poetics of the Middle Ages and critical choices in the final third of the twentieth century" (2). In fact, the two positions do not need to be seen as opposing, since it is perfectly coherent to argue for similarities between aspects of a medieval past and contemporary thought while at the same time maintaining the existence of fundamental differences between the Middle Ages and modernity. See below, footnote 52, for a detailed exposition of this argument in relation to medieval sign theory and modern semiotics.

3. Lee Patterson, "On the Margin: Postmodernism, Ironic History, and Medieval Studies," *Speculum* 65 (1990): 87–108, 92.

4. E. K. Chambers, *The Mediaeval Stage*, 2 vols. (London/Edinburgh/New York: Oxford, Clarendon Press, 1903).

5. Chambers v.

6. Chambers II, 180. See also II, 206, and Hardison's discussion, in O. B. Hardison, Jr., *Christian Rite and Christian Drama in the Middle Ages: Essays in the Origin and Early History of Modern Drama* (Baltimore: The Johns Hopkins University Press, 1965) 14.

7. Patterson 93.

8. Patterson 99–100.

9. A proponent of the continuity thesis, Jody Enders deals with the conundrum with disarming frankness, describing her approach as "emphasizing similarities over differences," and referring to that choice as a "preference" that "encourages more flexibility" in the use of nomenclature (*Theater of Cruelty* 17).

10. "The gap between medieval and Renaissance drama remains as wide as ever in spite of numerous demonstrations that in other areas of culture the contrast between Middle Ages and Renaissance is far less emphatic than Burkhart imagined" (Hardison 29)—a point already stressed in 1953 by Ernst Robert Curtius, *European Literature and the Latin Middle Ages*, trans. W. Trask (New York: Pantheon Books, 1953), and reiterated more recently by Rainer Warning: "Religious drama is perhaps the genre which demonstrates most forcefully the alterity of the Middle Ages" (266). It is worth pointing out that Hardison paved the way for contemporary studies of medieval theater first by opposing, with Karl Young, Chamber's attitude toward the medieval stage as merely preparatory for Shakespeare, and toward religious spectacle as being utterly anathematic to theater, and then further by undermining the distinction maintained by Young between the liturgy itself and drama. Contemporary theorists interested in de-emphasizing historical differences are thus indebted to him (indeed, Jody Ender's first book is dedicated to him) as a principal debunker of the kind of medieval exceptionalist theses they oppose. Nevertheless, as he makes clear in the quote above, even for him, in drama the exception stands.

11. See, for example, Paul Zumthor, *La lettre et la voix, de la "littérature" médiévale* (Paris: Éditions du Seuil, 1987). As Gumbrecht writes concerning what he perceives to be a renewed interest in things medieval, "Il me paraît donc que le regain d'interêt que nous manifestons pour le thème du masque marque une rupture avec l'obsession 'moderne' de percer les masques afin de parvenir à la plénitude du sens qu'ils dissimulent. Nous commençons plutôt à ressentir la nostalgie de leur matérialité et de leur sensualité, et nous sommes portés à désarticuler l'instance de l'auteur, garantie de la stabilité signifiante, pour retrouver derrière lui une corporalité opaque et une temporalité confuse qui avaient été refoulées pendant des siècles" [It seems to me, then, that the renewed interest we are

showing in the theme of the mask marks a rupture with the modern obsession of piercing through masks in order to arrive at the plenitude of the meaning they hide. We are beginning rather to feel the nostalgia of their materiality and their sensuality, and we are led to disarticulate the agency of the author, guarantor of the stability of signification, rediscovering behind him an opaque corporeality and a confused temporality that had been repressed for centuries]. Hans Ulrich Gumbrecht, "L'auteur comme masque. Contribution à l'archéologie de l'imprimé," *Masques et déguisements dans la littérature médiévale* (Montréal: Les Presses de l'Université de Montréal, 1988) 185–192, 192.

12. For an example of the former line of argumentation, see Gustave Cohen, *Le Théâtre en France au Moyen Âge*, 2 vols. (Paris: Les Editions Rieder, 1928) vol. 1, *Le Théâtre Religieux* 1; as regards the second, see Chambers I, 90, and *passim*, as well as Hardison's discussion, 16. For Wickham's thesis, see his *Early English Stages, 1300 to 1660*, 2 vols. (London: Routledge and Paul, 1959–1981), and its discussion in William Tydeman, *The Theatre in the Middle Ages: Western European Stage Conditions, c.800–1576* (Cambridge: Cambridge University Press, 1978) 128. Ender's thesis appears in *Rhetoric and the Origins of Medieval Drama* (Ithaca and London: Cornell University Press, 1992).

13. Hardison viii–ix.
14. Cohen I, 1–6.
15. Cohen I, 8.
16. As Enders says of legal discourse: "In other words, the same coexistence of ritual and representation that we now imbue with dramatic significance in the liturgy proves equally significant in legal ritual" (*Rhetoric* 9).

17. J. E. Gillet advances a similar thesis concerning the "confirmatory magic" of performances. See *Propalladia and Other Works of Bartolomé de Torres Naharro*, ed. J. E. Gillet (Bryn Mawr, Pa.: George Banter Publishing, 1961) introduction.

18. Hardison x, 12.
19. Hardison 12.
20. Chambers I, 183.
21. Chambers I, 187.
22. See Tydeman 4–5 for more on the connection between performance and sympathetic magic.

23. Sir James George Frazer, *The Golden Bough: A Study in Magic and Religion* (London/New York: Oxford University Press, World's Classics edition, 1994) 26.

24. Frazer 27.

25. For a survey of these ideas, see Alexandre Koyré's influential *From the Closed World to the Infinite Universe* (Baltimore/London: The Johns Hopkins University Press, 1957); and E. Grant, "Medieval and Seventeenth-Century Conceptions of an Infinite Void Space Beyond the Cosmos," *ISIS* 60 (1969): 39–60. Rpt. in E. Grant, *Studies in Medieval Science and Natural Philosophy* (London: Varorium Reprints, 1981).

26. For a detailed analysis of the conception of space in medieval thought and literature see my "On Dante, Hyperspheres and the Curvature of the Medieval Cosmos," *The Journal of the History of Ideas* 60.2 (1999): 195–216.

27. For a useful review of these theories, see Marvin Carlson, *Theories of the Theatre, A Historical and Critical Survey, from the Greeks to the Present* (Ithaca and London: Cornell University Press, 1984) 37–57.

28. Michael Taussig, *Mimesis and Alterity: A Particular History of the Senses* (New York/London: Routledge, 1993) xiii–xiv.

29. The fact that, as Heidegger argues, the very notion of "worldview" issues from the modern worldview should not diminish this argument in any way. After all, those reading these words are most likely just as modern as the one writing them. See my discussion of Heidegger in chapter 4.

30. Sigmund Mowinckel, *Das Weltbild der Primitiven* (München: Ernst Reinhardt, 1924), discussed in Rosalie and Murray Wax, "The Magical World View," *Anthropological Studies of Witchcraft, Magic and Religion*, vol. 1 of *Witchcraft, Magic and Demonology: a Twelve Volume Anthology of Scholarly Articles*, ed. Brian P. Levack (New York and London: Garland Pub., 1992) 180.

31. Wax 183.

32. Wax 184.

33. Jeffrey Burton Russell, *Witchcraft in the Middle Ages* (Ithaca and London: Cornell University Press, 1972) 5.

34. Michel Foucault, *The Order of Things: An Archaeology of the Human Sciences* (New York: Random House, Vintage Books Edition, 1994) 17. Despite this similarity, the differences between the present analysis and Foucault's should be sufficiently obvious to merely mention a few: Foucault's history posits a sudden rupture between epistemes, mine does not; his is an epistemological history, describing changes in the organization of knowledge within certain intellectual traditions, while mine is a phenomenological history, describing changes in the modes of experience associated with the practices and conventions of spectacle. Finally, see chapter 4 for my discussion of the Foucauldian version of subjectification theory.

35. Foucault 19.

36. Frazer 28.

37. Richard Kieckhefer, *Magic in the Middle Ages* (Cambridge: Cambridge University Press, 1990) 82. For further examples of harmful magical practices see also Russell, *passim*, and Jules Garinet, *Histoire de la Magie en France, depuis le commencement de la monarchie jusqu'à nos jours* (Paris: Chez Foulon et Compagnie, 1818) *passim*.

38. Kieckhefer 13.

39. Kieckhefer 15.

40. Johann Huizinga, *The Autumn of the Middle Ages*, trans. Rodney J. Paton and Ulrich Mammitzsch (Chicago: University of Chicago Press, 1996) 192.

41. Kieckhefer 78.

42. Kieckhefer 74. David Rollo makes the point that writing itself was often identified, at least rhetorically, with magic. *Glamorous Sorcery: Magic and Literacy in the High Middle Ages* (Minneapolis: University of Minnesota Press, 2000).

43. Kieckhefer 79.

44. Jean-Claude Schmitt, *La raison des gestes dans l'Occident médiéval* (Paris: Gallimard, 1990) 346.

45. Huizinga 177.

46. Schmitt 346. See also Miri Ruben, *Corpus Christi: The Eucharist in Late Medieval Culture* (Cambridge: Cambridge University Press, 1991) 53.

47. Schmitt 321.

48. Schmitt 329.
49. Schmitt 335.
50. Translations in brackets are mine.
51. Schmitt 336.
52. Schmitt 341.
53. Schmitt 343.
54. Schmitt 342.

55. The reigning metaphor in thinking about grammar at this time, as contained in the phrase "grammatica speculativa," was that of language mirroring thought and its relation with the world: "la metafora dello specchio contenuto nella parola, cioè occuparsi della capacità del linguaggio di rispecchiare il pensiero e il suo rapporto con la realtà" [the metaphor of the mirror contained in the word, treating of the capacity of language to reflect thought and its relation to reality]. *I filosofi e il linguaggio*, a cura di Ugo Volli, Cecilia Galloti, and Simona Bulgari (Bologna: Progetto Leonardo, 1993) 103. See also Theo Kobush, "Grammatica Speculativa (12.–14. Jahrhundert)," *Klassiker der Sprachphilosophie von Platon bis Noam Chomsky*, herausgegeben von Tilman Borsche (München: C. H. Beck, 1996): "Vielmehr betrachtet der Grammatiker auch den Laut nur als bedeutenden, insofern er in artikuliertem Zustand ein Zeichen der Sache selbst und Grundlage der Modi significandi ist" (81) [On the contrary, the grammatician also considers the sound as meaningful only insofar as it is, in an articulated state, a sign of the thing itself and a foundation of the Modi significandi].

56. The question that immediately presents itself is why, even in the context of western culture, should this magic worldview be understood as limited to the Middle Ages. The prevalence of the practice of and belief in witchcraft through the eighteenth century would seem to undermine this thesis considerably. However, it is precisely the obsessive scapegoating of witches in the early modern period that indicates the extent to which magic had been dislodged from its position as a normal aspect of nature. As Maravall argues, the rise in this kind of magic in the sixteenth century was another example of the urge, characteristic of modernity, to dominate nature (see José Antonio Maravall, *Culture of the Baroque: Analysis of a Historical Structure*, trans. Terry Cochran [Minneapolis: University of Minnesota Press, 1986] 230). But this urge betrays a separation between the human being and nature as object not present in the medieval conception of magic.

57. Frazer 30.
58. Frazer 666–675.
59. Frazer 557.
60. Frazer 30.

61. Gregory Dix, *The Shape of the Liturgy* (Westminster: Dacre Press, 1945) ch. 9; quoted in Wax 184. See also Russell 11. This view of transubstantiation as magic is hardly new to the twentieth century. Both Zwingli and Luther, despite their own differences concerning the nature of the communion, condemned the sacrament as "an unscriptural piece of priestly magic" (Geoffrey Rudolph Elton, *Reformation Europe, 1517–1559* [Cleveland: Meridian Books, 1964] 71).

62. David Bell, *Many Mansions: An Introduction to the Development and Diversity of Medieval Theology, West and East* (Spencer, Mass./Kalamazoo, Mich.: Cistercian Pubs., 1996) 289. For the history of the rituals surrounding the sacrament of the Eucharist, see Ruben.

63. Bell 290–297.
64. Bell 299.
65. Bell 299.
66. Bell 300.
67. At which point I, in a moment of flippancy that was intended to be funny but that I later regretted, suggested that what was more difficult to believe was that it was actually a piece of bread.
68. Jauss makes exactly this point about the difficulty of transferring oneself back "into cultic participation without the bridge of the Catholic faith which the liturgical drama presupposes" (185).
69. See Lucien Febvre's classic study, *The Problem of Unbelief in the Sixteenth century: the Religion of Rabelais*, trans. Beatrice Gottlieb (Cambridge Mass.: Harvard University Press, 1982).
70. Huizinga 189.
71. John Calvin, *Institutes of the Christian Religion*, trans. Ford Lewis Battles (Grand Rapids, MI: William B. Erdmans Publishing, 1975) 107.
72. Stephen M. Nadler, "Arnauld, Descartes, and Transubstantiation: Reconciling Cartesian Metaphysics and Real Presence," *Journal of the History of Ideas* 49.2 (April–June, 1988): 229–246, 238.
73. Nadler 232.
74. Nadler 232.
75. "Eucharist," *New Catholic Encyclopedia*, vol. V (New York: 1967) 599–609, 605.
76. Hans Ulrich Gumbrecht, "Form without Matter vs. Form as Event," *MLN* 111 (1996): 578–592, 588.
77. Gumbrecht, "Form without Matter" 588; see also Robert F. Company, "The Real Presence," *History of Religions* 32.3 Feb. 1993: 233–272, which, though not principally about the Catholic doctrine, makes the following point: "... our preoccupation (in its distinctly modern form) with the signifier/signified relationship in discourse on religion is surely rooted in the particular historical trajectory of the Protestant Reformation, with its arguments over the status of images and relics and over the presence ('real' or 'symbolic' or 'spiritual') of Christ in the elements of the Eucharist" (237). Rubin discusses the relation of transubstantiation to medieval grammar on 16ff.
78. Huizinga 1.
79. Recent studies of medieval sign theory have confirmed the thesis of an affinity between medieval sign theory and contemporary semiotics, particularly as regards the prevalence of a "language paradigm" such as has come to dominate philosophy in the wake of the "linguistic turn." The idea is that, whereas in the age of positivism language took a second place to the physical, metaphysical, or mental realities it was supposed to represent, in both the sign theory of the Middle Ages and the language philosophy of the twentieth century, language is understood to have a much more constitutive, intrusive, foundational relationship to both cognition and the world. For a discussion of the relation between semiotics and medieval sign theory, see Theresa Coletti, *Naming the Rose: Eco, Medieval Signs, and Modern Theory* (Ithaca and London: Cornell University Press, 1988) esp. 17–31. She discusses the term "language paradigm," which she quotes from György Márkus ("The Paradigm of Language: Wittgenstein, Lévi-Strauss,

Gadamer," *The Structural Allegory: Reconstructive Encounters with the New French Thought*, ed. John Fekete [Minneapolis: University of Minnesota Press, 1984] 105) on page 28. Howard Bloch's discussion of early medieval grammar is among the most insightful (*Etymologies and Genealogies: A Literary Anthropology of the French Middle Ages* [Chiacgo and London: University of Chicago Press, 1983]. See also Eugene Vance's collection of essays on the subject in *Mervelous Signals: Poetics and Sign Theory in the Middle Ages* (Lincoln: University of Nebraska Press, 1986). Foucault speaks of the "return of language," in *The Order of Things* (303–307), as characterizing the current epistemic situation. Finally, and in general, the philosophies of Heidegger and the later Wittgenstein, as well as those of neopragmatism (Rorty) and deconstruction (Derrida), can be described as entailing a suspicion for the "metaphysical" notion of a reality independent of the language we use to describe it. Whereas medieval thought can hardly be described as antimetaphysical in the same way, the metaphysics of medieval theology could also not be considered extra-linguistic, since the ultimate reality, that of God's being, was believed to be coterminous with his Word (Coletti, 33). It may appear that the affinity between medieval sign theory and contemporary language philosophy noted by so many scholars would jeopardize any exceptionalist thesis concerning the Middle Ages. But what must be stressed here is the fundamental difference in this regard between the Middle Ages and early and high modernity. If the twentieth century has "returned to language," to paraphrase Foucault, this only reinforces the idea that the culture of modernity had been, in some sense, "alienated" from it. Indeed, the theatrical spatiality described in this book is what underlies the very notion of a description-independent reality that modern epistemology takes as its ultimate axiom. That contemporary philosophy, starting perhaps most intensively with Heidegger, brings that reality into question is more an indication of modernity becoming aware of its situation than of escaping it or passing on to a new one.

80. Huizinga 47.
81. Huizinga 281.
82. Zumthor 288.
83. Karl Young, *The Drama of the Medieval Church*, 2 vols. (Oxford: The Clarendon Press, 1933) I, 80–81; quoted and discussed in Hardison 31.
84. Young I, 79–80.
85. Young I, 84–85; quoted and discussed in Hardison 24.
86. It should be noted that the Middle Ages tended to be quite loose with acting terminology. See, for example, Johannes de Janue's *Catholicon*, under the word *persona*: "A character [*persona*] is called an actor [*histrio*], the representator in a comedy, who in diverse ways impersonates various characters through representation." Allardyce Nicoll, *Masks, Mimes and Miracles: Studies in the Popular Theatre* (New York: Harcourt, Brace, 1931) 158. Clearly, just to assign exact correlates of our concepts of character, actor and impersonation to these medieval categories is already a thorny problem. See also Clopper's useful precisions concerning medieval usage (11–12).
87. Hardison viii.
88. Tydeman 38.
89. Tydeman 189–90.
90. Hardison 38–9.
91. Hardison 40.

92. Hardison 47–8.

93. Clopper concurs: "When we see the word 'drama' in a medieval text, therefore, we ought not to think of a script for an enactment by persons assuming roles; rather, we should think of it as a formal and visual presentation of responding voices" (9). See also Warning's support for this thesis as regards religious drama: "The 'absoluteness' of modern drama, i.e., the separation between the internal situation of performance and the external one of reception, does not come into consideration for religious drama. The 'as if' of these plays does not constitute what we call fiction, but remains a form of ritual." Nevertheless, Warning's ultimate point is to distinguish between the *kind* of ritual involved in liturgy and in drama.

94. Tydeman 214. It is also in this sense that we can understand the general trend toward prohibiting passion plays in the sixteenth century, as will be discussed in greater detail in the next chapter. As the public's skills and practices became more attuned to expectations of verisimilitude as opposed to ritual participation, the representation of religious themes became more and more a problem, given that these spectacles now ran the risk of *failing to correspond to the reality portrayed*. Such was the reasoning behind the Bishop of Evora's prohibition of the plays in 1534. See Erika Fischer-Lichte, *Geschichte des Dramas*, 2 vols. (Tuebingen and Basel: A. Francke Verlag, 1999) 1:88.

95. Tydeman 214.

96. Nicoll 208. For almost identical descriptions by Nicolas Trevet (c. 1258–c.1328) and John Lydgate (c.1412–20), see Tydeman 48, 49. See also Stephen Orgel, "The Play of Conscience," *Performativity and Performance*, eds. Andrew Parker and Eve Kosofsky Sedgwick (New York/London: Routledge, 1995) 133–151, for a discussion of medieval interpretations of the *Poetics* and its theory of tragedy.

97. Nicoll 170.

98. See Gumbrecht's argument concerning the "role" of the author in "L'auteur comme masque" *passim*.

99. George R. Kernodle, *From Art to Theatre: Form and Convention in the Renaissance* (Chicago: University of Chicago Press, 1944) 63.

100. Quoted and discussed in Natalie Crohn Schmitt, "The Idea of a Person in Medieval Morality Plays," *The Drama of the Middle Ages: Comparative and Critical Essays*, eds. Clifford Davidson, C. J. Gianakaris, and John H. Stroupe (New York: AMS Press, 1982) 304–15, 304.

101. Hardison 289.

102. Cohen I, 45.

103. Hardison 231.

104. Hans Ulrich Gumbrecht, "The Body vs. the Printing Press: Media in the Early Modern Period, Mentalities in the Reign of Castille, and Another History of Literary Forms," *Poetics* 14 (1985): 209–227, *passim*.

105. "Body vs. Printing Press" 226–227.

106. Nicoll 176. See also, Karl Young, "The Origins of the Easter Play," *PMLA* xxix (1914).

107. Text in Hardison 179.

108. Text in Ana María Alvarez Pellerito, ed., *Teatro medieval* (Madrid: Colección Austral, 1990) 39.

109. Tydeman 191.

110. Hardison 178.
111. Gustave Cohen, *Histoire de la mise en scène dans le théâtre religieux français du moyen âge* (Paris: Librairie Honoré Champion, 1951) 48.
112. Elie Konigson, *L'espace théâtral médiéval* (Paris: Éditions du Centre National de la Recherche Scientifique, 1975) 52; and Tydeman 53.
113. Chambers II, 83; Konigson 50; Hardison 266.
114. Konigson 51; Tydeman 46.
115. Tydeman 141.
116. Quoted in Tydeman 150.
117. Nicoll 195.
118. Nicoll 195.
119. Tydeman 57.
120. Tydeman 142–44.
121. Pellerito 47–8; Tydeman 99.
122. For more on the English pageant plays, see A. M. Nagler, *The Medieval Religious Stage* (New Haven and London: Yale University Press, 1976) 55–73; V. A. Kolve, *The Play Called Corpus Christi* (Stanford, CA: Stanford University Press, 1966); and Miri Rubin, *Corpus Christi*.
123. Tydeman 177.
124. Hardison 272.
125. Hardison 47.
126. Hardison 271.
127. Text in Chambers II, 80.
128. Chambers 83.
129. Indeed, the connection between presence and pain, or death, is more than casual, as I discuss below in the context of "the crypt." See Jody Enders discussion of torture and truth in medieval theater, in *The Medieval Theater of Cruelty*. See also Warning's discussion of the excessive representation of pain in passion plays (278).
130. For a survey and criticism of this common interpretation of Foucault's work, see Kevin Jon Heller, "Power, Subjectification and Resistance in Foucault," *SubStance* 79 (1996): 78–110.
131. A hypothesis developed during the colloquium on "Medieval Theatricality in a Culture of Performance," Yale, April 27-May 1, 1996, and elaborated during a Stanford Seminar devoted to the topic of medieval and early-modern spectacle in the fall of 1996.
132. P. G. Evans, "A Spanish Knight in Flesh and Blood—A Study of the Chivalric Spirit of Suero de Quiñones," *Hispania* 15 (1932): 141–152.
133. Bernard Guenée and Françoise Lehoux, *Les entrées royales françaises de 1328 à 1515* (Paris: Centre National de la Recherche Scientifique, 1968) 10.
134. Guenée 15–16.
135. Guenée 17.
136. Guenée 22–23.
137. Archives de la Mairie de Londres, registre K, fol. 101 v. 103; full text cited in Guenée 62–69, 63. As regards the importance of station, see Huizinga: "During medieval times the conception of the division of society into estates permeates all the fibers of theological and political reflections.... In medieval thought the term 'estate' or 'order' is held

together in all these cases by an awareness that each of these groups represents a divine institution, that it is an organ of the world edifice that is just as indispensable and just as hierarchically dignified as the heavenly throne and the powers of the angelic ranks" (62).

138. Notice that the same term is used for this pageant as is used for the liturgical and semiliturgical dramas of the fourteenth to sixteenth centuries.

139. Guenée 64–65.

140. As Kernodle also points out, the appearance of contemporary figures in tableaux depicting historical or biblical figures and vice versa could reinforce a certain meaning and its application to a present situation: "A scene of Louis de Nevers, Count of Flanders, granting privileges to the city of Bourges was more likely to impress Charles V because it was accompanied by a scene of Moses bringing the Tables of the Law down from the mountain" (65–66).

141. Elie Konigson stresses the contractual nature of such ceremonies, in which the king is effectively exchanging his presence for the promise of the city's ramparts should he ever need them (253).

142. For a brilliant analysis of the political function of masques in Elizabethan England, see Stephen Orgel, *The Illusion of Power* (Berkeley: University of California Press, 1975) *passim.*

143. "Body vs. Printing Press" 190. Jelle Koopmans has made this point more recently in the context of her discussion of the medieval theater of the excluded. Koopmans, *Le théâtre des exclus au Moyen Âge: hérétiques, sorcières et marginaux* (Paris: Editions Imago, 1997) 31. This would also be the place to mention the notion of play in the Middle Ages as developed by Gumbrecht, among others, on the basis of Huizinga's famous thesis *Homo Ludens: A Study of the Play Element in Culture* (London: Temple Smith, 1970). Gumbrecht's argument is that there was a practice of play peculiar to the Middle Ages which involved the generation of the very spaces that would normally distinguish the serious from the playful or fictional. These very boundaries, in other words, were themselves subject to the shifting of play. See Gumbrecht, "Laughter and Arbitrariness, Subjectivity and Seriousness: The *Libro de Buen Amor*, the *Celestina*, and the Style of Sense Production in Early Modern Times," *Making Sense in Life and Literature*, trans. Glen Burns (Minneapolis: University of Minnesota Press, 1992) 111–122. Sturges discusses the aspect of play in medieval interpretation in light of textual *mouvance*, whereby manuscripts changed from version to version, and interpreters were guided not by the fixed notion of authorial intention but by "something more closely resembling this free play" (Sturges 3). See also Clopper, *Drama, Play, and Game* 20, *passim*. Sarah Beckwith analyzes the York cycle of passion plays as an enactment or embodiment of specific political spaces in her "Making the World in York and the York Cycle," *Framing Medieval Bodies*, eds. Sarah Kay and Miri Rubin (Manchester and New York: Manchester University Press, 1984) 254–275.

144. Momos were, according to Eugenio Asensio, "mascarada y el enmascarado que en ella iba. Los enmascarados . . . eran la flor de la corte, desde el rey hasta el paje, y despeglaban un lujo asiático en vestidos y joyas" (50) [the mask and the one who was masked. The masked participants were the flower of the court, from the king to the page, and they displayed an Asiatic opulence in their dresses and jewels].

145. Pellerito 51.

146. Pellerito 46.

147. Juan de Mata Carriazo, ed. *Hechos del condestable Don Miguel Lucas de Iranzo* (Madrid: Espasa-Calpe, 1940) 47–48. See Enders' discussion of the space proper to legal discourse as a "privileged theatrical space of legal performance" (*Rhetoric* 72). For Enders, legal rhetoric becomes the prime candidate for an "origin" to medieval drama, because "the legal conflict was similarly enacted within a predisposing material space that nurtured the histrionic performance of primordial drama" (72). But what is striking in her analysis of legal discourse is precisely that its performance is so closely tied to such a "predisposing material space," a dependence that is negated in properly theatrical spaces from the sixteenth century on. What Enders sees in the dramatic nature of such legal performances is, in my mind, exactly what is at issue in the medieval political spectacle: the appropriation of a space of power through dramatic, participatory enactment. Enders herself stresses the participatory nature of this drama: "...like medieval drama, classical and medieval legal ritual drew its audience into its proceedings and fostered lively exchanges between participants and onlookers" (73).

148. Chambers II, 219.

149. Pellerito 52; see also, Angus Mackay, "Ritual and Propaganda in Fifteenth Century Castille," *Past and Present* 107 (1985): 3–43.

150. As Regueiro points out, strictly speaking, there was still no clear separation between the space of acting and that of viewing during the time of Encina. See José M. Regueiro, *Espacios dramáticos en el teatro español medieval, renacentista y barroca* (Kassel: Edition Reichenberger, 1996) 9. That characters should emerge before a clear architectural and spatial distinction is developed is evidence for the claim that the "screen," as I describe it below, is not merely an effect of a particular staging convention, but was rather the manifestation of a spatial ontological distinction emerging at the level of spatial experience.

151. Ronald E. Surtz, *The Birth of a Theater: Dramatic Convention in the Spanish Theater from Juan del Encina to Lope de Vega* (Madrid: Editorial Castalia, 1979) 9.

152. Surtz 11.

153. Surtz 32.

154. Surtz 9.

155. On this strategic aspect of Encina's writing, see Richard Andrews, *Juan del Encina, Promethesius in Search of Prestige* (Berkeley: University of California Press, 1959). For details concerning the relation of the eclogues to his situation in the court of the Dukes of Alba, see Robert Ter Horst, "The Duke and Duchess of Alba and Juan del Enzina: Courtly Sponsors of an Uncourtly Genius," *Studies in Honor of William C. Mc-Crary*, eds. Robert Fiore, Everett W. Hesse, John E. Keller, and José A. Madrigal (Lincoln: University of Nebraska Press, 1986) 215–220.

156. Juan Del Encina, *Obra Completa* (Madrid: Biblioteca Castro, 1996).

157. Encina 769.

158. Encina 772.

159. Encina 773.

160. Henry Sullivan, *Juan del Encina* (Boston: Twayne Publishers, 1976) 52, summarizing Bruce Wardropper, "Metamorphosis in the Theater of Juan del Encina," *Studies in Philology* 59 (1962): 41–51; 43. See also Daniel Altamiranda, "La constitución del personaje dramático: A propósito de las primeras églogas de Juan del Encina," *Romanistisches Jahrbuch* 41 (1990): 317–325; 317.

161. Surtz 43.
162. Surtz 77.
163. Encina 825.
164. Encina 826.
165. Encina 829.
166. Mingo's own words in the above passage also provide amusing support for this reading, in that he seems to be playing with the notion of being two separate characters, being "beside himself." At which point Gil instructs him to get back in himself, since being beside himself (and hence not playing his role very well) is not likely to help him get ahead.

CHAPTER 3

1. Donald Spoto, *Laurence Olivier: A Biography* (New York: Harper Collins, 1992) 382.

2. Diderot, *Paradoxe sur le comédien*, ed. Stéphane Lojkine (Paris: Armand Colin, 1992).

3. Diderot's dialogue needs to be seen in the context of the debate taking place in France at the time over the conventional gesticular code of the established style of acting, and whether naturalism in one's representation was best produced by experiencing the emotions one wants to portray within oneself or rather dissembling those emotions via the mastery of certain techniques. See Lionel Trilling, *Sincerity and Authenticity* (Cambridge, Mass.: Harvard University Press, 1972) 64.

4. Diderot 88.

5. Diderot is in fact speaking of an actress at this point.

6. Diderot 89.

7. Diderot 152.

8. Lope de Vega, *Comedias*, ed. Luis Guarner, 2 vols. (Barcelona: Editorial Iberia, 1955) vol. 1, 232.

9. Jean de Rotrou, *Le véritable Saint Genest*, ed. José Sanchez (Paris: Éditions Sand, 1988) 111; these lines are to be found in the appendix of Sanchez's edition, and were originally discovered by Jacques Scherer in a 1648 version of the play.

10. Alan S. Trueblood, in his "Role Playing and the Sense of Illusion in Lope de Vega," *Hispanic Review* 32 (1964): 305-318, 318, would seem to be suggesting otherwise, when he quotes Lopez Pinciano as suggesting that the actor ought to move the audience to tears without crying him or herself. However, in Pinciano's text the statement appears in the context of a dialogue between the characters Pinciano and Fadrique as a riposte to the claim that "mueva a sí primero, conuiene, como auemos dicho, el que huuiere de mouer a otro" [it behooves him who wishes to move others to be moved himself first]. The wisdom that "será bien que el trágico mueua a llanto sin llorar él" [it is well that the actor move to tears without crying himself], is countered by Fadrique, who claims that this is really only valid for comics. In any case, the entire debate is framed by the supposition that the purpose of acting is the exact imitation of real life, as Fadrique says, "conuiene, pues, que actor mire la persona que va a imitar y de tal manera se transforme en ella, que a todos parezca no imitación, sino propriedad . . ." [the actor should observe the person he is going to imitate and in such a way that he transforms

himself into that person, such that all believe it is not an imitation, but truth]. Lopez Pinciano, *Philosophía Antigua Poética*, v. 3, ed. Alfredo Carballo Picazo (Madrid: Marsiega, 1973), 282–283.

11. Jacques Lacan, *Ecrits: a Selection* (New York and London: W. W. Norton, 1977) 316.

12. To insist on this point is not to claim that human characters are "merely linguistic," or "composed only of signifiers," but rather that characters, in all their imaginary complexity, function like signifiers, attaining their coherence and meaning for us by implicitly referring to other characters, and to the field of knowable characters in general.

13. Lionel Abel, *Metatheatre: A New View of Dramatic Form* (New York: Hill & Wang, 1963). Abel's book sparked something close to a debate in Hispanic studies when Thomas A. O'Connor ("Is the Spanish *Comedia* a Metatheater?," *Hispanic Review* 43 [1975]: 275–289) latched onto the concept only to argue that the *comedia* could not be a metatheater on account of Spain's predominant theocentric worldview. Stephen Lipmann responded, correctly it seems to me, that the fact of Spain's theocentric worldview is pretty much unrelated to whether or not the comedia was a metatheater. See Stephen Lipmann, "'Metatheater' and the Criticism of the *Comedia*," *MLN* 91 (1976): 231–246. Lipmann also discusses Wardropper's contention that characters imagining scenes of their own dishonor in the *comedia* constitutes a metatheater of sorts (238), which would be a specific instance of precisely that metatheatrical potential I am claiming for all theater.

14. Abel 60.

15. Abel 60.

16. "Le procédé du théâtre dans le théâtre: questions de méthode," *Dix-septième Siècle* 36 (1984): 261–265, 261. Unless otherwise indicated, the rest of my references to Forestier are to his book, *Le Théâtre dans le Théâtre sur la Scène Française du XVIIe Siècle* (Genève: Librarie Droz, 1981).

17. See, for example, Forestier 39; Robert J. Nelson, *Play within a Play. The Dramatist's Conception of his Art: Shakespeare to Anouilh* (New Haven: Yale University Press, 1958), 43; Emilio Orozco Díaz, *El teatro y la teatralidad del barroco* (Barcelona: Editorial Planeta, 1969) *passim*. Curiously enough, each of these critics makes explicit that the technique of the play within the play is new to the baroque, while remaining perfectly aware that the metaphor of world as theater is not.

18. *As You Like It* 2.7.139–42. See Nelson 43.

19. See Frank J. Warnke, *Versions of Baroque* (New Haven: Yale University Press, 1972) 67.

20. "Le procédé du théâtre dans le théâtre: questions de méthode" 261.

21. *Le théâtre* 11.

22. *Le théâtre* 12.

23. Erving Goffman, *Frame Analysis* (Cambridge, Mass.: Harvard University Press, 1974).

24. "Social Representation and Mimesis," *New Literary History* 16.3 (1985): 447–466, 454.

25. Nelson 8; Forestier 9.

26. Nelson 8; Forestier 21.

27. Forestier 19.
28. For a detailed discussion of causality and the practice of cultural history, see my "A Wrinkle in Historical Time," *SubStance* 81 (1996): 30–55.
29. And, as I argue in the article cited above, such "retroactive causality" always comes into existence from the vantage of a particular historicizing gaze.
30. Emilio Orozco Díaz, *El teatro y la teatralidad del barroco* (Barcelona: Editorial Planeta, 1969) 15. Theoretical literature on the nature of the baroque is legion, so I will just list here those authors whose projects share a certain descriptive affinity with the notion of theatricality: Deleuze makes vibrant use of Leibniz's "fold that goes to inifinity" as the principal metaphor for his version of the Baroque, one that places an emphasis on the constant tension between a singularly inflected point of view and the infinity it inhabits (*The Fold: Leibniz and the Baroque*, trans. Tom Conley [Minneapolis: University of Minnesota Press, 1993]); Heinrich Wölfflin, *Renaissance and Baroque*, trans. Kathrin Simon (Ithaca, Cornell University Press, 1966); Warnke, *Versions of Baroque*, cited above.
31. Orozco Díaz 26.
32. Orozco Díaz 102.
33. Orozco Díaz 109.
34. Orozco Díaz 13.
35. Orozco Díaz 39.
36. Orozco Díaz 40.
37. Orozco Díaz 42.
38. "Velázquez, con decisivo gesto barroco, valorará el plano anterior al lienzo, contando con el espectador, para dar más fuerza de realidad a la ficción pictórica y enlazarla vigorosamente con el plano de la realidad, con el proprio ambiente del espectador. Su aspiración suma será que el cuadro no sea cuadro, sino un ámbito espacial que limita el marco como si fuese una puerta a través de la cual se puede salir y entrar; o, si queremos extremar la relación, como si fuese la embocadura de la escena teatral" (43; *passim* for more examples of this tendency en baroque painting) [Velázquez, with a decisive baroque gesture, animates the space behind the canvas, counting on the spectator to give greater realistic force to the pictorial fiction and attach it vigorously to the space of reality, with the spectator's own milieu. His great ambition is for the painting to not be a painting, but rather a spatial ambit limited by the frame, as if the frame were a door through which one could enter or leave; or, if we want to emphasize the relationship, as if it were the border of the theatrical stage].
39. The same dynamic occurs respecting the relation between theatrical time and the time of the actual representation, a relation that, as Forestier points out, only becomes problematic during this period (105).
40. The claim for the radical novelty of this space may seem objectionable—even for those who have accepted my argument concerning the nature of spectacle in the Middle Ages—in light of popular assumptions concerning the ancient Greek theater. The first answer to this objection is that as the story I am telling is not teleological, whether the ancient Greek did or did not experience space theatrically is not of crucial importance for describing the historical change at the threshold of modernity. The second answer is perhaps more to the point: although this is not the forum for a complete exploration of the question, there is evidence that the Greek theater also did not know

"character" in the peculiarly modern sense of the term. See John Jones' influential argument in *On Aristotle and Greek Tragedy* (Stanford: Stanford University Press, 1980).

41. Bibliothèque nationale, fonds français, manuscript no. 12537. The manuscript is also available in a nineteenth-century edition by W. Mostert and E. Stengel, eds., *L'Ystoire et la vie de Saint Genis* (Marburg: N. G. Elwert'sche Verlagsbuchhandlung, 1895).

42. See my discussion of the term *mimus* in chapter 2; see Mostert and Stengel 62, lines 800 to 823, for a routine played out by the four *mimi*, in which one breaks a string of his instrument and the rest proceed to make one pun after another on the word "corde."

43. Mostert 62, 833–37.

44. Mostert 65, 1116–22.

45. Mostert 71, 1704–24.

46. Mostert 81, 2528–35.

47. The conflict, again, lies in the fact that, for Descartes, the species were secondary properties, existing only for the beholder rather than intrinsic to the substance itself. This posed an insoluble problem for transubstantiation since, if the species are not a part of the substance of the bread, in the way that the color, smell, and taste of Genesius's apple are, then there is nothing specifically breadlike about the substance bread, and therefore nothing particularly miraculous about its transformation into Christ's body.

48. Rotrou IV, vii, 1324–1329.

49. Rotrou I, v, 307–308.

CHAPTER 4

1. D'Aubignac, *Practique du théâtre par l'Abbé*, 3 vols. (Amsterdam, 1715) I, 4, I,18; cited in Eugène Rigal, *Le Théatre Français Avant la Période Classique* (Paris: Hachette, 1901) 297.

2. An anonymous pamphlet circulating at the time of the *querelle du Cid* preached that "[t]he object of dramatic poetry is to imitate every action, every place, and every time, so that nothing of any sort which occurs in the world, no interval of time however long, no country of whatever size or remoteness should be excluded from what theatre can treat." Armand Gasté, *La querelle du Cid* (Paris, 1898) 255–256; quoted in Marvin Carlson, *Theories of the Theatre: A Historical and Critical Survey, from the Greeks to the Present* (Ithaca: Cornell University Press, 1984) 95. It continues: "Nature creates nothing that Art cannot imitate: any action, any effect can be imitated by the Art of Poetry. The difficulty is to imitate and make the measure and proportion of the imitations suitable to those things imitated." Gasté 360; Carlson 95.

3. Jean Jacquot, "Les types du lieu théâtral et leurs transformations de la fin du Moyen Âge au milieu du XVIIe siècle," *Le lieu théâtral à la Renaissance*, ed. Jean Jacquot (Paris: Éditions du Centre National de la Recherche Scientifique, 1964) 473–510; 475.

4. It may be objected that many of the claims I am advancing about the innovation of the theater could be more appropriately made about the invention of perspective in painting. I have written elsewhere about the importance of perspective, and will only add here that I do not consider these two themes to be incompatible or even entirely distinguishable; I merely choose to focus, in this book, on the vocabulary generated by an emphasis on the theater and its history. See David Castillo and William

Egginton, "The Perspectival Imaginary and the Symbolization of Power in Early Modern Europe," *Indiana Journal of Hispanic Literatures* 8 (1997): 75–94.

5. Jacquot 476; Phyllis Hartnoll, *The Concise History of Theatre* (New York: Harry N. Abrams, 1968) 51.
6. Jacquot 473.
7. Jacquot 501.
8. Carlson 37.
9. Carlson 37.
10. Carlson 39.
11. Bernard Weinberg, *A History of Literary Criticism in the Italian Renaissance*, 2 vols. (Chicago: University of Chicago Press, 1961) 1: 392; quoted in Carlson 39.
12. Weinberg 1: 389; Carlson 38.
13. Carlson 47.
14. Lodovico Castelvetro, *Poetica d'Aristotele vulgarizzata e sposta* (Basel, 1596) 109; Quoted and translated in Carlson 49.
15. Carlson 54.
16. Quoted and translated in Weinberg 1:412; Carlson 40.
17. Marvin Herrick, *Comic Theory in the Sixteenth Century* (Urbana: University of Illinois Press, 1964) 131.
18. Herrick 145.
19. Carlson 55.
20. Rigal 112.
21. Rigal 112.
22. Quoted in Rigal 234.
23. Rigal 236.
24. Carlson 71.
25. Carlson 73.
26. Quoted in Rigal 112.
27. Rigal 115.
28. Rigal 112.
29. Rigal 239.
30. *Opuscules critiques* (Paris, 1936) 119; quoted in Carlson 92.
31. Carlson 92.
32. Carlson 93.
33. Carlson 265.
34. Jacquot 500.
35. S. Wilma Deierkauf-Holsboer, *Histoire de la mise en scène dans le théâtre français à Paris de 1600 à 1673* (Paris: Nizet, 1960) 11.
36. Jacquot 483.
37. Jacquot 458.
38. Deierkauf-Holsboer 11.
39. Rigal 242.
40. Jacquot 489.
41. Rigal 38.
42. The anonymous *Remonstrances très humbles au roi de France et de Pologne*, quoted in Rigal 42–43.

43. Actors both in France and Spain suffered many slights at the hands of the clergy, players in France even being refused, on occasion, the right to marry (Rigal 22). All of which could lead us to believe that the pious gentleman's outrage might be merely due to his being, well, pious. See also Lopez Pinciano, *Philosophía Antigua Poética*, v. 3, ed. Alfredo Carballo Picazo (Madrid: Marsiega, 1973) 263: "¡Mirad, dixo el Pinciano, de que nos haze nueuos el señor Fadrique! Ay quien diga que los actores son gente infame y tanto, que no les deuían dar el Sanctíssimo Sacramento, como está decretado y ordenado por los sacros Cánones; ansí lo oy dezir a vn padre predicador" [Look, said Pinciano, señor Fadrique is really telling us something new! There are those who say that actors are such infamous people that they should not be given the Holy Sacrament, as is decreed and ordered by the sacred Canons; that's how I heard it once from a preacher].

44. Rigal 44.
45. Rigal 1–3; *passim*.
46. Rigal 135.
47. Rigal 138.
48. Deierkauf-Holsboer 45.
49. Rigal 82–83; *passim*.
50. Deierkauf-Holsboer 46.
51. Deierkauf-Holsboer 48.
52. Deierkauf-Holsboer 49.
53. Deierkauf-Holsboer 49.
54. Jacquot 499.
55. Deierkauf-Holsboer 58. At this time there was also a new amusement specializing in mechanical effects available for those who missed the more exciting visual spectacles of the older decor system, the *Pièces à machine*, allowing those with a taste for more psychological and poetic fare to go to the *Bourgogne* (60). In addition, in 1647, 300 box seats were installed, making the *Bourgogne*—which had until that point been frequented mostly by the bourgeois and lower classes—a place for a mixed audience, where people could be seated in a way that was differentiated according to their social position (19).
56. Deierkauf-Holsboer 18.
57. Deierkauf-Holsboer 15.
58. Jacquot 499.
59. Quoted in Rigal 299.
60. As Alberto Porqueras Mayo puts it, "[n]ingún país en el mundo, por estos siglos, puede ofercer una teoría dramática tan original y completa como España" [No country in the world, at that time, can offer a dramatic theory as original and complete as Spain]. Federico Sánchez Escribano y Alberto Porqueras Mayo, *Preceptiva dramática española del renacimiento y el barroco* (Madrid: Editorial Gredos, 1965) 31.
61. And his condemnation of theoretical poetics was not limited to this work. In the piece I examine in this chapter, *Lo fingido verdadero* (Lope de Vega, *Comedias*, ed. Luis Guarner, 2 vols., vol. 1 (Barcelona: Editorial Iberia, 1953), Lope takes yet another opportunity to poke fun at dramatic precepts, doing so all the while in the name of his own brand of verisimilitude. Diocleciano tells Ginés:

Dame una nueva fábula que tenga
más invención, aunque carezca de arte;

que tengo gusto de español en esto,
y como me lo dé lo verosímil,
nunca reparo tanto en los preceptos,
antes me cansa su rigor, y he visto
que los que miran en guardar el arte,
nunca del natural alcanzan parte. (230)

[Give me a new fable with
more invention, although it lack art;
since I am very Spanish in that regard,
and as long as it is verisimilar,
I never pay too much attention to the precepts,
but rather am wearied by their rigor, and have seen
that those who look to conform to artistry,
never achieve a degree of naturalness.]

 62. José Luis Canet Vallés, ed., *De la comedia humanística al teatro representable* (Valencia: UNED, 1993) 20.
 63. Canet Vallés 20.
 64. Canet Vallés 22–23.
 65. Pinciano 294.
 66. Pinciano 284–285.
 67. Pinciano 289.
 68. Quoted in Maxmiliano Cabañas, "Lope de Vega y Madrid: fiestas y celebraciones," *Edad de Oro* 14 (1995): 37–54; 48.
 69. See Jacquot 506–507.
 70. N. D. Shergold, *A History of the Spanish Stage from Medieval Times until the End of the Seventeenth Century* (Oxford: The Clarendon Press, 1967) 176.
 71. Unlike court productions and *autos*, productions in *corrales* were "almost destitute of scenery" (H. A. Rennert, *The Spanish Stage in the Time of Lope de Vega* [New York: The Hispanic Society of America, 1909] 76).
 72. It is also known that the values and interests of the court in all cultural matters were highly influential, which was certainly the case of the courtly theater's relation to the *comedia*. See Antonio Tordera, "El circuito de apariencias y afectos en el actor barroco," *Actor y técnica de representación del teatro español*, ed. José María Díez Borque (London: Tamesis Books Limited, 1989) 124.
 73. Othón Arróniz, *La influencia italiana en el nacimiento de la comedia española* (Madrid: Editorial Gredos, 1969) 14.
 74. Arróniz 21.
 75. Rennert 79.
 76. According to Menéndez y Pelayo, Rueda's merit lies not in his dramatic structure but in his "art of dialogue, which is a treasure of popular diction, picturesque and seasoned . . ."; quoted in Rennert 14.
 77. Shergold 175.
 78. Rennert 26.
 79. Rennert 27.
 80. José María Díez Borque, *Sociedad y teatro en la España de Lope de Vega* (Barcelona: Antoni Bosch, 1978) 156.

81. Rennert 29.
82. (Madrid, 1804), ed. J. M. Díez Borque (Barcelona: Ed. Labor, 1975); translation quoted in Rennert 40.
83. Rennert 85.
84. John J. Allen, "La escenografía en los corrales de comedia," *Studies in Honor of Bruce W. Wardropper*, eds. Dian Fox, Harry Sieber and Robert Ter Horst (Newark, DE: Juan de la Cuesta, 1989) 2.
85. Allen 3. For details on the staging in other theaters of the seventeenth century, see J.M. Ruano de la Haza and John J. Allen, *Los teatros comerciales del siglo XVII y la escenificación de la comedia* (Madrid: Editorial Castalia, 1994).
86. Díez Borque 217.
87. George R. Kernodle, *From Art to Theatre: Form and Convention in the Renaissance* (Chicago: University of Chicago Press, 1944) 57.
88. Kernodle 62.
89. Kernodle 63.
90. Kernodle 71.
91. Kernodle 76.
92. Kernodle 90.
93. Kernodle 90.
94. Kernodle 93.
95. Díez Borque 188; Rennert 89.
96. Rennert 76.
97. Díez Borque 196.
98. Díez Borque 190.
99. Rennert 88.
100. Díez Borque 217.
101. Rennert 92.
102. Díez Borque 218.
103. The notable and paradoxical exception is the actor, who necessarily transgressed not only public expectations of sartorial propriety, but the legal prohibitions against extravagance of dress as well.
104. Joan Copjec, *Read My Desire: Lacan Against the Historicists* (Cambridge, Mass. and London: The MIT Press, 1994) 21.
105. Copjec 22.
106. See Anthony Cascardi, "Subjects of Control," *Culture and Control in Counter-Reformation Spain*, eds. Anne Cruz and Mary Elizabeth Perry (Minneapolis: University of Minnesota Press, 1992) 231–254.
107. This function of the stage and its relation to Maravall's thesis of the guided culture of the Baroque is discussed in the next chapter.
108. See Jacques Lacan, *The Four Fundamental Concepts of Psycho-Analysis* (New York and London: W. W. Norton, 1981) 67–122.
109. Copjec 35.
110. Shergold 221–222.
111. Allen 9.
112. Allen 17.
113. Allen 8.

114. Deierkauf-Holsboer 49.
115. Deierkauf-Holsboer 49.
116. Deierkauf-Holsboer 52.
117. Jacquot 507.
118. Pinciano 280.
119. Lope de Vega, *Comedias*. Page number references will refer to this edition.
120. Lope 206.
121. Lope 213–214.
122. Lope 286.
123. Lope 242.
124. Lope 243.
125. Lope 248.
126. Lope 269.
127. Lope 273.
128. Lope 266.
129. Lope 274.
130. Lope 275.
131. Recall that, in chapter 1, I argued that the reason the liar's paradox ("I am lying") is not paradoxical is because of the speaking subject's ability to negotiate between him or herself as character and as actor, an elaboration of Lacan's distinction between the subject of the utterance and the subject of the enunciation.

CHAPTER 5

1. See my discussion of his argument in chapter 2.
2. A curtailed list, to be sure, to which one might add endlessly, but certainly including such thoughts and tendencies as structuralism, Deleuzian schizoanalysis, cybernetics and proponents of artificial intelligence, etc. Slavoj Žižek would certainly object to psychoanalysis being put on this list, since he perceives it as presenting a bulwark against this concerted attack on subjectivity (*The Ticklish Subject* [London: Verso, 1999]), but Lacanian subjectivity already constitutes a critique of the strong, centered subject, as I elaborate below.
3. Pragmatism might be said, in this context, to lie somewhere between deconstruction and historicism. Richard Rorty, for example, denies that he is claiming that the Cartesian "cogito" is an incorrect foundation for philosophy (such a formulation would imply that there is such a thing as a correct foundation for philosophy), but rather that it no longer provides a useful vocabulary for dealing with the problems that it was originally produced to deal with: "One may wish to say, as I do, that the seventeenth-century image is outworn—that the tradition which it inspired has lost its vitality. But that is quite a different criticism from saying that this tradition misunderstood something or failed to solve a problem" (Richard Rorty, *Philosophy and the Mirror of Nature* [Princeton: Princeton University Press, 1979] 114).
4. Martin Heidegger, "The Age of the World Picture," *The Question Concerning Technology and Other Essays*, trans. William Lovitt (New York: Harper Torchbooks, 1977) 115–154, 127.
5. "World Picture" 128.

6. "World Picture" 128.
7. "World Picture" 131.
8. "World Picture" 153.
9. I defend the importance of this distinction against the neopragmatist insistence on its nonexistence in "Keeping Pragmatism Pure: Rorty avec Lacan," *The Pragmatic Turn in Philosophy: Contemporary Engagements Between Analytic and Continental Thought*, eds. William Egginton and Mike Sandbothe (Albany: SUNY Press, forthcoming).
10. As Rorty points out, Heidegger ignored many different social practices "because he never really looked outside of philosophy books. His sense of the drama of European history was confined to his own 'Sketches for a History of Being as Metaphysics.'" Richard Rorty, *Essays on Heidegger and Others, Philosophical Papers Volume 2* (Cambridge: Cambridge University Press, 1991) 49.
11. I intentionally avoid quoting or discussing Descartes directly in any detail in this chapter, since I have no desire to enter into a debate concerning his merits or failings as a founder of modern philosophy. Rather, my interest is to demonstrate how Descartes has been used and positioned in order to construct, criticize or defend certain notions of what it is to be a subject.
12. Charles Taylor, "Inwardness and the Culture of Modernity," *Philosophical Interventions in the Unfinished Project of Enlightenment*, eds. Axel Honneth, Thomas McCarthy, Claus Offe, and Albrecht Wellmer, trans. William Rehg (Cambridge, Mass. and London: The MIT Press, 1992).
13. Taylor 94.
14. Taylor 94.
15. Taylor 99.
16. Taylor, of course, is very much a part of the movement in philosophy that considers "subjectivity" to be an adequate term for a pan-cultural, pan-generic phenomenon: "But now the source we have to connect with is deep within us. This fact is part of the massive subjective turn of modern culture, a new form of inwardness, in which we come to think of ourselves as beings with inner depth." Charles Taylor et al., *Multiculturalism*, ed. Amy Gutmann (Princeton: Princeton University Press, 1994) 29. The key phrase here is "come to think of ourselves," which indicates a level of experience that might be otherwise—or at least further—explained. None of this is to say that I disagree with the story Taylor tells, most famously in *Sources of the Self* (Cambridge, Mass.: Harvard University Press, 1989), of a modern form of identity developing the characteristic of inwardness, a concept of ordinary life, and an ethics of self expression. Furthermore, Taylor is right when he says we have to avoid thinking of philosophers as merely epiphenomenal in respect to their cultural milieu; philosophers certainly did have an enormous influence on political life, for instance. Nevertheless, as he puts it, "the temptation to give the priority to the philosophical formulation comes from the fact that it is a formulation. The movement through the culture is something diffuse and ambiguous, hard to pick out and define" (307). Describing the self as described by philosophy is one part of the equation; the sort of material cultural matrix provided by the skills and practices of spectacle cannot be ignored.
17. Taylor 98.
18. Anthony J. Cascardi, *The Subject of Modernity* (Cambridge: Cambridge University Press, 1992); I refer to his work here because it is one of the most thoroughgoing

examples of the use of the subjectivity thesis to explain modernity in an interdisciplinary way. Cascardi also makes connections to the sociological understanding of modernity, particularly that of Weber. Gidden's notion of Modernity as describing "the idea of the world as open to transformation by human intervention" has a strong resonance with the "instrumentality" ascribed to subjectivity below. See Anthony Giddens and Christopher Pierson, *Conversations with Anthony Giddens: Making Sense of Modernity* (Cambridge: Polity Press, 1998) 94. Also, Claude Lévi-Strauss' distinction between the traditional "bricoleur" and the modern "engineer" is in clear conformity with this thesis. *The Savage Mind* (Chicago, University of Chicago Press, 1966).

19. Cascardi 2.

20. Martin Heidegger, *Being and Time*, trans. John Macquarrie and Edward Robinson (San Francisco: HarperSanFrancisco, 1962) 55.

21. In fact, Cascardi specifically rejects such an interpretation when he claims that "what is most significant about the emergence of the subject can be uncovered not from the history of events but from the modes of discourse and consciousness that were evolved in response to the process of social change" (54), thereby positioning the status of the subject within the realm of the reflective, or of "second-order" observation, rather than in that of lived experience.

22. "[W]hat is at stake in our engagement with the problem of modernity is essentially a description of the subject" (2).

23. The reference is to Jürgen Habermas' *The Philosophical Discourse of Modernity* (Oxford: Oxford University Press, 1987), a book which, from my perspective, has the advantage of precisely not trying to stake a claim for subjectivity outside of the discourse of philosophy. I discuss where Habermas does seem to be staking such a claim in the section on political subjectivity below.

24. Cascardi 10.

25. Factors such as the discovery of a new world, the formation of states, the global marketplace, urbanization, etc. "may collectively be regarded as the historical 'conditions of possibility' to which the recentering of selfhood in the form of subjectivity was a response" (42).

26. "But as we see in the philosophical writings of Descartes, the understanding of selfhood as subjectivity came to acquire a normative and legitimizing force, and served to validate under the semblance of a false necessity what must in the first instance be seen as an historically contingent phenomenon" (5).

27. Cascardi 61.

28. Cascardi 126.

29. Cascardi 70.

30. Edmund Husserl, *Cartesian Meditations: An Introduction to Phenomenology*, trans. Dorian Cairns (The Hague: M. Nijhoff, 1977).

31. Martin Heidegger, *The Basic Problems of Phenomenology*, trans. Albert Hofstadter (Bloomington: Indiana University Press, 1982) 297. His opposition to Husserl is even clearer in his contention that "[t]he idea of a subject which has intentional experiences merely inside its own sphere and is . . . encapsulated within itself is an absurdity which misconstrues the basic ontological structure of the being that we ourselves are" (63–64). I am indebted for drawing my attention to this text and for much of this interpretation of Heidegger's version of phenomenology to Hubert L. Dreyfus's remarkable

commentary, *Being-in-the-World: A Commentary on Heidegger's* Being and Time, Division I (Cambridge, Mass./London: The MIT Press, 1991); the above quotations with his commentary can be found on pages 67 and 51 respectively.

32. Dreyfus 19.
33. Dreyfus 22.
34. Dreyfus 30.
35. *Being and Time* 60.
36. *Being and Time* 55.
37. *The End of Philosophy* (New York: Harper and Row, 1973) 15; quoted in Dreyfus 127.
38. *Being and Time* 41.
39. Cascardi 55.
40. Dreyfus 47.
41. "In particular we must show how the aroundness of the environment, the specific spatiality of entities encountered in the environment, is founded upon the worldhood of the world, while contrariwise the world, on its part, is not present-at-hand in space" (*Being and Time* 135).
42. Dreyfus 129. For an exhaustive philosophical discussion of the problem of space, see Henri Lefebvre, *La production de l'espace* (Paris: Éditions anthropos, 1974).
43. This is not problematic for quite trivial reasons: namely, the definition of any concept will be, at least in part, not historically variable, because if all the predicates of a concept were to change from one period to the next, the concept would simply be conceived of as having a different referent.
44. *Being and Time* 138.
45. *Being and Time* 140.
46. Marshall McLuhan, *Understanding Media: The Extensions of Man* (Cambridge, Mass./London: The MIT Press, 1994): "This is merely to say that the personal and social consequences of any medium—that is, of any extension of ourselves—result from the new scale that is introduced into our affairs by each extension of ourselves, or by any new technology" (7).
47. McLuhan 31.
48. Taylor unconsciously reflects on this injection of spatiality into philosophical language when, in his discussion of the inwardness that serves as the focus of his discussion he writes: "What we turn to in radical reflexivity seems to demand description as something 'inner.' This spatial metaphor is irresistible to describe the 'space' opened by self-scrutiny" (103).
49. Taylor 98.
50. Rorty 50.
51. Descartes, *Meditation III*, Alquié edition, II, 193; quoted in Rorty 56.
52. "World Picture" 150.
53. "World Picture" 131.
54. This notion of the picture that includes within it a copy of the representer is also central to the psychoanalytic idea of the "fantasy screen," which I discuss below.
55. Étienne Balibar, "Citizen Subject," *Who Comes After the Subject?* eds. Eduardo Cadava, Peter Connor, and Jean-Luc Nancy (London and New York: Routledge, 1991) 33–57, 33.

56. Balibar 35.
57. Balibar 35.
58. René Descartes, *Meditations on First Philosophy*, 3rd ed., trans. Donald A. Cress (Indianapolis/Cambridge: Hackett Publishing, 1993) 13.
59. Elias, *The Civilizing Process* (New York: Pantheon Books, 1982) 8; quoted in Oscar Pereira, *Del cortesano al actor: literatura y representación pública en la primera modernidad española*, diss., University of Minnesota, 1993) 79.
60. See David Parker, *Class and State in* Ancien Régime *France* (New York: Routledge, 1996) for such a criticism.
61. Charles Tilly, "Reflections on the History of European State-Making," *The Formation of National States in Western Europe*, ed. Charles Tilly (Princeton: Princeton University Press, 1975) 18.
62. Tilly 21.
63. Tilly 24.
64. See Kenneth H. F. Dyson, *The State Tradition in Western Europe* (Oxford: Martin Robertson, 1980) 29; Tilly *passim*; José Antonio Maravall, *Estado moderno y mentalidad social*, 2 vols. (Madrid: Ediciones de la Revista de Occidente, 1972) vol. 1, 105, 108.
65. Dyson 25.
66. Dyson 27.
67. Dyson 28.
68. Tilly 27.
69. Dyson 55.
70. *Estado moderno* 33; my translation.
71. See also my article with David Castillo, "The Perspectival Imaginary and the Symbolization of Power in Early Modern Europe," cited above. The point is not that the feudal relationship is not mediated, but rather that the mediation is one of *reference* (the lord is always available to the senses) as opposed to *signification* (the sovereign culls allegiance via a network of representatives, and distributes power via the same network, a network of symbols referring back to symbols). Cf. Benedict Anderson, *Imagined Communities* (London: Verso, 1983): "It is *imagined* because the members of even the smallest nation will never know most of their fellow members, meet them, or even hear of them, yet in the minds of each lives the image of their communion" (15); quoted and discussed in Pereira 69. For the reasons cited above, I prefer symbolic to imagined, although our reference point, the nation-state is the same in both cases; and, indeed, below I refer to as imaginary the space in which the nation and its other inhabitants exist, in order to accentuate the fact that it cannot be real.
72. Dyson 29; *Estado moderno* 250, 420. The theory of sovereignty, of course, achieves its greatest renown in the work of Bodin in France: "every citizen is a subject, his freedom being somewhat diminished by the majesty of the one to whom he owes obedience." Jean Bodin, *Les six livres de la République* 1.6 (Paris, 1986) 114; quoted and discussed in Balibar 44.
73. The nature of these methods will be discussed in greater detail below.
74. *Estado moderno* 250.
75. *Estado moderno* 463. Du Bellay speaks of "L'afféction naturelle envers ma patrie" (465) [the natural affection toward my fatherland; *my translation*]; this new word

expressed, in addition, the fellowship of sharing one's domain, *patria*, with another being, for that very reason one's relation. *Compatriota*, the term expressing this relation, begins to appear as well in the sixteenth century (466). On protonational bonds, see also José Antonio Maravall, *Culture of the Baroque: Analysis of a Historical Structure*, trans. Terry Cochran (Minneapolis: University of Minnesota Press, 1986) 103.

76. *Estado moderno* 486.
77. *Estado moderno* 490.
78. *Culture of the Baroque* 14.
79. Jürgen Habermas, *The Structural Transformation of the Public Sphere: An Inquiry into a Category of Bourgeois Society*, trans. Thomas Burger (Cambridge, Mass.: The MIT Press, 1991).
80. Habermas 7. A point also argued by Georges Duby, "Introduction: Private Power, Public Power," *A History of Private Life: vol. 2, Revelations of the Medieval World*, trans. Arthur Goldhammer (Cambridge, Mass. and London: Harvard University Press, 1988) 3–32.
81. Habermas 5.
82. Habermas 4.
83. Habermas 11.
84. Habermas 26.
85. Balibar 52.
86. Balibar 45.
87. Balibar 40.
88. Habermas 43.
89. Habermas 49.
90. Habermas 28, 49.
91. Thomas Hobbes, *Leviathan: Parts I and II* (New York: Macmillan Publishing, 1958).
92. Hobbes 132; emphasis in original.
93. Hobbes 132; emphasis in original.
94. Hobbes 133.
95. Hobbes 135.
96. Hobbes 143.
97. While Hobbes may use the words author/actor, his derivation of the pairing from the Greek *persona* as disguise or outward appearance, as he explains above, makes it clear that his distinction and mine are one and the same.
98. Such a model becomes fundamental for many of the most influential thinkers of democracy. Rousseau, for instance, depends on it insofar as his notion of the *volonté générale* involves the ability of the individual to "alienate" his or her private and public selves, to have, in effect, two separate selves, one who acts in accordance with private desires and another who supports, in his or her role as citizen, the body of the state: "En effet chaque individu peut comme homme avoir une volonté particulière contraire ou dissemblable à la volonté générale qu'il a comme Citoyen" [In effect each individual can, as a man, have a private will contrary to, or that he can dissemble to, the general will that he has as a Citizen]. Rousseau, *Du Contrat Social* (Genève: Les Éditions du Cheval Ailé, 1947) 196.
99. Michel Foucault, "The Subject and Power," *Critical Inquiry* 8 (1982): 777–795.

100. Foucault 781.
101. Foucault 782.
102. Foucault 785.
103. Judith Butler, *The Psychic Life of Power: Theories in Subjection* (Stanford: Stanford University Press, 1997).
104. Butler 2.
105. Butler 3.
106. Butler 7.
107. See Jacques-Alain Miller's introductory lecture in *Reading Seminars I & II* (New York: State University of New York Press, 1996).
108. See, for example, Lacan, *Écrits: A Selection* (New York: W. W. Norton, 1977) 300.
109. For a particularly cogent analysis of the "temporal" paradoxes associated with this model of subjectivity, see Slavoj Žižek, *The Metastases of Enjoyment: Six Essays on Woman and Causality* (London: Verso, 1994) 37, in which he defines the subject as an "effect that entirely posits its own cause."
110. These two forms of "investment" are in fact Lacan's two modes of identification: symbolic identification (identification with what Freud called the ego-ideal, or that point from which one is gazed at), and imaginary identification (with what Freud called the ideal ego, that ideal form that one imagines and desires for oneself, precisely because one imagines that it is what the other desires). See Jacques Lacan, *The Four Fundamental Concepts of Psychoanalysis* (London & New York: W. W. Norton, 1981) 270.
111. I am aware that the stock historicist reply is to point out that whatever aspect of one's theory one claims is not historical is in fact the unwitting universalization of a particular quality. But such a reaction misses the point and engenders disagreement where there need be none. When a historicist defines subjectification as *this*, and then goes on to show how *this* differs in different times and places, he or she is making a *pragmatic* distinction between the term's definition—its "essence"—and what changes about it—its accidents—without ever needing to accept that this "essence" would be defined in the same way from the perspective of a different time and place. I am merely pointing out that as the Foucauldians are apparently drawing their distinction in a similar way to that of the psychoanalysts, it would make sense not to use one and the same word for the one's "essence" and the others' accidents.
112. See Judith Butler, *Gender Troubles: Feminism and the Subversion of Identity* (New York/London: Routledge, 1990) 124, and *passim*.
113. Butler, *Psychic Life* 11.
114. See Slavoj Žižek, *The Sublime Object of Ideology* (London: Verso, 1989) ch. 3, *passim*.
115. Žižek 122. It is important to note here that "breathing space," at least as I am using it, should not be taken as some Archimedean point, outside of ideology, from which the subject exercises its autonomous agency. It could not ground such an exercise of agency because it is not a "space" in which a "subject" could be situated, but rather refers to the incompatibilities, slips, inconsistencies, and failures, and ultimate desire for self-identity that constitute the core experiences of selfhood.
116. Concealment and revelation also became a leitmotif of baroque literature and the arts, a leitmotif Maravall names the technique of "incompletion." See Maravall,

Culture of the Baroque 217–220. On this aspect of Gracián's thinking, see my "Gracián and the Emergence of the Modern Subject," *Hispanic Issues* 14 (1997): 151–169, which, needless to say, would be differently titled were it written today . . .

117. Pereira 164.
118. See Americo Castro, *De la edad conflictiva*, 2nd ed. (Madrid: Taurus, 1963).
119. From a letter from Castro to Maravall, reprinted in *Culture of the Baroque* xxxiv.
120. *Culture* xvii.
121. *Culture* 3.
122. Castro's and Maravall's disagreement concerning the role "purity of blood" played in social advancement is an example of such a debate. See Maravall, *Poder, honor y élites en el siglo XVII* (Madrid: Siglo XXI, 1979).
123. *Culture* 10.
124. *Culture* 19.
125. *Culture* 27.
126. *Culture* 46.
127. *Culture* xix. See also Maravall, *Teatro y literatura en la sociedad barroca* (Barcelona: Ed. Crítica, 1990), for a more explicit analysis of the theater's ideological role in baroque society.
128. Mitchell Greenberg, *Subjectivity and Subjugation in Seventeenth-Century Drama and Prose, the family romance of French classicism* (Cambridge: Cambridge University Press, 1992) 18. See also Jean-Marie Apostolidès's work on spectacle and political power in seventeenth century France: *Le roi machine: spectacle et politique au temps de Louis XIV* (Paris: Éditions de Minuit, 1981), and *Le prince sacrifié: Théâtre et politique au temps de Louis XIV* (Paris: Éditions de Minuit, 1985).
129. Greenberg 19.
130. "Rather it is the illusion of totality, an illusion that is the 'hailing' of a necessarily split, divided subject sutured in the reflection of his own narcissism" (20); but if the subject is already split, is there anything new about this subject?
131. Mitchell Greenberg, *Canonical States, Canonical Stages: Oedipus Othering, and Seventeenth-Century Drama* (Minneapolis/London: University of Minnesota Press, 1996) xii.
132. Pereira 1.
133. Pereira 3.
134. Pereira 77.
135. Pereira 2.
136. See Stephen Greenblatt, who, in *Renaissance Self-Fashioning: From More to Shakespeare* (Chicago and London: The University of Chicago Press, 1980), disputes this claim: "there is considerable empirical evidence that there may well have been less *autonomy* in self-fashioning in the sixteenth century than before, that family, state, and religious institutions impose a more rigid and far-reaching discipline upon their middle-class and aristocratic subjects. Autonomy is an issue but not the sole or even the central issue: the power to impose a shape upon oneself is an aspect of the more general power to control identity—that of others at least as often as one's own" (1).
137. Pereira 4.
138. Pereira 42.

139. Pereira 151.

140. That the theater was in fact instrumentalized in this way I have no doubt, although it is not my purpose to argue that here. For an example of this argument as it pertains to the Golden Age theater, see Castillo and Egginton, "All the King's Subjects: Honor in Early Modernity," *Romance Language Annuals* 6 (1995): 422–427, and Egginton and Castillo, "The Rules of Chanfalla's Game," *Romance Language Annuals* 6 (1995): 444–449.

141. Theories in literary studies about the distinction of modernity are legion, and while the use of "subjectivity" as an explanatory device has become popular as of late, it is certainly not universal. Lionel Trilling briefly surveys some of the traditional theories in his *Sincerity and Authenticity* 19–20, where he says as well: "Historians of European culture are in substantial agreement that, in the late sixteenth and early seventeenth centuries, something like a mutation in human nature took place." Before this time, Trilling adds, a man was not what we would call an individual, with an internal space. He did not "imagine himself in more than one role, standing outside or above his own personality" (24). Such claims, as well as Trilling's brilliant history of the emergence of the theme of sincerity in the sixteenth century, are further evidence for the notion that the mutation in question was that of people becoming theatrical. Indeed, sincerity and theatricality will produce, when followed to their logical extremes, the same absurdity, one best expressed by Gide when he said, "One cannot both be sincere and seem so" (Trilling 70).

142. Luiz Costa Lima, *Control of the Imaginary: Reason and Imagination in Modern Times*, trans. Ronald W. Sousa (Minneapolis: University of Minnesota Press, 1988) 19.

143. *Control* 4.

144. *Control* 5.

145. *Control* 5.

146. *Control* 8–10. Of course, these same authors are also and at the same time undermining the uniformity of some historical change from presubjective to subjective organizations of selfhood, since their chronologies tend not to support the modernity/subjectivity thesis. Recent scholarship has continued to demote this thesis, as attested to by Claire Sponsler: "But recent work in medieval history has eroded the notion of a harmonious Middle Ages within which individual identities were unproblematic. Instead, the communities that took shape from 1200 to 1500 are now increasingly imagined by historians to have been distinctly disharmonious and the subjects inhabiting them to have been anything but secure, stable, and unaware of themselves as subjects." Sponsler, *Drama and Resistance: Bodies, Goods, and Theatricality in Late Medieval England* (Minneapolis: University of Minnesota Press, 1997) xii.

147. *Control* 17.

148. Luiz Costa Lima, "Social Representation and Mimesis," *New Literary History* 16.3 (1985): 447–467; 452.

149. "Social" 454.

150. John Austin, *How to Do Things with Words*, 2nd ed. (Cambridge, Mass.: Harvard University Press 1975, 1977 printing).

151. Austin 22.

152. Costa Lima makes the same connection, quoting John Searle, Austin's student: "Literature 'imitates' the illocutionary and, by virtue of this, suspends the latter's

normative force, thereby allowing the recipient to see from afar the relationship between the enunciation and its social context" ("Social" 460).

153. "Social" 460.

154. Charles Palliser, *Betrayals* (New York: Ballantine Books, 1994) 202.

155. Giambattista Vico, *The New Science*, trans. Thomas Goddard Bergin and Max Harold Fisch (Ithaca and London: Cornell University Press, 1970) 90. See also Robert Pogue Harrison's commentary in *Forests: The Shadow of Civilization* (Chicago and London: The University of Chicago Press, 1992): "Vico reminds us that prior to its ability to think abstractly, the primitive mind was unable even to conceive of a distinction between truth and falsehood (so many centuries does it take even to become aware of such a dichotomy). But once the mind fully develops its powers of abstraction, critical reason becomes ironic" (12). My point is, of course, that this distinction between primitive literalness and modern, ironic abstraction can be described in a less evaluative way as the phenomenological distinction between presence and theatricality.

156. *Écrits* 20; see also my article, "Keeping Pragmatism Pure," cited above.

157. *Écrits* 20, my paraphrase.

158. In the case of Don Quixote, Costa Lima argues that Cervantes invents the fictional as a sort of third way between the fantastic or fictitious—at that time feeling the first winds of its future prohibition by the priests of verisimilitude—and the quotidian or verisimilar. The new genre, fictionality, is made possible by an ironic distancing that allows the author to "place himself outside of his narrative" and in a sense liberates him from the pure prohibition of the fictitious. See Costa Lima, *The Dark Side of Reason: Fictionality and Power* (Stanford, CA: Stanford University Press, 1992) 7.

159. Wolfgang Iser, *The Fictive and the Imaginary: Charting Literary Anthropology* (Baltimore: Johns Hopkins University Press, 1993) xiv–xv.

160. A real, historical correlate in this sense to Don Quixote would be Menocchio, the miller burned for heresy whose life is the subject of Carlo Ginzburg's *The Cheese and the Worms* (trans. John and Anne Tedeschi [Baltimore: The Johns Hopkins University Press, 1980]. Ginzburg's thesis is that Menocchio's heresy is the result of a conflict in the mind of one man between two cultures, an oral and a written one. As Ginzburg says of Menocchio, "[i]n his mental and linguistic world, marked as it was by the most absolute literalism, even metaphors must be taken in a rigorously literal sense" (62). See Costa Lima's own discussion of this text in his *Limits of the Voice* (Stanford, CA: Stanford University Press, 1996).

161. Michel Foucault, *The Order of Things: An Archaeology of the Human Sciences* (New York: Random House, Vintage Books Edition, 1994) 48–49.

162. As it happens, many of the voices Costa Lima turns to in order to support his subjectivity thesis are engaged in refuting, from the vantage of medieval studies (Howard Bloch is an excellent example) the claim that subjectivity is particular to a Modern Age born in the Renaissance. By citing such scholars, Costa Lima is indicating that he too refuses to subscribe to such a limitation of the notion; and yet it seems that for the "development of subjectivity" to be a substantial part of his explanation for the historically specific prohibition of fictionality in sixteenth century poetics, he would *perforce* have to defend such a historically specific notion of subjectivity, one that appears quite a bit later than that described by Howard Bloch.

163. McLuhan 19.

164. McLuhan 22.

165. Jay David Bolter and Richard Grusin, *Remediation: Understanding New Media* (Cambridge, Mass.: The MIT Press, 1999).

166. Bolter and Grusin 11.

167. Bolter and Grusin 24–25.

168. For a more detailed exploration of the ramifications of theatricality on media studies, see my "Reality is Bleeding: A Brief History of Film from the Sixteenth Century," *Configurations* 9 (2001): 207–229.

169. McLuhan 31.

170. *Culture* 220.

171. *Culture* 218.

EPILOGUE

1. As I indicated in chapter 2, the "return to language" in philosophy seems more a case of modernity's self awareness than of escaping or superceding the condition of modernity.

2. As Turkle documents, a frequent Web surfer reports: "I split my mind. I'm getting better at it. I can see myself as being two or three more. And I just turn on one part of my mind and the other when I go from window to window.... And then I get a real-time message (which flashes on the screen as soon as it is sent from another system user), and I guess that's RL. It's just one more window." Turkle, Sherry, *Life on the Screen: Identity in the Age of Internet* (New York: Simon & Schuster, 1995) 13.

3. Which is precisely the meaning of Heidegger's famous phrase, made into the title of his posthumously published interview with *Der Spiegel*, "Only a God can Save us Now." "The Spiegel Interview, 1966," trans. William J. Richardson, *Heidegger: The Man and the Thinker*, ed. Thomas Sheehan (Chicago: University of Chicago Press, 1981).

INDEX

Abel, Lionel, 75
Alberti, Leon Battista, 88, 165
Alexander III, Pope, 43
Allen, John J., 111
Altamiranda, Daniel, 184 n160
Althusser, Louis, 141
Amalarius of Metz, 48
Anderson, Benedict, 197 n71
Andrews, Richard, 184 n155
Apostolidès, Jean-Marie, 200 n128
Aquinas, Saint Thomas, 48
Aristotle, 37, 89–91, 100
Arróniz, Othón, 191 n73
Artaud, Antonin, 168
Asensio, Eugenio, 183 n144
Asimov, Isaac, 169
Aubignac, Abbé de, 86, 92, 94
Austin, John, 6, 13, 17–19, 76, 77, 118, 160
Averroës, 89

Balibar, Étienne, 131, 139, 140, 145
Bandinelli, Rolando, 43
Baudouin, Francisco, 144
Barbara, Saint, 54
Beckwith, Sarah, 183 n143
Bell, David, 178 n62
Bentham, Jeremy, 22
Bloch, Howard, 159, 180 n79, 202 n162
Boccaccio, Giovanni, 174 n1
Bodin, Jean, 197 n72
Bolter, Jay David, 165
Borsche, Tilman, 178 n55
Brownlee, Kevin, 174 n2
Brownlee, Marina S., 174 n2
Bulgari, Simona, 178 n55
Butler, Judith, 5, 12–19, 141, 149, 150, 172 n15

Cabañas, Maxmiliano, 191 n68
Cadava, Eduardo, 196 n55
Calderón de la Barca, Pedro, 75, 113
Calvin, Jean, 44
Canet Vallés, José Luis, 191 n62
Carlos V, 60
Carlson, Marvin, 176 n27
Cascardi, Anthony, 110, 130–312
Castelvetro, Lodovico, 89, 90
Castillo, David, 189 n4, 197 n71, 201 n140
Castro, Américo, 153, 154
Cervantes y Saavedro, Miguel de, 163
Chambers, E.K., 34–36, 53, 55
Chapelain, Jean, 93
Charlemagne, 59
Charron, Pierre, 142
Chobham, Thomas de, 41
Christ, Jesus, 39–41, 43–45, 47, 48, 51–53, 64, 81, 107
Clopper, Lawrence, 174 n2, 181 n93, 183 n143
Cohen, Gustave, 35, 36, 50
Coletti, Theresa, 179 n79
Company, Robert F., 179 n77
Connor, Peter, 196 n55
Copjec, Joan, 110, 172 n19
Corneille, Pierre, 2, 98, 99
Costa Lima, Luiz, 76, 158–160, 162, 164
Cruz, Anne, 192 n106
Curtius, Ernst Robert, 175 n10

Dante Alighieri, 76
Deierkauf-Holsboer, S. Wilma, 97, 189 n35
Deleuze, Gilles, 168, 187 n30
Derrida, Jacques, 17, 18, 76, 77
Denis, Saint, 54

205

Descartes, René, 6, 30, 44, 125–127, 129, 131, 132, 135, 138, 139, 156, 157
Diderot, Denis, 68–72
Díez Borque, José-María, 109
Diocletian, Emperor, 1, 80, 82, 116, 117
Dix, Gregory, 43
Dreyfus, Hubert, 195 n31
Du Bellay, Joachim, 92
Duby, Georges, 198 n80
Dürer, Albrecht, 165
Dyson, Kenneth, 143

Egginton, William, 189 n4, 194 n9, 197 n71, 200 n116, 201 n140, 203 n168
Elias, Norbert, 141
Elizabeth of Thuringia, Saint, 39
Encina, Juan del, 6, 60–66, 103
Enders, Jody, 35, 174 n2, 175 n9, 176 n12, n16, 182 n129, 184 n147
Enrique IV, 59, 60
Evans, P.G., 182 n132

Febvre, Lucien, 179 n69
Fischer-Lichte, Erika, 181 n94
Flitterman-Lewis, Sandy, 172 n19
Forestier, Georges, 75, 77, 78
Foucault, Michel, 16, 22, 33, 36, 38, 46, 56, 127–129, 140, 141, 148, 150, 159, 163, 168, 172 n15
Frazer, James, 36–38, 40, 42
Freud, Sigmund, 9, 12, 16, 24–26, 31, 70, 149, 172 n34

Galloti, Cecilia, 178 n55
Garnier, Robert, 92
Gasté, Armand, 188 n2
Genesius, Saint, 1, 6, 67, 71, 80–83, 113, 161
Giddens, Anthony, 195 n18
Gillet, J.E., 176 n17
Ginzburg, Carlo, 202 n160
Gracián, Baltasar, 200 n116
Grant, Edward, 176 n25
Greenberg, Mitchell, 155, 156, 158

Greenblatt, Stephen, 33, 200 n136
Grusin, Richard, 165
Goffman, Erving, 20, 21, 26, 76, 159, 160
Guarini, Battista, 91
Guenée, Bernard, 57, 58
Gumbrecht, Hans Ulrich, 35, 45, 56, 59, 174 n2, 175 n11
Gutmann, Amy, 194 n16

Habermas, Jürgen, 130, 144–146, 195 n23
Hardison, O.B., 35, 36, 47, 48, 50, 52, 55, 108
Hardy, Alexandre, 92, 93, 97, 98
Harrison, Robert Pogue, 202 n155
Hector of Troy, 59
Hegel, Georg Wilhelm Friedrich, 3, 22, 125, 150, 169
Heidegger, Martin, 4, 124–128, 130–140, 151, 164, 168, 171 n1
Heller, Kevin Jon, 182 n130
Henri III, 95
Herrick, Marvin, 189 n17
Hobbes, Thomas, 146, 147
Hoffman, Dustin, 67
Horace, 89, 91, 100
Huizinga, Johann, 39, 44–46, 51
Husserl, Edmund, 132, 133, 135, 195 n30

Innocent III, Pope, 48
Iranzo, Miguel Lucas de, 59
Iser, Wolfgang, 162
Isidor of Seville, 49

Jacquot, Jean, 87, 98
Janue, Johannes de, 180, n86
Jauss, Hans Robert, 174 n2, 179 n68
Jodelle, Étienne, 92
John of Salisbury, 76
Jones, Inigo, 103
Jones, John, 188 n40
Jonson, Ben, 103
Julia of Liège, Saint, 43
Juan II, 59

Kant, Immanuel, 4, 132, 145
Kay, Sarah, 183 n143
Kernodle, George, 50, 107, 108
Kieckhefer, Richard, 177 n37
Kierkegaard, Søren, 44
Kobush, Theo, 178 n55
Kolve, V.A., 182 n122
Konigson, Elie, 182 n112
Koopmans, Jelle, 183 n143
Koyré, Alexandre, 176 n25

Lacan, Jacques, 6, 12, 16, 24–31, 74, 110, 125, 150, 151, 162
Lacoue-Labarthe, Philippe, 173 n36
Lefebvre, Henri, 196 n42
Lehoux, Françoise, 57, 58
Lévi-Strauss, Claude, 195 n18
Lipmann, Stephen, 186 n13
Locke, John, 138
Lombardi, Bartolomeo, 90
Lombardi, Peter, 43
Lotti, Cosmo, 102
Louis XI, 46
Luther, Martin, 44, 178 n61

Mackenzie, Roy, 50
Maggi, Vincenzo, 90
Mahelot, 97, 98, 111, 112
Mairet, Jean, 112
Manuel, Juan, 159
Maravall, José-Antonio, 143, 144, 153–155, 158, 165, 178 n56
Mariana, Juan de, 144
Marx, Karl, 140
McLuhan, Marshall, 137, 164, 165
Merleau-Ponty, Maurice, 46
Menéndez Pidal, Ramón, 159
Menéndez y Pelayo, Marcelino, 191 n76
Mowinckel, Sigmund, 38

Nadler, Stephen M., 179 n72
Nagler, A.M., 182 n122
Nancy, Jean-Luc, 196 n55
Nazero de Ganassa, Alberto, 104
Nelson, Robert, 76

Nichols, Stephen G., 174 n2
Nicoll, Allardyce, 180 n86
Nietzsche, Friedrich, 150

O'Connor, Thomas A., 186 n13
Olivier, Laurence, 67
Orgel, Stephen, 181 n96, 183 n142
Orozco Díaz, Emilio, 78–80

Parker, Andrew, 19
Parker, David, 197 n60
Palliser, Charles, 160, 161
Patterson, Lee, 33–35, 123
Pellerito, Ana María Álvarez, 59, 181 n108
Pellicer, Casiano, 104
Pereira, Oscar, 152, 156–158
Perry, Mary Elizabeth, 192
Picolomini, Alessandro, 90
Pierson, Christopher, 195 n18
Pinciano, López, 100, 112, 120, 186 n10
Philip of Burgundy, 46
Plato, 76
Plautus, 49
Porqueras Mayo, Alberto, 190 n60

Racine, Jean, 50
Ratramnus, 43
Reguiero, José M., 184 n150
Rennert, H.A., 191 n71
Richardson, William J., 203 n3
Rigal, Eugène, 91–93, 97
Robortello, Francesco, 89
Ronsard, Pierre de, 92
Rorty, Richard, 127, 138, 162, 193 n3, 194 n10
Rotrou, Jean, 1, 2, 68, 71, 72, 80, 82
Rousseau, Jean-Jacques, 164, 198 n98
Ruano de la Haza, J.M., 192 n85
Rubin, Miri, 182 n122, 183 n143
Rueda, Lope de, 103, 104
Russell, Jeffrey Burton, 177 n33

Sánchez Escribano, Federíco, 190 n60
Sandbothe, Mike, 194 n9
Sartre, Jean-Paul, 6, 22–25, 27, 135

Scaligero, Julius Caesar, 89
Schlesinger, John, 67
Schmitt, Jean-Claude, 40, 41
Schmitt, Natalie Crohn, 181 n100
Searle, John, 18
Sedgwick, Eve Kosofsky, 19
Segni, Bernardo, 90
Seneca, 49
Serlio, Sebastiano, 88, 98
Shakespeare, William 2, 34, 50, 75
Sheehan, Thomas, 203 n3
Shergold, N.D., 191 n70
Silverman, Kaja, 29, 30
Sponsler, Claire, 201 n146
Spoto, Donald, 185 n1
Stanislavski, Konstantin, 67
Stelarc, 168
Sturges, Robert S. 174 n2, 183 n143
Suero de Quiñones, 56
Sullivan, Henry, 64
Surtz, Ronald, 61, 62, 64

Taille, Jean de la, 92
Taussig, Michael, 6, 38
Taylor, Charles, 128, 129, 137, 194 n16
Terence, 49, 88
Ter Horst, Robert, 184 n155
Tilly, Charles, 142
Tordera, Antonio, 191 n72
Torres Naharro, Bartolomé de, 100, 103
Trilling, Lionel, 185 n3, 201 n141

Trueblood, Alan S., 185 n10
Turkle, Sherry, 203 n2
Tydeman, William, 48

Valla, Giorgio, 89, 100
Vance, Eugene, 180 n79
Vega, Lope de, 1, 2, 7, 50, 61, 68–71, 80, 82, 83, 96, 100, 102, 112–122, 162
Velázquez, Diego, 187 n38
Vico, Giambattista, 161, 162
Villegas, Alonso, 144
Vitruvius, 88, 98
Volli, Ugo, 178 n55

Wardropper, Bruce, 64, 186 n13
Warning, Rainer, 174 n2, 175 n10, 181 n93
Warnke, Frank J., 186 n19
Wax, Rosalie and Murray, 177 n30
Weinberg, Bernard, 189 n11
Wittgenstein, Ludwig, 180 n79
Wölfflin, Heinrich, 187 n30

Young, Karl, 36, 47, 48

Zink, Michel, 174 n2
Žižek, Slavoj, 12, 24, 26, 27, 151, 168, 171 n4, 173 n40, 193 n2, 199 n109
Zumthor, Paul, 35, 46, 159, 175 n11
Zwingli, Huldrych, 44, 178 n56